EVALUATION FOR PERSONAL INJURY CLAIMS

BEST PRACTICES IN FORENSIC MENTAL HEALTH ASSESSMENT

Series Editors
Thomas Grisso, Alan M. Goldstein, and Kirk Heilbrun

Series Advisory Board
Paul Appelbaum, Richard Bonnie, and John Monahan

Titles in the Series
Foundations of Forensic Mental Health Assessment, *Kirk Heilbrun, Thomas Grisso, and Alan M. Goldstein*

Criminal Titles
Evaluation of Competence to Stand Trial, *Patricia A. Zapf and Ronald Roesch*

Evaluation of Criminal Responsibility, *Ira K. Packer*

Evaluating Capacity to Waive Miranda Rights, *Alan M. Goldstein and Naomi E. Sevin Goldstein*

Evaluation of Sexually Violent Predators, *Philip H. Witt and Mary Alice Conroy*

Evaluation for Risk of Violence in Adults, *Kirk Heilbrun*

Jury Selection, *Margaret Bull Kovera and Brian L. Cutler*

Evaluation for Capital Sentencing, *Mark D. Cunningham*

Evaluating Eyewitness Identification, *Brian L. Cutler and Margaret Bull Kovera*

Civil Titles
Evaluation of Capacity to Consent to Treatment and Research, *Scott Y. H. Kim*

Evaluation for Guardianship, *Eric Y. Drogin and Curtis L. Barrett*

Evaluation for Personal Injury Claims, *Andrew W. Kane and Joel A. Dvoskin*

Evaluation for Civil Commitment, *Debra Pinals and Douglas Mossman*

Evaluation for Harassment and Discrimination Claims, *William Foote and Jane Goodman-Delahunty*

Evaluation of Workplace Disability, *Lisa Drago Piechowski*

Juvenile and Family Titles
Evaluation for Child Custody, *Geri S.W. Fuhrmann*

Evaluation of Juveniles' Competence to Stand Trial, *Ivan Kruh and Thomas Grisso*

Evaluation for Risk of Violence in Juveniles, *Robert Hoge and D.A. Andrews*

Evaluation for Parenting Capacity in Child Protection, *Karen S. Budd, Mary Connell and Jennifer R. Clark*

Evaluation for Disposition and Transfer of Juvenile Offenders, *Randall T. Salekin*

EVALUATION FOR PERSONAL INJURY CLAIMS

ANDREW W. KANE
JOEL A. DVOSKIN

OXFORD
UNIVERSITY PRESS

OXFORD
UNIVERSITY PRESS

Oxford University Press, Inc., publishes works that further
Oxford University's objective of excellence
in research, scholarship, and education.

Oxford   New York
Auckland   Cape Town   Dar es Salaam   Hong Kong   Karachi
Kuala Lumpur   Madrid   Melbourne   Mexico City   Nairobi
New Delhi   Shanghai   Taipei   Toronto

With offices in
Argentina   Austria   Brazil   Chile   Czech Republic   France   Greece
Guatemala   Hungary   Italy   Japan   Poland   Portugal   Singapore
South Korea   Switzerland   Thailand   Turkey   Ukraine   Vietnam

Published by Oxford University Press, Inc.
198 Madison Avenue, New York, New York 10016
www.oup.com

_____

Library of Congress Cataloging-in-Publication Data

Kane, Andrew W.
   Evaluation for personal injury claims / Andrew W. Kane and Joel A. Dvoskin.
      p. cm.
   Includes bibliographical references and index.
   ISBN 978-0-19-532607-9
   1. Personal injuries—United States—Trial practice. 2. Evidence, Expert—
United States. 3. Forensic psychology—United States. I. Dvoskin, Joel A.
(Joel Alan) II. Title.
   KF8925.P4K36 2011
   346.7303'23—dc22   2010048455

_____

9 8 7 6 5 4 3 2 1

Printed in the United States of America
on acid-free paper

About Best Practices in Forensic Mental Health Assessment

The recent growth of the fields of forensic psychology and forensic psychiatry has created a need for this book series describing best practices in forensic mental health assessment (FMHA). Currently, forensic evaluations are conducted by mental health professionals for a variety of criminal, civil, and juvenile legal questions. The research foundation supporting these assessments has become broader and deeper in recent decades. Consensus has become clearer on the recognition of essential requirements for ethical and professional conduct. In the larger context of the current emphasis on "empirically supported" assessment and intervention in psychiatry and psychology, the specialization of FMHA has advanced sufficiently to justify a series devoted to best practices. Although this series focuses mainly on evaluations conducted by psychologists and psychiatrists, the fundamentals and principles offered also apply to evaluations conducted by clinical social workers, psychiatric nurses, and other mental health professionals.

This series describes "best practice" as empirically supported (when the relevant research is available), legally relevant, and consistent with applicable ethical and professional standards. Authors of the books in this series identify the approaches that seem best, while incorporating what is practical and acknowledging that best practice represents a goal to which the forensic clinician should aspire, rather than a standard that can always be met. The American Academy of Forensic Psychology assisted the editors in enlisting the consultation of board-certified forensic psychologists specialized in each topic area. Board-certified forensic psychiatrists were also consultants on many of the volumes. Their comments on the manuscripts helped to ensure that the methods described in these volumes represent a generally accepted view of best practice.

The series' authors were selected for their specific expertise in a particular area. At the broadest level, however, certain general principles apply to all types of forensic evaluations. Rather than repeat those fundamental principles in every volume, the series offers them in the first volume, *Foundations of Forensic Mental Health Assessment.* Reading the first book, followed by a specific topical book, will provide the reader both the general principles that the specific topic shares with all forensic evaluations and those that are particular to the specific assessment question.

The specific topics of the 19 books were selected by the series editors as the most important and oft-considered areas of forensic assessment conducted by mental health professionals and behavioral scientists. Each of the 19 topical books is organized according to a common template. The authors address the applicable legal context, forensic mental health concepts, and empirical foundations and limits in the "Foundation" part of the book. They then describe preparation for the evaluation, data collection, data interpretation, and report writing and testimony in the "Application" part of the book. This creates a fairly uniform approach to considering these areas across different topics. All authors in this series have attempted to be as concise as possible in addressing best practice in their area. In addition, topical volumes feature elements to make them user friendly in actual practice. These elements include boxes that highlight especially important information, relevant case law, best-practice guidelines, and cautions against common pitfalls. A glossary of key terms is also provided in each volume.

We hope the series will be useful for different groups of individuals. Practicing forensic clinicians will find succinct, current information relevant to their practice. Those who are in training to specialize in forensic mental health assessment (whether in formal training or in the process of respecialization) should find helpful the combination of broadly applicable considerations presented in the first volume together with the more specific aspects of other volumes in the series. Those who teach and supervise trainees can offer these volumes as a guide for practices to which the trainee can aspire. Researchers and scholars interested in FMHA best practice may find researchable ideas, particularly on topics that have received insufficient research attention to date. Judges and attorneys with questions about FMHA best practice will find these books relevant and concise. Clinical and forensic administrators who run agencies, court clinics, and hospitals in which litigants are assessed may also use some of the books in this series to establish expectancies for evaluations performed by professionals in their agencies.

We also anticipate that the 19 specific books in this series will serve as reference works that help courts and attorneys evaluate the quality of forensic mental health professionals' evaluations. A word of caution is in order, however. These volumes focus on best practice, not what is minimally acceptable legally or ethically. Courts involved in malpractice litigation, or ethics committees or licensure boards considering complaints, should not expect that materials describing best practice easily or necessarily translate into the minimally acceptable professional conduct that is typically at issue in such proceedings.

Kane and Dvoskin offer a concise description of a range of issues relevant to the forensic evaluation of personal injury claims. They cover the foundational tort law under which such evaluations are conducted, the particular duties of the forensic evaluator, and the supporting scientific evidence. They also provide step-by-step guidance, from the first contact with the attorney to the completion of all evaluative tasks (including possible expert testimony), in the assessment of personal injury claims. The broadly-applicable forensic assessment components and the elements specific to personal injury are blended in a clear, masterful fashion.

Kirk Heilbrun
Alan M. Goldstein
Thomas Grisso

Acknowledgment

We would like to thank Kirk Heilbrun, Alan Goldstein and Jon Gould for the immense help they gave us by reviewing the manuscript for this book, and the suggestions they made for improving it. Dr. Kane would also like to thank his wife, Carole, who has been incredibly understanding about the need to spend long hours on the manuscript. All of these people have helped greatly to enhance the quality of this book. Finally, we want to thank our parents for empowering us, and our children (Betsy and Dan Kane, Lori and Mike Kraft, Jenn and Mike Dvoskin) for inspiring us.

Contents

EVALUATION FOR PERSONAL INJURY CLAIMS

FOUNDATION

The Legal Context | 1

Introduction

As is the case with all of the volumes in this series, this book seeks to serve as a bridge between the vastly different worlds of psychology and psychiatry, and the law, and specifically to guide those boundary spanners—forensic mental health experts—who regularly set foot in both worlds at once. In this case, we turn to the civil law, which establishes a set of rights and duties that govern the daily business of life, and the manner in which citizens interact with one another.

Unlike criminal law, which focuses on the behavior of the perpetrator, and in which crimes typically result in the loss of freedom and are determined by a prohibited act, in civil law the consequences of a breach of duty are far more likely to be determined by the harm suffered by the victim. When these losses are concrete, for example the destruction of a vehicle, there may be no need for psychological expertise in deciding what is required to make the victim whole. However, this is not the case when the harms suffered are psychological in nature.

Generally, the consequences of civil wrongs, called *torts*, are simply designed to make the victim whole, or to restore the person to his or her condition prior to the commission of the tort. Thus, when the harms claimed are psychological, that is, when the victim experiences emotional harm, cognitive impairment, or a loss of behavioral control, the courts turn to mental health professionals to advise them about the degree to which the plaintiff has been harmed, and what can be done to restore functioning and to compensate the victim for his or her suffering, especially when the impairment or disability is permanent.

This first chapter explains the fundamental components of tort law, including the definition of duty, an explanation of various theories of causation, how harms are identified and compensated as damages, as well as the basic elements of civil process that forensic experts will need to know from the first phone call they receive regarding a case. We conclude with a discussion of the nature and admissibility of psychological expert testimony, and the duties owed to the court by the testifying expert to the court.

Chapter 2 addresses the basic duties of a forensic mental health expert witness, and how to approach cases in general, including the duty to be objective and the common sources of error and bias that threaten accuracy and objectivity. Chapter 3 discusses the nature of psychological evidence, and the difficulty in coming to sound conclusions when psychological harms are largely based on the plaintiff's subjective experience of distress. Special emphasis is placed on the evidentiary foundation of inferential opinions, and especially on the process of evaluation and psychological testing, as well as the thorny issue of malingering. Chapter 4 addresses a variety of professional and ethical rules for forensic mental health experts, and explains the process by which cases are conducted, offering step-by-step guidance, from the first phone call from an attorney until the case has been decided. Chapter 5 explains in detail the various ways of collecting reliable and valid data, including psychological interviews, sources of collateral information, and especially the strengths and weaknesses of various psychological instruments commonly used to assess psychological harms. The data having been gathered, Chapter 6 discusses the interpretation of various sources of data toward conclusions about the legal questions that will be posed, especially the determination of diagnosis, describing impairment, and deciding the degree to which it has caused disability in the plaintiff. Finally, Chapter 7 provides a useful process and structure for writing reports and preparing testimony.

We now turn toward description of the process of civil law, and define the terms and concepts that will be used throughout this volume.

Tort Law

Personal injury is an area of *tort* law, involving a "private or civil wrong, or injury, other than a breach of contract, for which the court will provide a remedy in the form of an action for damages" (Black's Law Dictionary, 5th ed., 1979, p. 1335). A tort requires that the defendant owed a duty to the plaintiff, that the duty was breached, that the plaintiff was injured as a result of the breach, and that the plaintiff's injury was proximately caused by the defendant. The defendant's breach may have involved *negligence*, *malpractice*, deliberate indifference, or another legal theory. The purpose of tort law is to distribute costs of harmful events based on social policies. "The commonly understood goal of tort compensation is to restore the injured to their pre-accident condition, to make them whole" (Shuman, 1994). Tort law attempts to deter unreasonable or negligent conduct and to compensate individuals who are injured with money for treatment or other means of achieving compensation (Shuman & Daley, 1996).

Definition of a duty usually rests on the *standard of care*. In a negligence case, the usual standard is the "reasonable person test"—that is, would a reasonable person have done what the defendant did? In a malpractice case, the standard of care is typically defined as whether the professional (e.g., physician, psychologist) acted as would a reasonable professional of the same type under the same or a similar set of circumstances (Greenberg, Shuman, Feldman, Middleton & Ewing, 2007; Young and Kane, 2007).

When a plaintiff has been physically harmed, courts have traditionally had no difficulty allowing claims to be made. When the harm was solely psychological or emotional, however, until fairly recently it was difficult to get courts to accept these cases. The concern was "that claims for psychological harm are easy to feign, difficult to verify, potentially limitless in frequency and amount, or somehow less deserving" than claims involving physical injuries (Shuman & Hardy, 2007, p. 529; see also Chamallas & Kerber, 1990). Currently, all jurisdictions permit recovery of damages for emotional or mental injuries that are proximately associated with physical injuries (Shuman, 2005).

Accordingly, for many years, cases alleging psychological or emotional damages were generally allowed to proceed only if there was a physical impact (under the *"impact rule,"* e.g., the plaintiff was hit by someone or something). This gradually gave way in the first part of the 20th century to a *"zone of danger"* test in which the plaintiff was alleged to have been placed in danger or fear of physical injury by virtue of the defendant's behavior. This was expanded to include a *"bystander rule"* under which an individual who wasn't in physical danger but who witnessed (and suffered significant psychological or emotional trauma from) a negligent action could sue for damages (Campbell & Montigny, 2004; Gabbay & Alonso, 2004; Shuman, 2005). Shuman and Hardy (2007) cite the 1968 California Supreme Court case of *Dillon v. Legg*, in which a mother witnessed a negligent injury to her child, as the landmark case in this area. After this case, courts increasingly focused on proximate cause as the basis on which psychological or emotional damage cases may be brought (Shuman). Even so, courts still tend to question the validity of claims for psychological and emotional harm far more than those for physical harm (Chamallas & Kerber, 1990; Shuman & Hardy). Courts may, however, welcome expert psychological and psychiatric testimony that helps the judge and jury understand mental disorders and psychological stress (Shuman).

It was not until 1993, in *Harris v. Forklift Systems, Inc.,* the Supreme Court indicated that evidence of psychological or emotional harm to an individual could be a substantial factor in determining whether an employer is responsible for sexual harassment. This was the first case in which the Supreme Court ruled that a psychological or emotional injury, in the

CASE LAW

Dillon v. Legg (1968)

The Supreme Court of California ruled that in determining whether the defendant owes a duty of care to the plaintiff, the court should consider the following: 1) the proximity of the plaintiff to the accident, 2) whether the plaintiff directly witnessed the accident, and 3) whether the plaintiff was closely related to the victim. Established the tort of negligent infliction of emotional distress absence of a physical injury, could be presented in the liability phase of a trial to demonstrate that a tort had occurred (Call, 2003).

Harris v. Forklift Systems, Inc. (1993)

The first case in which the U.S. Supreme Court ruled that a psychological injury, in the absence of a physical injury, could be presented as evidence in a civil suit.

Causality and Proximate Cause

Causality or *causation* involves the establishment of some direct link or relationship between an event and a subsequent consequence of that event. However, it does not necessarily indicate that it is the sole, primary or predominant cause; it may simply be a contributing factor. In contrast, *proximate cause* involves "that which, in a natural and continuous sequence, unbroken by any efficient intervening cause, produces injury, and without which the result would not have occurred" (Black's Law Dictionary, 5th ed., 1979, p. 1103). Proximate cause, therefore, is the event or behavior *but for* which the result would not have occurred. In most cases, proximate cause is implied if it was reasonably foreseeable that a first action or event would lead to the actual outcome, although one event or action could proximately cause a harm that was unforeseeable. Causation is also supported if the first action or event is a substantial factor leading to the actual outcome (Melton, Petrila, Poythress, & Slobogin, 2007).

Ackerman and Kane (1998) indicate that the cause need not be unique or exclusive for liability to be associated with it. For example, the event or behavior that was proximately causal may have either directly caused an injury or may have simply made an existing problem worse. However, "[t]he law of torts indicates that the tortfeasor is liable whether the stressor caused the injury or aggravated a preexisting condition" (p. 578).

Damages

The legal definition of "damages" refers to the compensation received by the plaintiff. Koocher (1998, p. 510) defines damages as "[m]oney received through judicial order by a plaintiff sustaining harm, impairment, or loss to his or her person or property as the result of the accidental, intentional, or negligent act of another." Damages may include compensation for "past and future loss of earning capacity, past and future medical and other care costs, as well as past and future pain and suffering" (Douglas, Huss, Murdoch, Washington, & Koch. et al., 1999). *Punitive damages* may be assessed to punish the defendant if the defendant's conduct was "outrageous or recklessly indifferent to the interests of the claimant" (Melton et al., 2007, p. 410).

"Traumatic" vs. "Tortious"

Throughout this book, we will use the terms "traumatic" or "allegedly traumatic" to refer to the events that are alleged to have been the cause of the psychological harm. Some authors would prefer the term "tortious," but we believe the variations on "traumatic" to be better in this context. Generally, the definition of "traumatic" typically refers to any event that places serious stress, shock, or injury to the body; similarly, emotional trauma includes an event that creates substantial emotional distress, psychological pain, or (especially in children) disruption to psychological development. Thus, for our purposes, any event that is deemed to be the cause of psychological harm is presumptively traumatic.

General vs. Specific Causation

Courts usually distinguish between *general* and *specific causation* in cases involving medical or psychological issues. The former refers to the question of whether a substance, material or event can cause a physical disorder (e.g., cancer.) The latter refers to whether the alleged causal agent produced a specific disorder in a specific person. According to Faigman and Monahan (2005), the parallel in psychology would be in terms of "social authority, social facts, and social frameworks" (p. 648). The first is analogous to a legal precedent, but in the form of prior research. Examples would include psychological research that bears on major social questions presented to the courts—for example, abortion, segregation, or whether juveniles should be subject to the death penalty, all issues on which the United States Supreme Court has ruled, in part based on the social authority of the research. The second, social facts, would be in the form of specific facts relevant to a case (e.g., the results of a survey commissioned for that case). One area in which this has been relevant is in determining whether the average person would find that a specific work, taken as a whole, appeals to prurient interests in obscenity cases. Forensic mental health experts also address issues of mental illness, competencies, risk of violence, and so forth. The last, social frameworks, would be a combination of the two—that is, social facts that are alleged to be specific examples of social authorities. Examples include a "battered woman syndrome" or "rape trauma syndrome," each of which entails both a general component (social authority) and a specific component (whether the alleged syndrome category applies to a specific individual in the instant case).

Summary Judgment

Federal Rule of Civil Procedure 56 and state equivalents address "summary judgment." A motion for summary judgment requests that the court consider the evidence admitted up to the point at which the motion for summary judgment is made (e.g., affidavits, statements under oath during depositions, responses to interrogatories). Under Federal Rule of Civil Procedure 56(C), the party moving for summary judgment must allege "that there is no genuine issue as to any material fact and that the moving party is entitled to a judgment as a matter of law." In other words, even if all of the factual allegations of the opposing party were true, the moving party would still prevail. Potential bases for a summary judgment include proof that the plaintiff signed a legally binding document preventing the plaintiff from suing the defendant; that a given defendant was not involved in the accident that caused the plaintiff's injury; or that the expert evidence offered by the plaintiff so seriously violated the *Daubert* (1993) requirements that the expert would not be permitted to testify in the trial, leaving the plaintiff without an expert. *Daubert* itself was initially decided by the trial court on the last basis, that is, that the evidence offered by eight well-credentialed experts for the plaintiff "did not meet the applicable [*Frye v. United States*, 1923] 'general acceptance' standard for the admission of expert testimony" (*Daubert*, p. 509).

Standards for Testimony: *Daubert, Frye,* and *Mohan*

For many years, the dominant standard for admitting expert testimony in American courts was *Frye v. United States* (1923). *Frye* required that "the thing from which the deduction is made must be sufficiently established to have gained general acceptance in the particular field in which it belongs" (p. 1014).

As indicated in the first book in this series (Heilbrun, Grisso & Goldstein, 2009), the U.S. Supreme Court indicated that the Federal Rules of Evidence (most-recent version, December 1, 2009) had superseded *Frye* in its ruling in *Daubert v. Merrell Dow Pharmaceuticals* (1993). The Supreme Court also specified a number of criteria that might be used by trial courts to assess the reliability (i.e., "trustworthiness," *Daubert*, 1993, footnote 9) of expert testimony. The Court emphasized that "[a]ll relevant evidence is admissible" (p. 587), specifically required that an "expert's testimony pertain to 'scientific knowledge'" (p. 590), and that expert testimony must "assist the trier of fact to understand or determine a fact in issue" (p. 592), among other possible requirements. In *Kumho Tire Co. v. Carmichael* (1999, p. 137), the Supreme Court "noted that *Daubert* discussed four factors — testing, peer review, error rates, and "acceptability" in the relevant scientific community — which

CASE LAW

Frye v. United States (1923)
The Court held that expert opinion based on a scientific technique is admissible only where the technique is generally accepted in the relevant scientific community.

Daubert v. Merrell Dow Pharmaceuticals (1993)
The Court ruled that judges be given the role of "gatekeeper," using a number of criteria (e.g., testing, peer review, error rate, and underlying science) to determine admissibility of expert testimony.

might prove helpful in determining the reliability of a particular scientific theory or technique." Specifically:

(1) "whether it can be and has been tested... [and] can be falsified;"

(2) whether the "theory or technique has been subjected to peer review and publication;"

(3) that consideration be given to the "known or potential rate of error;" and

(4) that there is "general acceptance of the particular technique within the scientific community."
[*Daubert*, 1993, pp. 593–594]

Many states have adopted the criteria from *Daubert* and its progeny by statute or case law, some have adopted portions of it, some continue to adhere primarily to *Frye*, and some have their own distinct criteria for expert testimony. The expert is obligated to know what the criteria are in any jurisdiction in which he or she testifies.

The Supreme Court remanded *Daubert* to the Ninth Circuit Court of Appeals, which indicated, in *Daubert v. Merrell Dow Pharmaceuticals, Inc.*, (1995), a number of additional criteria that might be applied to expert testimony.

Frye was often criticized as being too conservative and too arbitrary, leading to novel evidence being excluded while permitting unreliable evidence to be admitted simply because it was generally accepted (Melton et al., 2007). The Supreme Court indicated that the Federal Rules of Evidence "displaced" Frye, replacing it with the "liberal thrust" of the Federal Rules and their "general approach of relaxing the traditional barriers to 'opinion' testimony [*Daubert*,

INFO

The Daubert standard replaced the Frye standard at the federal level, but states are free to choose either, or a combination of both, or another method, to determine the standard for admissibility of testimony. It is your responsibility to know what criteria are used in the jurisdiction in which you are testifying.

1993, p.588]. Indeed, the Supreme Court's ruling in *General Electric Co. v. Joiner* (1997) ensured that trial judges would have wide discretion in the application of the *Daubert* standard (Dvoskin & Guy, 2008).

As a result of the combined influence of *Daubert, Joiner* and *Kumho*, Rule 702 of the Federal Rules of Evidence was amended in 2000 to read:

> Testimony by Experts: If scientific, technical, or other specialized knowledge will assist the trier of fact to understand the evidence or to determine a fact in issue, a witness qualified as an expert by knowledge, skill, experience, training, or education, may testify thereto in the form of an opinion or otherwise, if (1) the testimony is based upon sufficient facts or data, (2) the testimony is the product of reliable principles and methods, and (3) the witness has applied the principles and methods reliably to the facts of the case. [Underlined portion was added to the old Rule 702.]

To the factors specified by the Supreme Court in *Daubert*, the Advisory Committee on the Federal Rules of Evidence (2000) added five additional suggested areas of consideration based on court rulings after *Daubert*:

(1) Whether experts are "proposing to testify about matters growing naturally and directly out of research they have conducted independent of the litigation, or whether they have developed their opinions expressly for purposes of testifying." *Daubert v. Merrell Dow Pharmaceuticals, Inc.,* (9th Cir., 1995, p. 1317).

(2) Whether the expert has unjustifiably extrapolated from an accepted premise to an unfounded conclusion.

(3) Whether the expert has adequately accounted for obvious alternative explanations.

(4) Whether the expert "is being as careful as he would be in his regular professional work outside his paid litigation consulting." *Sheehan v. Daily Racing Form, Inc.,* (7th Cir., 1997, p. 942).

(5) Whether the field of expertise claimed by the expert is known to reach reliable results for the type of opinion the expert would give.

It should be noted that the Supreme Court, in *Barefoot v. Estelle* (1983), ruled that the testimony of a psychiatrist on the basis of clinical experience was admissible, because "the rules of evidence generally extant at the federal and state levels anticipate that relevant, unprivileged evidence should be admitted and its weight left to the fact finder, who would have the benefit of cross-examination and contrary evidence by the opposing party" (p. 898). Sales and Shuman (2005) suggested that a Texas federal court decision provides criteria that could be used in a *Daubert* analysis of clinical testimony [*Antoine-Tubbs v. Local 513 Air Transp. Div.* (N.D. Texas, 1998]:

(1) personal examination of the plaintiff by the doctor;

(2) personally taking a detailed medical history from the plaintiff;

(3) using differential diagnosis and etiology;

(4) reviewing tests, reports and opinions of other doctors;

(5) reviewing other facts or data reasonably relied on by medical experts in forming opinions or inferences as to medical causation;

(6) reference to medical literature; and

(7) utilizing the doctor's training and experience.

Similarly, a forensic mental health expert would be expected to do a personal examination, take a detailed history, construct a differential diagnosis, review tests, reports and opinions of relevant clinicians, review information reasonably relied upon by psychological experts in assessing causation, referring to the psychological and medical literature, and utilizing the expert's training and experience.

The Supreme Court made it clear in *Daubert* and its two progeny [*General Electric Company v. Joiner* (1997) and *Kumho Tire Co. v. Carmichael* (1999)] that trial court judges are to exercise their gatekeeping functions. It should be noted, though, that trial judges are not required to question expert testimony. It is up to attorneys to bring *motions in limine* [i.e., a motion to exclude "matters which are irrelevant, inadmissible and prejudicial" (*Black's Law Dictionary*, 1979, p. 914)] if they wish to have proposed testimony excluded, or to address the proposed testimony during trial testimony. Finally, it should be noted that the Supreme Court of Canada, in *R. v. Mohan* (1994), indicated that trial judges are to act as gatekeepers for expert evidence, that evidence be relevant, that experts are to assist the trier of fact in understanding the issues and evidence, and that experts must have specialized knowledge.

Put simply, courts applying *Daubert* are encouraged to ask two questions of experts: "Why should we believe you?" and "Why should we care?" The first speaks to the credibility, reliability, and validity of experts' opinions and the facts and logic upon which they are based. The second addresses the need for the expert to identify the relevance of the opinions to be offered to the specific questions at bar. Consistent with long traditions of Anglo-American law, this probative value must then be weighed against any prejudicial effects of the opinions to be offered (Dvoskin & Guy, 2008).

We would advise forensic experts to base their testimony on both the prevailing standards of their jurisdictions and on broader bases such as research published in peer-reviewed journals. Experts should note, however, that the Supreme Court commented in *Kumho* on the potential for some of the best research to be found in non-peer-reviewed journals, so such journals should not be excluded from the expert's search of the professional literature. The same is true of books, monographs, government reports, and so forth. Experts should also be aware of evidence that peer review is a flawed assumption of trustworthiness, despite its prominent place in the Supreme Court decisions (Kane, 2007c). *Peer review* should not be taken as incontrovertible evidence of validity or reliability. Peer review probably improves the accuracy of most published articles, but peer review offers no guarantee of trustworthiness. Peer review is also better than no peer review — though even "non-peer reviewed" articles are very often informally peer reviewed by one's colleagues, and many non-peer reviewed articles contain valid, reliable, and useful information. The "best practice" is to critically evaluate every source, not to uncritically assume that any source is trustworthy, even if formally peer reviewed, and regardless of how prestigious the journal. Experts should also be familiar

BEST PRACTICE

Do not automatically exclude non-peer reviewed journals or books from your search of the professional literature. Often, articles in these journals contain valid, reliable, and useful information.

with the Federal Rules of Evidence, even if they do not testify in federal courts and if the states in which they testify do not follow the Federal Rules. An expert whose work and testimony meets the standards of the Federal Rules is likely to do well in meeting the standards of his or her own jurisdiction(s).

Workers' Compensation versus Tort Litigation

Torts involve allegations of civil wrongs that are presented to juries (in most cases) for a determination as to whether there was a duty, the duty was breached, the breach was the proximate cause of an injury, and the plaintiff should receive damages for his or her suffering. Such litigation is guided by the Federal Rules of Evidence or their state equivalents.

However, in many states, if the allegation of injury involves a work-related incident or accident, the adjudication may take place in an administrative setting (e.g., workers' compensation cases) rather than a civil court (Shuman, 2005). In such cases, the trier of fact is generally an administrative law judge, and many of the rules of evidence are suspended to facilitate the efficiency of the process. Juries are rarely involved. Because the decision-maker is likely to be familiar with the types of compensable injuries, expert testimony may be more limited than in civil court litigation, and it may be presented in written form rather than through testimony. Expert testimony substantiating a claim is generally required, however. Several issues are the same as in a tort case, including whether there is a psychological injury and, if so, whether it can be attributed to the incident in the workplace (Walfish, 2006).

However, there may be no requirement of negligence or breach of a duty, so long as the injury was work-related.

Craig (2005) discussed workers' compensation injuries in three categories of interest to mental health experts: (1) *physical-mental* injuries, in which a physical injury is exacerbated by psychological factors; (2) *mental-physical* injuries, in which extreme psychological stress or another psychological factor causes physical difficulties; or (3) *mental-mental* injuries, in which both the injury and the response to it are exclusively psychological. In the first type, the presence of a physical injury gives credibility to the psychological injury (Melton et al., 2007). In the second, the credibility of the mental component is enhanced by the subsequent physical injury—for example, when fright leads to a heart attack, or when physical injuries result from a sudden or long-term stressor (Melton et al.). The third category, lacking a major physical component, is compensable in most jurisdictions, but not all. It may involve either intentional or negligent infliction of emotional distress (Melton et al.). Stress must be exceptional in order for many jurisdictions to permit compensation, and some will permit compensation only if the stressor was sudden as well (Melton et al.). The third category may involve either intentional or negligent infliction of emotional distress (Melton et al.), and generally is more difficult to prove.

The expert may be a treating professional or an independent psychologist or psychiatrist retained specifically for the evaluation. Causality must be established between the accident and the worker's injury, but, as noted earlier, there need not be a finding of fault. There is also generally a significant limit on damages for psychological or emotional injuries. Most administrative law courts permit recovery for psychological or emotional injuries without requiring an additional physical cause, but they require more than the ordinary stress of the workplace before awarding damages (Melton et al., 2007). Because research indicates that psychological problems may impede recovery from physical harm, psychological services may be authorized as part of the treatment (Walfish, 2006). Experts may generally express conclusions about the degree of disability or harm in probabilities rather than asserting that the injury is more likely than not ("reasonable medical/ psychological certainty") because many states do not require proof that an employment-related injury is the only cause of the psychological or emotional injury.

INFO

Workers' comp injuries fall into one of the following four categories

- Physical only

- Physical-mental injuries

- Mental-physical injuries

- Mental-mental injuries

1
chapter

Process of a Case

A personal injury claim may be filed whenever an individual (a plaintiff) has been injured, or feels injured, by the behavior (action or failure to act) of another individual or entity (the defendant), provided that the plaintiff can assert that the defendant owed a duty to the plaintiff, that the defendant breached that duty, that the plaintiff was injured as a result, that the defendant's action or behavior was the proximate cause of the plaintiff's injury, and that the plaintiff suffered as a result of the defendant's action or failure to act. The plaintiff typically retains an attorney to file the case and to ensure that the many required legal steps are followed.

Most personal injury cases are filed in state courts, some in federal courts. Depending on the nature of the case, the location of the defendant (in the same state, out-of-state, or both), and other factors, the case will be filed in the appropriate state or federal trial court. There are statutes of limitations on most cases, typically two or three years from the date of the alleged tort. However, there are many variations. In most jurisdictions, the statute of limitations period begins when the plaintiff discovers the injury, which may be significantly after the traumatic behavior if the plaintiff suffers from a delayed Posttraumatic Stress Disorder. In cases of sexual misconduct by professionals (e.g., therapists, clergy, physicians), the plaintiff may not associate his or her psychological problems with the sexual misconduct until years after the last sexual contact. In some jurisdictions, the statute of limitations period does not begin until a minor reaches the age of majority, typically 18 (Daller, 2009). These complexities make it essential in nearly every case for the plaintiff to have an attorney.

The plaintiff's attorney will generally investigate the case to determine that a tort in fact exists, and that statutes and case law support bringing the personal injury suit. Since attorneys normally take personal injury cases on a contingency basis, they don't want to invest a great deal of time or money in a case with minimal likelihood of success. If there is an issue of psychological damages and/or professional negligence, the attorney may retain a psychologist or other mental health professional as a consultant. Professionals retained as consultants work under the attorney-client privilege, meaning that all information is privileged – unless the expert testimony is introduced as part of the claim, in which case the information ceases to be confidential and the consultant could be deposed, called to testify, or both.

Forensic mental health experts may be retained by attorneys in one of two roles: (1) as a potential testifying expert; or (2) as a part of the advocacy team, with a goal of winning the case, but without a plan for the expert to testify. Because expert psychological witnesses have an ethical duty to strive for objectivity, it is generally inappropriate to move from the second category (advocacy/consulting role) to a testifying role. Expert witnesses have a duty to accurately inform the trier of fact, whether it helps or hurts their client's chances to win at trial. Early on, a forensic mental health expert might be asked to consult with either attorney regarding the validity of the plaintiff's claim. In the case of plaintiff's potential attorney, this consultation might occur even before the attorney accepts the plaintiff as a client. However, experts must always be very careful to maintain their objectivity unless and until it is decided that they will not testify.

If the case is accepted by the attorney, and it passes muster in the attorney's investigation, the plaintiff's case is filed in court and the defendant is served with the complaint, a list of the allegations in the case. Each side then requests information from the other side, to investigate the evidence and witnesses that may be utilized at trial, a process known as pre-trial discovery. There will typically be questions posed in writing (interrogatories) and requests for documents believed to be relevant to the case. The plaintiff's medical (including psychotherapy) records are likely to be requested, as well as work, financial, and other records. The defense may seek to have the plaintiff examined by its own psychologist or physician. The plaintiff, defendant, and other potential witnesses may be deposed, as each side seeks, and has a right to learn, what evidence the other side is potentially going to present at trial. The discovery process typically takes at least a number of months, and it is not exceptional for it to take years.

BEWARE It is unethical to go from a advocacy/consulting role, where you work together with the plaintiff's legal team to try to win the case, to a testifying expert role, which requires you to strive for impartiality and objectivity.

Once discovery is complete, there may be settlement discussions, or mediation, to try to avoid a trial. The vast majority of cases are settled prior to trial. Those that are not proceed to trial, either before a judge or (in most cases) both a judge and jury.

Professional Negligence Cases and Experts' Immunity

If there is an allegation of negligence by a professional (e.g., psychologist, physician, engineer), the professional's conduct will be considered using two sets of standards: the *standard of practice* and the *standard of care*. According to Heilbrun, DeMatteo, Marczyk and Goldstein (2008),

> Standards of care are judicial determinations that establish minimally acceptable standards of professional conduct in the context of specific disputes (American Law Institute, 1965). By contrast, standards of practice are generally defined either as the customary way of doing things in a particular field (the "industry standard")

or as aspirational "best practices" in a particular field (Caldwell & Seamone, 2007). Second, standards of practice are internally established by the field itself. This can occur informally, for instance, when a particular practice becomes 'adopted' as the customary way of doing things. It can also occur more formally, for example, through development of practice guidelines applicable to practitioners in the specific field, such as the "Specialty Guidelines for Forensic Psychologists" (Committee on Ethical Guidelines for Forensic Psychologists, 1991, pp. 2–3.)

Standards of care may have a basis in statute or administrative code, and adherence is mandatory. Standards of practice, in contrast, are generally aspirational rather than required. Failing to adhere to a standard of care is considered negligence, making the professional liable to malpractice claims. Failing to adhere to a standard of practice does not automatically open the professional to legal liability, but may cause the professional to be sanctioned by an ethics committee or a state licensing board (Heilbrun et al., 2008). Violations of a standard of practice, e.g., the *Ethical Principles of Psychologists and Code of Conduct* (American Psychological Association, 2002) may be raised as an issue in a malpractice case. However, what the judge (or jury) must decide in malpractice litigation is whether the defendant has violated the standard of care. This decision may be informed by evidence on standard of practice, either concerning the existing standards of practice in the field or the defendant's history of standards of practice violations. It should also be noted that a number of states have adopted the APA ethics code by reference in statute or administrative code or by case law, making adherence mandatory under the standard of care. A number of states have criminal statutes that address sexual misconduct by psychotherapists, indicating that it is automatically a breach of the standard of care, and prescribing criminal penalties (see, for example, Wisconsin statute 940.22)(2), making sexual misconduct a Class F felony). It is not unusual for a professional convicted of violation of the standard of care regarding sexual contact with a patient or client to have to also face a malpractice suit involving the same issue.

Shuman and Greenberg (2003) suggest that experts often receive pressure from retaining attorneys to conclude, and to state in testimony, that the data accumulated by the expert and the conclusions based on that data support the attorney's theory of the case. The psychologist must resist this pressure, remaining impartial and advocating for his or her data, not for the retaining attorney, as required by professional ethics and the *Specialty Guidelines for Forensic Psychologists* (1991). All witnesses, including experts, are to assist the fact finder, not any party (Saks & Lanyon, 2007). A possible area of confusion for psychologists is that few statutes or adminstrative codes specify whether expert testimony is included under the specified areas of "the practice of psychology" (Cohen, 2004). Psychologists should determine, for each jurisdiction in which they intend to testify, whether testimony is part of the practice of psychology in that jurisdiction, in part to ensure that they are not breaching statutory or administrative code requirements for the practice of psychology if they are practicing in a jurisdiction in which they are not licensed.

It should also be noted that the Washington Supreme Court, in *Deatherage v. Washington Examining Board of Psychology* (1997), held that a psychologist did not have immunity from discipline by the state's psychology licensing board for failure to qualify statements made in child custody evaluations, failing to verify information, mischaracterizing information, and misinterpreting test data (Cohen, 2004; Ewing, 2003). Similarly, neurosurgeon Gary Lustgarten's license was suspended for one year by the North Carolina Medical Board in 2002 because of his testimony in a medical malpractice suit. The Board held that Dr. Lustgarten misstated facts and the appropriate standard of care, thereby constituting unprofessional conduct (North Carolina Medical Board Web site, http://glsuite.ncmedboard.org/DataTier/Documents/Repository/LegacyImages/00/01/07/00010779.tif, retrieved October 13, 2005). Lustgarten appealed to a Superior Court, which affirmed the Board's action in 2003 (http://www.ncmedboard.org/images/uploads/disciplinary_reports/ba43.pdf, retrieved September 20, 2009).

Further, although witness and/or quasi-judicial immunity prevents civil

BEWARE
Never agree to an attorney's request to only present evidence and conclusions that support his or her case. You must always remain impartial and objective.

lawsuits against experts by nearly anyone, a few courts have permitted litigants to sue their own experts for malpractice, alleging that the expert was negligent and/or practiced below the minimum standard for his or her profession (Cohen, 2004; Ewing, 2003; Goldstein, 2007). In *Howard v. Drapkin*, (1990) and *Susan A. v. County of Sonoma*, (1991), California courts of appeal indicated that quasi-judicial immunity was based upon the expert's being retained as an independent, neutral party, and may not apply if the expert is retained by only one side, even though the expert's actual testimony is protected by witness immunity and quasi-judicial or judicial immunity (Weinstock & Garrick, 1995). Other than these types of examples, a perjury prosecution is the only potentially viable legal solution if an expert makes statements shown to be untrue. However, according to the Illinois Supreme Court, "It is virtually impossible to prosecute an expert witness for perjury" (*Sears v. Rutishauser*, 1984).

Malpractice litigation proceeds on the same basis as other torts. It must be established that the professional owed a duty to his or her patient or client, that the duty was breached, that the patient or client was injured as a direct result of the breach, and that the patient or client is due damages as compensation for the injuries suffered. Although expert testimony is possible in most personal injury cases, in malpractice cases it is very likely, since the expert's testimony helps establish the standards of practice that are relevant to the standard of care at issue. That is, "the plaintiff must prove through expert testimony that the care or skill exercised by a defendant physician was inferior to that exercised by comparable professionals in the community" (Slovenko, 1988, p. 353).

The Expert's Duty

Experts generally owe legal duties to the court, the retaining attorney, and third parties, with each involving a professional duty as well. The duty to the court, in essence the standard of care, includes the offering of testimony that is reliable, helpful, honest, and objective. The professional and ethical duty, more akin to the standard of practice, is to strive to provide assistance to the fact finder in a way that is consistent with the field's articulation of the components of good practice.

When testifying, experts will take an oath to tell "the truth, the whole truth, and nothing but the truth." While the retaining attorney has the right to decide which questions to ask of an expert, the expert's legal and ethical obligation is to present opinions fairly and with sufficient foundation, and to resist any attempt to distort, misrepresent, or leave out information that may be contrary to the position of the retaining attorney.

Of course, absolute objectivity is impossible to achieve, as every expert brings certain biases to each case. Instead of pretending to be free of bias, experts should take steps to correct for bias so as to maximize their objectivity. These steps include (a) transparency, or showing one's work; (b) humbly acknowledging the limitation's of one's expertise; (c) inclusion of contrary findings or authorities; (d) seeking consultation; and (e) a willingness to admit when one does not know the answer to a question (Dvoskin, 2007). See the section on *biases* in Chapter 4.

A therapist may testify in the role of a "treating expert." The treating expert may not, however, function as an independent witness, because he or she owes a duty to the patient as well as to the court and professional standards. The treating expert is ethically required to be primarily a fact witness, unless there are extenuating circumstances. See pp. 85-91 of the first book of this series (Heilbrun et al., 2009) for extensive discussion of the differences between clinical and forensic roles.

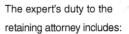

INFO

The expert's duty to the retaining attorney includes:

- Clear articulation of the referral questions; i.e., what the expert will likely be asked on direct examination at trial

- Accurate and careful review of relevant facts

- Formulation and clear articulation of opinions

- Clear articulation of the (especially evidentiary) foundation and limitations of each opinion

- Performing his or her duties at the level of the standard of practice, aiming for best practices.

A recent decision of the Fifth Circuit Court of Appeals (*U.S. v. Cooks*, 2009) addressed the difference between lay and expert witnesses in a criminal case, but the decision should be applicable in personal injury cases as well. The Court indicated that, "[b]efore a district court may allow a witness to testify as an expert, it must be assured that the proffered witness is qualified to testify by virtue of his 'knowledge, skill, experience, training or education.' Fed. R. Evid. 702...."

If the witness is only testifying as a lay witness, the witness's testimony in the form of opinions or inferences is limited to those opinions or inferences which are (a) rationally based on the perception of the witness, (b) helpful to a clear understanding of the witness' testimony or the determination of a fact in issue, and (c) not based on scientific, technical, or other specialized knowledge within the scope of rule 702. Fed. R. Evid. 701. "[T]he distinction between lay and expert witness testimony is that lay testimony results from a process of reasoning familiar in everyday life, while expert testimony results from a process of reasoning which can be mastered only by specialists in the field." [citation omitted] Moreover, any part of a witness's opinion that rests on scientific, technical, or specialized knowledge must be determined by reference to Rule 702, not Rule 701. Fed. R. Evid. 701 advisory committee's note. [pp. 4–5]

At least for federal trial courts under the Fifth Circuit, this would appear to make much, if not all, of therapists' testimony expert testimony (e.g., diagnosis, prognosis, or etiology), since it is based upon the "knowledge, skill, experience, training or education" of the therapist. This poses a likely ethical dilemma for therapists who are psychologists, as discussed in Heilbrun et al. (2009), given that therapists have not assumed a forensic role when conducting therapy and are therefore not prepared to provide the kind of data and conclusions that can only flow from a forensic evaluation. Until this dilemma is resolved by the courts, our advice is to clearly label each and every response as fact or opinion, and to explicitly list its limitations, to allow the court to make a determination regarding which rules apply. More importantly, if the mental health professional has not conducted the inquiry that would be required in order to adequately form and support a forensic opinion, then it is often the best course to simply say so. In other words, when asked if he or she has an opinion on the forensic question, the answer might very well be "no."

Learned Treatises

Federal Rule of Evidence 803(18) defines "learned treatises" as "statements contained in published treatises, periodicals, or pamphlets on a subject of history, medicine, or other science or art, established as a reliable authority by the testimony or admission of the witness or by other expert testimony or by judicial notice. If admitted, the statements may be read into evidence but may not be received as exhibits...."

Learned treatises are expected to be trustworthy because professionals with knowledge, training and skills have written them with the intent of having other professionals read and rely on them. Because other professionals will point out inaccurate information, and because professionals want their writings to be accepted in the professional community, it is expected that they will strive for accuracy and trustworthiness (Kirkpatrick & Mueller, 2003). *Daubert* indicates that peer review is of special value, though peer review is not a guarantee of quality, and many articles in non-peer-reviewed sources are of high quality (Kane, 2007c). Most professionals also have colleagues informally review their articles for accuracy and readability. As discussed previously, formal peer review is desirable, but the emphasis should be on the quality of the publication.

Experts must have great familiarity with the professional literature in the areas covered by a specific case, including books and professional journals that address issues in the case (Goldstein, 2007). It is that literature that provides the nomothetic (population) data upon which the expert depends for a comparison with the idiographic (individual) data from the assessment he or she conducts of the plaintiff. Both codes of ethics and forensic guidelines require experts to have this familiarity, and courts understandably expect experts to *be* expert in the areas in which they testify in order to assist the trier of fact.

Conclusion

In this chapter, we have explained the fundamental components of tort law, explained theories of duty, causation, and damages, and discussed the nature and admissibility of psychological expert testimony, and the duties owed by a testifying expert to the court. We now turn, in chapter 2, to the roles and duties of a psychological expert, the common threats to the objectivity and competence that is required of testifying experts, and how to guard against these threats.

Forensic Mental Health Assessment Concepts | 2

Heilbrun et al. (2009) discuss forensic mental health assessment concepts at great length in the first book in this series. The following discussion will, therefore, be relatively brief.

Heilbrun (2001), Heilbrun et al. (2002), Heilbrun et al. (2003), Heilbrun, Marczyk, DeMatteo and Mack-Allen (2007) and Heilbrun et al. (2009) discuss at length principles of Forensic Mental Health Assessment (FMHA) that deal with causality, a central issue in personal injury evaluations. They note that human behavior is multidimensional, and that numerous sources of information should be utilized in order to fully assess an individual. Similarly, Schultz (2003b) and Young, Kane & Nicholson (2007) emphasize the need for integration of a multifactorial process of determining causality.

Heilbrun and his co-authors emphasize the need to address functional abilities, and to place them in the context of *nomothetic (group) evidence*—that is, evidence empirically derived from (usually large) populations that are similar to that of the plaintiff. Methods utilized must be both valid and reliable, including use of psychological instruments appropriate for the population and the individual being assessed. Nomothetic data are scientifically and empirically based upon questionnaires and tests with forensic value, as well as on base rates and outcome data. It furnishes normative data on the performance of groups in various areas, providing the basis for making assertions regarding the functioning and impairment, if any, of an individual. Further, population-level research addresses the prediction of outcomes, suggesting how specific interventions may assist with the management of the course of symptoms.

This is contrasted with *idiographic evidence*, which addresses information collected regarding a specific individual who is being assessed, usually the plaintiff. The assessment of the individual should resemble a scientific study, producing the simplest explanation for the data collected that accounts for all of the essential variables in the case. The forensic mental health evaluator then proceeds to address all reasonably likely explanations for the data assembled in order to arrive at conclusions that make scientific sense. This usually includes addressing the individual's personal and psychosocial history, his or her functional capacities prior to and following the allegedly traumatic event or events, and the individual's response style and the possibility that the person may be exaggerating, feigning, or otherwise malingering. Greenberg (2003) noted that most individuals will exaggerate their difficulties to some degree, and that the evaluator should not assume that this is an indication of malingering.

There is some key terminology that must be addressed.

- "Exaggeration" may be either conscious or unconscious. As used here, it suggests relatively mild overstatement of problems that is within or outside of conscious awareness, with no psychodynamic meaning intended here or elsewhere in this book.

- "Feigning" is "the deliberate fabrication or gross exaggeration of psychological or physical symptoms without any assumptions about its goals" (Rogers, 2008a, p. 6). Psychological tests are able to demonstrate feigning, but not malingering (Rogers).

- "Malingering" is "the intentional production of false or grossly exaggerated physical or psychological symptoms, motivated by external incentives such as avoiding military duty, avoiding work, obtaining financial compensation, evading criminal prosecution, or obtaining drugs" (DSM-IV-TR, 2000, p. 739). The only unequivocal way to identify malingering is to have the individual admit to it, but there are various means of assessing malingering that permit a strong inferential statement to be made regarding its likelihood. Malingering, involving an attempt to consciously gain an external goal such as money, is discussed at length in Chapter 3. Further, even when there is clear evidence that symptoms have been exaggerated or feigned, it is important for the expert evaluator to consider the likely reasons. Finally, it is important to remember that the presence of malingering does not preclude the presence of real psychological distress or disability (Ackerman & Kane, 1998; Drob, Meehan & Waxman, 2009; Kane, 2007a; Rogers, 2008a).

2
chapter

More specifically, the FMHA in a personal injury context addresses (a) any mental disorders identified, (b) the legally-relevant functional abilities affected by the allegedly traumatic incident(s), and (c) the nature and strength of any causal connection between the allegedly traumatic event(s) and the resultant functional abilities of the plaintiff (Heilbrun, 2001; Vore, 2007). One must also operationalize legal requirements into psychological terms, so that the professional literature can be searched and an appropriate evaluation conducted. Schultz (2003b) suggests that best practices include: (1) applying a biopsychosocial model, (2) utilization of standardized procedures, (3) using numerous information sources, including standardized tests and other instruments and collateral sources, (4) comparing the individual with relevant group data and base rates, (5) considering iatragenic and litigation-related factors, and (6) comparison of current and premorbid levels of functioning. Caution must be exercised to ensure that one follows the data closely, attributing neither too much nor too little importance to the incident, accident, or allegedly tortious behavior (Faust & Heard, 2003b).

Expert Witness vs. Consultant

When serving as a consultant to attorneys, an expert may be retained for a number of reasons; for example, to help the attorney understand the psychological issues in a case, help the attorney decide whether or not to claim psychological damages, to review documents (including reports by other experts), to help the attorney prepare questions for experts on the other side of the case, or otherwise to help the attorney prepare for depositions and the trial. As long as there is no plan for the expert consultant to testify, he or she is typically bound by the attorney work product privilege, and may not reveal any aspect of the case to anyone other than the attorney or someone designated by the attorney without explicit instruction to the contrary by the retaining attorney or court order. The retaining attorney does not usually have to tell anyone that the consultant has been retained, and the consultant cannot ordinarily be called to testify in a deposition or trial. The primary exception is if the consultant has information that the opposing attorney cannot reasonably obtain from any other source, in which case the consultant may be required to release that information (Federal Rules of Civil Procedure, Rule 26 (b)(4)(B) (ii) or state equivalents, 2009).

The expert who is going to testify in a case should be capable of fulfilling the requirements proposed by Heilbrun et al. that

Opinions should be data based, including thorough consideration given to all sources of information: comprehensive notes of litigant's interview responses; results of all psychological tests and instruments; information provided by third parties; and a review of records. Relevant studies, published in peer review journals on issues related to the specific case should be considered as well. Findings should be examined for consistency within and between data sources.... Whenever possible, opinions should incorporate sources with established reliability, and with validity for purposes

INFO

Consulting experts may be retained by attorneys for a variety of reasons including

- To help the attorney understand the psychological issues of the case
- To help the attorney decide whether to seek psychological damages
- To review documents
- To help the attorney prepare questions for cross-examination of other experts
- To help the attorney prepare for deposition and trial

consistent with the present evaluation. Alternative opinions conflicting with the opinions reached should be considered, and rejected when they are less consistent with all of the information available to the expert (2009, p. 55).

A testifying expert should do a comprehensive, impartial evaluation using a biopsychosocial approach that considers all of the pertinent evidence, uses valid and reliable methods of assessment and interpretation, considers the professional literature in coming to conclusions, and proffers testimony that is relevant, reliable, and helpful to the trier of fact (Kane, 2007b).

Skills Needed by the Testifying Expert

In addition to the types of skills just discussed, the testifying expert must be good at explaining sometimes complicated information and subjects to the trier of fact in a manner that will assist with understanding. There is often an advantage if the expert is skilled in teaching or training, experienced in helping others understand information and issues. Romano and Romano (1993), the editors of *Trial Diplomacy Journal,* identified a number of other attributes that are often important: that the expert be articulate, credible, sincere, authoritative, correct, should use common sense, be wise, and be strong on cross-examination.

Potential Sources of Bias and Error

It is nearly impossible for anyone to avoid all sources of bias when conducting an assessment (Dvoskin, 2007). Being human, we each have some personal biases that must not be allowed to interfere. It is, therefore, essential that forensic experts be aware of potential sources of bias and try to ensure that none of them significantly interferes with one's assessments or testimony. According to Kane (2007c, pp. 332–333), one must be aware of the following kinds and sources of bias:

> *Anchoring bias* describes the tendency for information received early in the diagnostic process to be remembered better and used more than information received later in the

BEWARE
Take heed
of any personal bias or
preconceived notions that
may interfere with your
objectivity in a particular
case. Specifically,

● Anchoring bias

● Attribution bias

● Confirmation bias

● Conformity effects

● "Halo effect"

● Observer effects

● Overconfidence bias

process. If the clinician begins the evaluation by getting information about the traumatic event and the individual's response to it, this may bias the whole evaluation (Bowman, 2003; Risinger, Saks, Thompson, & Rosenthal, 2002).

Attribution bias involves "discounting contextual factors accounting for behavior and imputing it instead to a permanent characteristic of an individual" (Sageman, 2003, p. 325). For example, an individual may be aggressive in a situation in which he or she has been attacked, or passive in a situation in which he or she is fearful. In the other 99% of his or her life, however, neither is a common characteristic.

Confirmation bias refers to evaluators giving more weight to information that is consistent with their own beliefs. For example, a clinician who believed that no one could be psychologically unscathed by a serious motor vehicle accident, or being a soldier in active combat, or enduring some other major traumatic event, may selectively attend to information confirming that bias, and disregard contrary information. Because evaluators, like everyone else, have hypotheses and expectations, they must take great care not to let them color the results of an evaluation (Bowman, 2003; Risinger et al., 2002).

Conformity effects refer to "our tendency to conform to the perceptions, beliefs, and behavior of others" (Risinger et al., 2002, p. 20). The evaluator may have difficulty arguing against the theory of the attorney who has retained the expert, or against the findings of another expert whom the evaluator respects, regardless of the actual findings of the evaluator.

"Halo effect" refers to "the tendency for a general evaluation of a person, or an evaluation of a person on a specific dimension, to be used as a basis for judgments of that person on other specific dimensions" (*APA Concise Dictionary of Psychology*, 2009, p. 220).

Hindsight bias occurs when people who are aware of how an incident turns out believe that that outcome was more likely than objective prediction would indicate. Since both experts and juries generally know the end of the story, their attempt to objectively judge foreseeability may be compromised (Shuman, 1995a; Wayte, Samra, Robbennolt, Heuer, & Koch, 2002). Experts must make every effort to judge the decision and actions of various parties based solely on what the party knew or should have known at the time.

Observer effects refer to the fact that the thoughts, feelings, experiences, and expectations of people, including scientists, influence their perceptions and conclusions. It is well-documented that scientists make errors of various kinds (Allchin, 2008; Committee on Science, Engineering and Public Policy, 1995), including simple counting errors, when they have a conscious or unconscious reason to skew the data in a given direction (or even when there is no evident motivation for skewing the data). This is why double-blind research is important in any area of science in which observer effects may bias the results—provided it is possible in the given research project. It is essential in research on medications, but is often difficult or impossible in psychological research (Risinger et al., 2002).

Overconfidence bias results when the clinician feels certain of his or her conclusions and therefore assumes they are valid. Research, however, has found that confidence in and validity of conclusions are not well-correlated. Regardless of his or her level of confidence, the clinician must keep an open mind while examining all of the relevant data (Bowman, 2003).

In addition, there are a number of other errors an expert may make. According to Risinger (2002), one may misperceive an individual or situation, make errors when recording information, remember information incorrectly, and/or incorrectly interpret data when forming conclusions. The expert who is committed to performing an impartial evaluation will keep these biases and sources of error in mind, working to minimize their potential negative affect on the evaluation and testimony.

Requirement to Specify Causation if Possible

An expert who does not specify the likely cause(s) of impairment and disability may not be permitted to testify.

> Experts must do something more than just "rule out" other possible causes. They must explain how they were able to "rule in" the product [in a product liability case] in question. If all the expert does is rule out other possible causes, he or she may fail to account for other potential (and sometimes unknown or unthought of) causes. When an expert only rules out causes, the trier of fact knows only what did not cause the harm. This does not necessarily aid the trier of fact in determining what did cause the harm—and that is what the law requires in tort cases, especially those that involve allegedly toxic products. [*Siharath v. Sandoz Pharmaceuticals Corp*, 131 F. Supp.2d 1347 (N.D.Ga. 2001), pp. 1371–1372.]

It is, therefore, incumbent on the expert to try to identify probable causes of any psychopathology or psychological harm identified.

BEWARE
If you cannot specify the likely cause of the claimant's injury, you may not be permitted to testify if the case goes to court.

Conclusion

In Chapter 2 we have laid out the foundational expectations of competence and objectivity, and explained the common sources of bias and prejudice that can affect an expert. We now turn in Chapter 3 to the nature of psychological evidence and the difficulty in coming to sound conclusions when psychological harms are largely based on the plaintiff's subjective experience of distress.

2
chapter

Empirical Foundations and Limits | **3**

The purpose of an evaluation in a personal injury case is to ascertain *whether an individual has been psychologically injured by a traumatic event and, if so, to what extent.* Broadly speaking, if there is evidence of a psychological injury, there are five possibilities: (1) the event is the sole cause of the psychological injury (rarely the case); (2) the event was the primary cause of the psychological injury (that is, the proximate cause), and *but for* the traumatic event the person would not have his or her present level of psychopathology, disability, or other psychological distress (e.g., grief); (3) the traumatic event materially contributed to the assessed psychopathology or other psychological distress but was not the primary cause; (4) the traumatic event had little identifiable affect on the individual; or (5) the traumatic event had no identifiable affect on the individual (Ackerman & Kane, 1998; Melton et al., 2007; Young, 2007).

While there is no gold standard for conducting a personal injury evaluation, this section provides guidance on best practices. Each evaluation must be designed to comprehensively address the issues identified by the referral question(s) in a given case. There are, however, various models suggested by various authors (e.g., Greenberg, 2003; Grisso, 2003; Heilbrun, 2001; Melton et al., 2007; Wilson & Moran, 2004), any of which will provide a starting point for conducting an evaluation.

A comprehensive evaluation is necessary because the evaluator is comparing

INFO

The purpose of a psychological evaluation in a personal injury case is to determine whether an individual has been psychologically injured by a traumatic event and, if so, to what extent.

the individual's pre-trauma functioning with his or her post-trauma status. The issue is not the individual's current status, *per se*, but *the degree to which, and ways in which, the individual differs from how he or she was before the traumatic event.* Toward this end, the evaluator should consult multiple data sources, including records that address the individual's functioning prior to the trauma, to create a baseline against which post-trauma changes may be assessed (Faust & Heard, 2003a; Goldstein, 2003, 2007; Heilbrun et al., 2009; Kane, 2007b; Melton et al., 2007; Young & Kane, 2007). Records may include medical, psychotherapy, school, arrest, employment, military, personnel, pharmacy, tax, and any other records that may identify the individual's ability to function prior to and after the traumatic event. The changes identified may not have been caused by the traumatic event but, rather, by other major life events in the individual's life. At the very least, the records review should go back three to five years prior to the traumatic event. For many people, however, going further back will yield additional relevant information. Other information that may be of value includes evidence of lifestyle changes [e.g., through reviewing checkbook registers or credit card statements (Greenberg, 2003) and personal diaries (Heilbrun et al., 2003)]. Medication records may identify pharmacological effects that are part of the clinical picture. Depositions and other legal documents will provide a variety of potentially important data. In addition to providing important information about the plaintiff, the records provide independent information about the individual, which may be compared with information furnished by the individual in interviews, questionnaires, and tests, as well as objective information about the allegedly traumatic event(s) (Wilson & Moran, 2004).

INFO

The key factor in a personal injury case is the degree to which, and ways in which, an individual differs from the way he or she was prior to the allegedly traumatic event.

Attorneys may offer to give the expert summaries of records that the attorney has reviewed. This is no substitute for the expert's reading of the original records. The expert should request copies of all pertinent records, and should read them rather than relying on any summary or highlighting by the attorney (Hess, 2006). Because handwritten medical records are often barely legible and thus time-consuming to review, experts may ask a nurse or medical records technician to transcribe them into typewritten form. While this practice saves time and money and can improve accuracy, it is imperative for the expert to look closely at the original records, at least as they relate to relevant or probative pieces of data, to confirm that the transcription is accurate and complete.

The review of records is, in part, to generate questions and hypotheses that may be addressed in the direct assessment of the individual. Accordingly, the best practice is, ideally, to review all of the available records prior to conducting the evaluation. This is especially true if one is retained by the defense, since defense-retained experts frequently have only one opportunity to interview the plaintiff. Although other records may later come to light, by reading as many as possible of the relevant records prior to the interview, the expert (plaintiff or defense) is likely to be able to address most, if not all, of the relevant issues in the interview.

Contributing factors must also be considered. Social support, the individual's perception of support from his or her employer, and the individual's overall life satisfaction are likely to affect his or her level of adjustment (Koch, O'Neill & Douglas, 2005). These and other factors may be assessed through testing and interviews of the individual, collateral interviews, diaries, and questionnaires.

According to Heilbrun et al. (2009, p. 95),

[f]orensic assessment instruments are tools that have been developed specifically for use in litigation. They measure constructs that are central to specific legal questions and are used only in the context of that specific kind of litigation. Their validation is conducted with those in the population associated with this specific legal question [italics in original].

In contrast,

[c]linical assessment instruments are those developed for assessment, diagnosis, and treatment-planning in therapeutic contexts,

INFO

The MMPI-2 is the most frequently used assessment instrument in personal injury evaluations.

but do not measure constructs that are typically of central importance in forensic assessment. By contrast, *forensically relevant instruments* were developed in the same way, but address constructs that are more central in criminal and civil litigation (such as response style) and may have undergone additional validation with these populations [italics in original].

Although there are no forensic assessment instruments specific to personal injury evaluations, there are a number of instruments that are forensically relevant (see pp. 95–96 and elsewhere in the first volume in this series by Heilbrun et al., 2009). The most frequently used forensically-relevant instrument is the Minnesota Multiphasic Personality Inventory, Second Edition (MMPI-2, Butcher, Graham, Ben-Porath, Tellegen, Dahlstrom & Kaemmer, 1989), which has a substantial professional literature establishing patterns of responses associated with malingering, defensiveness, and numerous clinical factors that may be relevant to a specific personal injury evaluation (Butcher, 1995; Butcher & Miller, 2006; Goldstein, 2007; Pope, Butcher & Seelen, 2006). However, in using this or other psychological instruments, it is important for the expert to know the underlying research upon which inferences about the test are based.

Review of Relevant Research

Once the evaluator becomes aware of the nature of the alleged tort, it is incumbent on that expert to become extremely familiar with the state of the art of research in the particular area (Goldstein, 2007; Kane, 2007a;). The research gives the expert the nomothetic data describing the typical victim of a particular type of traumatic experience, addresses base rates of various disorders, and may suggest which specific psychological tests will be most relevant to the assessment of the particular case. Similarly, review of research on assessment instruments appropriate to a given type of case will help ensure that the assessment is relevant to understanding the plaintiff and what he or she experienced, and also help the evaluator form hypotheses regarding the case that can be tested out in the course of the assessment.

BEST PRACTICE
Once the referral question is clarified and confirmed, you must familiarize yourself with the relevant research, including group data, base rates, and appropriate assessment measures.

Clinical versus Actuarial Assessment

Psychologists have long debated the relative pros and cons of actuarial (statistical) vs. clinical assessment. Actuarial assessments are those that are statistically-based, involving the "use of data about prior instances, in order to estimate the likelihood or risk of a particular outcome" (APA Concise Dictionary of Psychology, p. 8), such as the MMPI-2, rather than such clinical methods as unstructured interviews and some projective methods. A third alternative, structured professional judgment (SPJ), utilizes standardized lists of questions that have been independently and empirically validated. The difference between actuarial and SPJ methods is that actuarial instruments require pre-assigned weights to each item, while SPJ instruments allow the evaluator to consider each item and weigh it according to the specifics of the instant case. Unfortunately, we do not know of any SPJ instrument for personal injury evaluations at this time. Research comparing actuarial and unstructured clinical assessments indicates that the actuarial method is better about half of the time, while there is no difference the other half of the time. "While these results provide no evidence for the superiority of clinical over actuarial approaches for any predictive task, they also do not provide a compelling consistent advantage for actuarial approaches" (Heilbrun, 2001, p. 126). Further, "[t]here is a 50+ year history of research comparing the accuracy of unstructured clinical judgment with actuarial approaches, with a consistent, modest advantage in predictive accuracy observed for the latter (Heilbrun, Yasuhara & Shah, 2010, p. 5). When a valid and reliable actuarial instrument is available and appropriate, it is good practice to use it. However, the

3
chapter

BEWARE ⚠️
There is little scientific support for unstructured, inferential clinical judgments standing alone. Be sure to tie your opinion to the evidence and logic on which it is based to the degree possible.

current state of the art also calls for clinical assessment methods to be used for a significant portion of a personal injury evaluation.

It is important to understand the difference between clinical interviews as one (among several) sources of information, as opposed to unstructured and unsupported clinical judgments. There are as yet very few actuarial instruments that will likely apply to the assessment of psychological injury, and none that we know of that speaks to the ultimate issues before the court. As a result, clinical interview is and will likely remain an important and acceptable method of gathering information, especially when combined with the other sources (e.g., collateral information, psychological tests) that we have described. However, unstructured clinical judgments have little empirical support. Thus, we recommend that each and every inferential opinion be explicitly tied to the evidence and logic upon which it is based. In other words, experts should not ask triers of fact to "take their word" for any opinion. By spelling out the evidence and logic upon which opinion is based, experts allow triers of fact to scrutinize, weigh, and evaluate the strength of the opinion for themselves.

Requirements for Correct Administration of Psychological Instruments

For a psychological test or other instrument to be valid and reliable, it must be correctly administered. Most tests and other instruments are developed under standardized conditions to address specific populations. To the degree that there is deviation from the standardized conditions or the population on which the test or other instrument was standardized, there is less reason to believe that the assessment will be valid.

Location

Tests, other assessment instruments, and interviews should be administered in an area that is free from distractions and relatively quiet. If this is not possible, the examiner must decide whether the conditions are acceptable (e.g., noise level not excessive, relative privacy) and proceed with the assessment only if the conditions

BEST PRACTICE
Always try to administer assessment measures and conduct interviews in a quiet environment, free of distractions.

are satisfactory. The report should include comments regarding any environmental factors that may have affected the results (Ackerman & Kane, 1998; Heilbrun, 2001; Kane, 2007b).

Third-Party Presence

Numerous observers have concluded that the individual being assessed should be alone with the examiner. Attorneys often want to be present during an assessment, or to have someone else present. However, assessment instruments are standardized with only the examiner present, and there is no research literature identifying the degree to which the results of a nonstandardized administration may alter the results of a particular instrument. This is also true with regard to audio- or video-recording. There is research indicating an adverse impact on the validity of some psychological tests when a third party is present or the assessment is recorded (Ackerman & Kane, 1998; Constantinou, Ashendorf, & McCaffrey, 2002; Constantinou & McCaffrey, 2003; Greiffenstein quoted in Heilbronner, 2005; Kehrer, Sanchez, Habif, Rosenbaum, & Townes, 2000; Lees-Haley quoted in Heilbronner, 2005; Lezak, Howieson, & Loring, 2004). There is no research, however, indicating that testing is as valid when a third party is present or the assessment is recorded as when it is not.

When it comes to interviews, the situation is less clear. Social facilitation research indicates that people's responses very often change when they know (or believe) that an interview is being observed or recorded (Barth, 2007; Bond, 2000; Gavett, Lynch & McCaffrey, 2005; McCaffrey, Lynch & Yantz, 2005;). The American Psychological Association Committee on Psychological Tests

BEST PRACTICE
It is best if only you and the individual being assessed are present. A third-party presence, such as an attorney, can adversely impact testing validity.

3
chapter

and Assessment (2007b) indicated that, "[b]ecause some examinees may be less likely to share personal information if the examinee believes that others are observing or could observe the examinee's actual statements or behavior..., the validity of non-standardized or non-test assessment procedures such as interviews or observations may also be affected by the perceived or actual presence of a third party.... [Also], [e]xaminees who are aware that their assessment is being recorded, either in audio only or in combined audio and video, may also alter their assessment behavior" (p. 2). On the other hand, the adversary process typically requires transparency— for example, to allow an opposing expert to comment upon the questions asked during an interview, or the manner in which the interview was conducted. For this reason, Pitt, Spiers, Dietz and Dvoskin (1999) have argued for preserving the interview on audio- or video-tape whenever possible. Further, unlike most psychological tests, psychological interviews are typically unstructured, allowing for vast individual differences in style and content, including, for example, whether the examiner has asked leading questions. Absent an observer or recording of the interview, there is no way for opposing counsel or their expert witnesses to comment upon the interview.

The U.S. Supreme Court did not differentiate between interviews and psychological tests—they are lumped together as "evaluations"—in addressing this issue. In *Estelle v. Smith* (451 U.S. 454, 470, n. 14, 1981) the Supreme Court held that the physical presence of an attorney during an evaluation "could contribute little and might seriously disrupt the examination."

INFO

There are advantages and disadvantages of using audio tape or video tape for your interview with the claimant. Transparency calls for taping, while the social facilitation research indicates that taping may adversely affect the validity of the data acquired.

A number of lower court cases have also ruled that the presence of a third party, including audio- or video-taping of a psychological evaluation, is not appropriate. For example, in *Shirsat v. Mutual Pharmaceutical Co.* (169 F.R.D. 68,

p. 70, E.D. Pa. 1996), the court found that "an observer, court reporter, or recording device, would constitute a distraction during the examination and work to diminish the accuracy of the process." In *Tomlin v. Holocek* (1993), the court ruled that "to require a recording of Dr. Aletsky's interview would potentiate toward invalidating her evaluatory technique" (p. 631), and that "the presence of third parties would lend a degree of artificiality to the interview technique which would be inconsistent with applicable, professional standards" (p. 632). In *Hertenstein v. Kimberly Home Health Care, Inc.* (1999), the court indicated that the "plaintiff has no right to have her attorney present.... [T]he court also finds that she has no right to the presence of any third person or mechanical recording device at the examination" (p. 629). Quoting from *Ragge v. MCA/Universal Studios* (165 F.R.D. 605, 609–10; C.D. Cal. 1995), the court indicated that "[t]hird parties may, regardless of their good intentions, contaminate a mental examination."

In *In re air crash at Tapei, Taiwan*, the United States District Court for the Central District of California (2003) indicated that

> [T]he majority of federal courts have rejected the notion that a third party should be allowed, even indirectly through a recording device, to observe a Rule 35 examination. Holland v. United States, (1998). "Several factors militate against allowing any third person or recording device at the mental [or physical] examination of [a] plaintiff."

CASE LAW

Shirsat v. Mutual Pharmaceutical Co. (1996)

- Third Circuit Court of Pennsylvania held that an observer, court reporter, or recording device would constitute a distraction during the examination and work to diminish the accuracy of the process.

- Other lower-court cases have ruled that the presence of a third-party during evaluations is inappropriate including, Tomlin v. Holocek (1993), Hertenstein v. Kimberly Home Health Care, Inc. (1999), and Ragge v. MCA/Universal Studios (1995).

3
chapter

Hertenstein, 189 F.R.D. at 630; Holland, 182 F.R.D. at 495–96; Tomlin, 150 F.R.D. at 631–33. These factors include: First,... the presence of a third party during the examination under Rule 35 "would lend a degree of artificiality to the interview technique which would be inconsistent with applicable professional standards." Second,...one of the purposes of Rule 35 is "to provide a 'level playing field' between the parties in their respective efforts to appraise" the plaintiff's condition. Therefore, the party requesting the examination should be free from oversight by the opposing party....[B]oth the plaintiff's and defendants' experts were "bound by the methodologies of their discipline and by the same formal or informal principles of professional integrity." Third,...[such an intrusion would] promote "the infusion of the adversary process into the...examining room[.]" Holland, 182 F.R.D. at 495–96 (citations omitted); Hertenstein, 189 F.R.D. at 630–31; Tomlin, 150 F.R.D. at 631–34. Additionally, "the presence of a[n audiotape] could influence [plaintiff], even unconsciously, to exaggerate or diminish his reactions to [the examiner's] physical examination." Holland, 182 F.R.D. at 496; see Sreenivasan Decl., 4–5. Finally, the infusion of the adversary process into the examining room by a recording device is "inconsistent with the just, speedy and inexpensive resolution of civil disputes [under Rule 1], and with the dictates of Rule 35." Hertenstein, 189 F.R.D. at 631 (quoting Tomlin, 150 F.R.D. at 634). The Court finds the above reasoning to be persuasive. "Weighing the concerns of the parties and the physicians, the court finds the presence of a mechanical recording device inappropriate under the facts of this case. Plaintiff[s] ha[ve] demonstrated no need for it. Its presence may invalidate the results of the examination[s], as it may consciously or unconsciously influence plaintiff[s] 'to exaggerate or diminish [their] reactions' to the examination[s]." Hertenstein, 189 F.R.D. at 631 (quoting Holland, 182 F.R.D. at 496).

When it comes to the administration of psychological tests, ethical standards also suggest that validity may be compromised if there is a third party present or if other nonstandard conditions are present. Ethical Standard 9.02 of the *Ethical Principles of*

Psychologists and Code of Conduct (2002) indicates that "(a) Psychologists administer, score, interpret, or use assessment techniques, interviews, tests, or instruments in a manner and for purposes that are appropriate in application of the techniques." Ethical Standard 9.06 indicates that "When interpreting assessment results..., psychologists take into account... various test factors.... They indicate any significant limitations of their interpretations." Ethical Standard 9.11 indicates that "Psychologists make reasonable efforts to maintain the integrity and security of test materials and other assessment techniques consistent with law and contractual obligations, and in a manner that permits adherence to this Ethics Code." Similarly, Standard 1.4 of the *Standards for Educational and Psychological Testing* (1999) indicates that "if a test is used in a way that has not been validated, it is incumbent on the user to justify the new use, collecting new evidence if necessary." Standard 5.4 refers to a need for "minimal distraction." Standard 12.19 indicates that the examiner "should take cognizance of the many factors that may influence a particular testing outcome." The argument is even stronger if the third party observer is not a psychologist. Ethical Standard 9.11 indicates that "Psychologists make reasonable efforts to maintain the integrity and security of test materials and other assessment techniques consistent with law and contractual obligations, and in a manner that permits adherence to this Ethics Code." Non-psychologists have no such duty.

The *Specialty Guidelines for Forensic Psychologists* (Committee on Ethical Guidelines for Forensic Psychologists, 1991) offers relevant, non-mandatory, guidelines. Neither third party observers nor transparency are directly addressed. Guideline A.2.a. indicates that, "[w]hen required to disclose results to a nonpsychologist, every attempt is made to ensure that test security is maintained and access to information is restricted to individuals with a legitimate and professional interest in the data" (p. 664). Guideline VI.A. indicates that

> forensic psychologists have an obligation to maintain current knowledge of scientific, professional and legal developments

within their area of claimed competence. They are obligated also to use that knowledge, consistent with accepted clinical and scientific standards, in selecting data collection methods and procedures for an evaluation, treatment, consultation or scholarly/empirical investigation [p. 661].

This would suggest that forensic psychologists be familiar with third party observer, social facilitation, and transparency research and principles, and that this research and these principles be weighed in each situation in which a third party observer (including audio- or videotaping) is considered.

Guideline VI.B. indicates that

forensic psychologists have an obligation to document and be prepared to make available, subject to court order or the rules of evidence, all data that form the basis for their evidence or services. The standard to be applied to such documentation or recording *anticipates* that the detail and quality of such documentation will be subject to reasonable judicial scrutiny…. When forensic psychologists conduct an examination or engage in the treatment of a party to a legal proceeding, with foreknowledge that their professional services will be used in an adjudicative forum, they incur a special responsibility to provide the best documentation possible under the circumstances [p. 661, emphasis in original].

This Guideline could be taken to suggest that audio- or videotaping be utilized to facilitate transparency.

The current revision of the *Specialty Guidelines* is undergoing review by several committees of the American Psychological Association at the time this is being written. The revision being circulated contains stronger statements favoring transparency than does the 1991 version of the *Guidelines*. The final language of the revision will not be known until the review process is completed. The anticipated completion date is 2011. The sixth revision of the draft *Specialty Guidelines* was issued on March 18, 2011. Final approval is anticipated to be no later than early 2012 (Personal communication from Randy Otto, April 12, 2011).

Otto and Krauss (2009, page 363) indicated that states have four approaches to the presence of an attorney during an evaluation in civil proceedings. They summarized various state court holdings as follows:

> Some states offer an absolute right to have an observer present during an examination (e.g., *Acosta v. Tenneco Oil Company*, 1990; *Langfeldt-Haaland v. Saupe Enterprises*, 1989; *Tietjen v. Department of Labor & Industry*, 1975), some direct that there is a presumptive right to have counsel present (e.g., *US Security Insurance Company v. Cimino*, 2000), some hold that there is no presumptive right to have counsel present (*McDaniel v. Toledo, Peoria & Western Railroad*, 1983; *Dziwanoski v. Ocean Carriers Corporation*, 1960), and some grant the trial court discretion to make this decision based on consideration of case specific factors (e.g., *Hayes v. District Court*, 1993; *Wood v. Chicago, Milwaukee, St. Paul & Pacific Railroad*, 1984)

Otto and Krauss (2009) concur that having a third party present may affect the interview and test responses of someone being evaluated. In particular, "the presence of a third party observer during psychological test administration can affect normative comparisons and threaten test security," (p.364) though test security would not be threatened if the observer is a psychologist. Further, "[b]ecause the presence of third party facilitators during the administration of psychological testing will certainly affect normative comparisons, their participation should only be considered when necessary to proceed with test administration…" (pp. 364–365). The problems engendered by third party observers may involve "(a) negative effects on the examinee's responses and participation, (b) interruption of the flow of information from the examinee to the examiner, (c) threats to the validity of conclusions that can be drawn from the evaluation, and (d) threats to the security (and future utility) of psychological assessment techniques and tests. All of these concerns are legitimate and should lead examining psychologists to make decisions about the presence of third parties only after serious deliberation" (p. 366).

Otto and Krauss (2009) take issue, however, with the positions of the National Academy of Neuropsychology (NAN) and the American Academy of Clinical Neuropsychology (AACN) that would exclude "involved" parties, such as attorneys or psychologists retained by attorneys, while permitting "uninvolved" individuals, such as psychology students or trainees, the parent of an anxious child, psychologists observing the work of psychometrists, or an interpreter. Both "involved" and "uninvolved" observers, as defined, are deviations from standard clinical practice, can cause distortion of the individual's response style, are not consistent with instructions for some tests, may threaten test security, and may cause problems with the reliability and validity of test results. They suggest that the most salient factor is not the above problems with the presence of third parties but, rather, "that almost all psychological and neuropsychological instruments have not been normed on individuals involved in legal proceedings" (p. 368). In particular, people being evaluated in forensic contexts "are much more likely to adopt a response style that, broadly conceived, can be characterized as 'less than candid and forthcoming'" (p. 368). The authors find it "inconsistent" that psychologists and neuropsychologists could hold that the presence of third parties would be a significant issue, while the fact that most instruments were not developed for forensic purposes would not necessarily be an issue.

Otto and Krauss are, of course, correct that few psychological tests or other instruments were developed and standardized for forensic use, and correct in indicating that numerous problems are engendered when third parties are present. However, some psychological tests, especially the MMPI-2, have very substantial research bases indicating how various response styles and forensic situations may affect the results of the test. Rather than demonstrating that psychologists and neuropsychologists put too much emphasis on the presence of third parties, Otto and Krauss are primarily suggesting that NAN and AACN rewrite their policy statements regarding the presence of third parties to reflect that most tests are not developed and standardized in forensic situations, and that the effects of third parties may be variable under various circumstances. This would reduce or eliminate the inconsistencies the authors note, while reinforcing the substantial research base that indicates that the presence of third parties in evaluations during psychological testing may have a sufficiently adverse affect to reduce the validity of the test results.

Finally, according to Dean (2004), "[I]n theory, a medical examination itself is not part of the adversarial proceedings, so generally, federal courts do not permit a party's attorney to be present at a Rule [Federal Rules of Civil Procedure] 35 physical examination unless there is some compelling reason to do so" (p. 141). We would expect the same to be true of a psychological examination. States that model their rules of civil procedure after the Federal Rules would be expected to have similar provisions.

There is generally only one circumstance, in our experience, in which there is a benefit to the presence of a third party and/or audio- or videotaping when administering psychological tests as part of a personal injury evaluation. That occurs when any individual refuses to be examined without that third party, whether it is an attorney, a family member, a therapist, or someone else. If the evaluator believes that it would be better to have the third party's presence than to request a court order or forego testing, he or she may allow the person (or recording device) to be present in the interview after indicating that the third party must be as inconspicuous as possible. While the test data may be open to some question regarding its validity, it is generally better to have the individual tested rather than have information only from secondary sources or under the duress of a court order. The American Psychological Association Committee on Psychological Tests and Assessment (2007a) indicated that *failing* to include a third party could, under some circumstances, undermine the validity of the results of an assessment.

It should be noted that some evaluators, including one of the present authors, in an attempt to have the forensic evaluation be as transparent as possible or to enhance the quality of the documentation, would prefer having the interview audiotaped or videorecorded (see Pitt, Dietz, Dvoskin, & and Spiers, 1999). They note that there is no "validity," per se, to psychological or psychiatric interviews; they have not been validated under standardized conditions like most psychological tests. As noted above, there is thus room for great variation in the method, style, and content of such

3
chapter

BEST PRACTICE
If you are unable to personally administer some assessment measures, you may have someone on your staff who is well-trained, or a consulting psychologist, administer the instruments for you. You must directly supervise the work, however.

interviews, and thus more reason for them to be available for scrutiny. This is a valid position, though one on which the present authors disagree. However, this position applies only to the interview, not to any formal psychological testing, since the test materials must be protected to try to ensure that they remain valid and reliable assessment tools.

Expert Administration

The psychologist should personally administer all formal instruments (including tests), if possible, to ensure that standard testing conditions are adhered to and to record extra-test behavior (e.g., reactions, expressions, side comments). If this is not possible, testing may be done by the psychologist's well-trained staff or a consulting psychologist, provided the psychologist directly supervises the work (Ackerman & Kane, 1998).

Direct Observation

No standardized test should ever be taken home by, or left with, the individual being assessed. If the administration is not directly observed, the psychologist cannot be certain that the test or other instrument was in fact answered by the person being assessed, nor that the individual was not intoxicated while taking the test, nor that other people did not contribute to the individual's responses to the test (Ethics Committee, American Psychological Association, 1993, 1994). The evaluator must also be certain that the evaluatee does not use a cell phone to consult with anyone during the administration of any test or other instrument.

BEWARE
Never allow the evaluatee to complete assessments at home or away from your (or your well-trained staff's) presence. Always directly observe the completion of tests.

Suitability

Tests and other assessment instruments must be suitable for the individual being assessed. If reading level is a concern, it must be assessed (e.g., with the Wide Range Achievement Test,

Fourth Edition (WRAT-4) prior to administering any instrument that will be read by the individual. The MMPI-2, for example, has a minimum of a sixth-grade reading level (Butcher et al., 2001), though some authors claim it requires a 7th or 8th grade reading level, and some questions require a high-school graduate or even college reading level. A test or other instrument that is only available in English should not be administered to someone who is not fluent in English. While a translator could be used in an interview, there is no research indicating that a translator can correctly translate each test item or would not otherwise influence the person's responses, and few if any psychological tests have been standardized under such conditions.

Psychologists should also make sure that tests have been normed on populations that are similar to that of the subject being examined. This requires that psychologists be aware of the underlying studies upon which the tests rely, and the nature of normative groups, to ensure that inferences from the tests are reasonable.

If the preceding requirements are not followed, the burden is on the psychologist to demonstrate that the test or other instrument remains reliable and valid despite the changes from standardized procedures. If the psychologist cannot ensure that the changes did not have an adverse effect, he or she also cannot testify to a reasonable degree of psychological or scientific certainty (or whatever is required in the given jurisdiction) that the results are valid (Ackerman & Kane, 1998).

Base Rates

"Base rate [is] the naturally occurring frequency of a phenomenon in a population. This rate is often contrasted with the rate of the phenomenon under the influence of some changed condition in order to determine the degree to which the change influences the phenomenon" (APA Concise Dictionary of Psychology, p. 49). Both diagnosis and prognosis may be made in error if relevant base rates are not considered. Lees-Haley and Brown (1993) identified base rates for problems that are common among personal injury claimants (170 people) and a control group of 50 outpatients from a group family practice clinic. Ninety-three percent of claimants reported nervousness or anxiety, as did 54% of the control group. Thus, the presence of nervousness alone would not justify an inferential opinion regarding psychological damages. Other common complaints among claimants in personal injury suits included headaches (88% for claimants, 62% for controls), problems concentrating (78% vs. 26%), and problems with memory (53% vs. 20%). The probative value of the expert's testimony is limited if he or she is not aware of the base rate for each problem or symptom (Fleishman, Jackson & Rothschild, 1999). The expert should have relatively objective evidence, e.g., a high score on Scale 7 of the MMPI-2 or reliable collateral reports as an indication of "nervousness," if the expert is citing "nervousness" as a consequence of the alleged psychological injury. The same principle would hold for the other characteristics noted.

According to *Mental Health: A Report of the Surgeon General* (U.S. Department of Health and Human Services, 1999), the base rate for mood disorders (Major Depression, Bipolar Disorder, Dysthymia, Cyclothymia) in one year in the United States is 7%. The base rate for an anxiety disorder is over 16% for adults 18–54 years old during one year, while the base rate for Posttraumatic Stress Disorder is 3.6%. The lifetime prevalence of exposure to serious trauma in the United States ranges from 40% to 70%, while the lifetime prevalence of PTSD is between 8% and 14% (Frueh, Elhai, & Kalouopek, 2004). Using DSM-IV criteria, the conditional probability of PTSD over a lifetime is 13% for women and 6.2% for men (Kimerling, Prins, Westrup & Lee, 2004). The presence of a mood or anxiety disorder, in and of itself, is not sufficient evidence that an individual is suffering from the trauma claimed in a given legal case. It is necessary to conduct a comprehensive evaluation to ascertain whether the individual's claims are legitimate, focusing particularly on the extent to which psychological problems and disabilities appear to be caused by the traumatic event.

BEST PRACTICE
Always consider relevant base rates when conducting the evaluation.

Error Rates

"Error rates" primarily refer to the likelihood of false positive and false negative errors, respectively, though other definitions exist (Krauss & Sales, 2003; Youngstrom & Busch, 2000). Evaluators should, therefore, use multiple sources to assess a given individual, while noting any significant questions that arise in the course of assessing whether that individual appears to have suffered from the event alleged to have caused his or her disability, and the diagnosis (or diagnoses) associated with his or her condition.

The U.S. Supreme Court, in *Daubert* and its progeny, offered no guidance to trial court judges in determining what error rate is acceptable. Since the consequences of error will vary from case to case, different error rates may be acceptable in different situations. Accordingly, each judge will utilize his or her own conceptualization of what error rate is involved in an evaluation, and may permit or exclude specific evidence on the basis of that notion. Each judge will also assign some value to the other *Daubert* factors (e.g., peer review and publication of supportive literature, degree of acceptance in the scientific community). According to Kraus and Sales,

3
chapter

Under the present conceptualization of the *Daubert* standard, eventual admissibility decisions will be a product of… what scientific information the forensic expert offers during the testimony, the pragmatic reliability, considerations chosen by the judge to evaluate that testimony, the manner in which the judge weighs the different chosen reliability considerations, and the level at which the judge attempts to fit the science to the legal question (2003, p. 552).

Similarly, Faust, Grimm, Ahern and Sokolik (2010) indicate that admissibility requires that

expert testimony be based on sufficient facts so as to not be speculative. Therefore, the judge requires a straightforward presentation of the facts the expert considered—data, documents, discovery materials, treatises, studies, calculations, analyses, and the like. The judge is not seeking a regurgitation of the underlying facts or data, merely an inventory of them. After presenting this information, the expert should explain how this basis was sufficient to support the opinions that will be expressed [p. 59].

We believe that it is incumbent on forensic psychologists to be familiar with the underlying empirical basis for conclusions suggested by each psychological test upon which the expert has relied in forming his or her opinion, including reason to believe that the test results apply to the plaintiff in the instant case. The MMPI-2, for example, was standardized on the basis of the 1990 U.S. census, but Hispanics were under-represented (Butcher et al., 2001). If the plaintiff is Hispanic, the expert would be expected to address how this might have affected the results of the test administration.

It is essential that the expert does not rely exclusively on "cookbooks" or computerized interpretations, or interpretations suggested by single sources. "Cookbooks" offer lists of statements about people who have scale scores or test protocols similar to the evaluatee, but offer little or no information regarding how those statements were obtained. Computerized interpretations tend to focus on one or at most a few high scores of the evaluatee on a given test, leaving out potentially essential information regarding the evaluatee from other scales. Most tests have more than one source of interpretive information (e.g., there are a number of books on interpretation of the MMPI-2, and thousands of articles on aspects of interpreting this test), making utilization of a single source inappropriate unless that source identifies a range of other studies, effectively incorporating multiple sources of information that are specifically identifiable (see, e.g., the MMPI-RF). Ideally, the expert can identify research involving assessment of injuries and subjects similar to the ones in the instant case. If so, that research should be weighed more heavily than more general sources, and cited. Overall, the interpretation should be based on a consensus among the foremost sources available—and those sources should be specifically identifiable. Only sources that cite research supporting the diagnostic and behavioral statements offered should be considered acceptable. The cited research should ideally include the nature of the populations studied, when the empirical research was conducted, the error rates of particular findings, and the strength of the correlational relationship between the test profile and the diagnosis. It should be noted that personality profiles (e.g., the MMPI-2) do not have "error rates" or validity coefficients, as they are used to assist in a number of different personality, psychopathology, and diagnostic decisions. However, their use for particular purposes (e.g., the diagnosis of depression) will typically have some empirical foundation for which these questions may appropriately be addressed. As with all sources of data, the expert ultimately integrates information from multiple sources (e.g., tests, interviews, and records) into a cohesive inferential opinion regarding the plaintiff's psychological condition.

Further, with the possible exception of the best measures of IQ, no single test by itself is sufficient to permit a strong conclusion regarding most characteristics of the plaintiff. If the test suggests depression, for example, it essential that there be supportive information from some combination of other tests, medical and other records, clinical interview(s), collateral interviews, and DSM-IV-TR (and/or ICD-9-CM) diagnostic criteria.

Differential Diagnosis

The most common diagnosis in personal injury cases is Posttraumatic Stress Disorder (PTSD) (Ackerman & Kane, 1998; Koch, Douglas, Nicholls & O'Neill, 2006). The most common diagnostic system in North America is the *Diagnostic and Statistical Manual of Mental Disorders, Fourth Edition, Text Revision* (DSM-IV-TR) (American Psychiatric Association, 2000). It should be noted that there is an International Classification of Diseases and Related Health Problems (World Health Organization), with ICD-9-CM (for "clinical modification") used for billing purposes in the U.S.A. and ICD-10 in Canada. Neither is commonly used for day-to-day diagnostic use in either country (Young & Kane, 2007), although ICD-10 has been available since 1992 and is used throughout most of the world. *Mental and Behavioural Disorders* is Chapter 5 of ICD-10.

The American Psychiatric Association is currently working on the fifth edition of the diagnostic manual, now scheduled for publication in 2013 (www.dsm5.org). The strengths of DSM-IV-TR have been its standardization and comprehensiveness, as well as its frequent usage in the United States and Canada. Its weakness is that diagnoses are explanatory constructs that are designed as a shorthand to permit professionals to discuss characteristics of an individual's disorder(s). Further, each revision of the DSM was adopted by vote of a group of psychiatrists on the basis of their understanding of research, thereby representing a value judgment rather than a careful scientific analysis (Shuman, 2002a; State Justice Institute, 1999). Adding a caveat that is frequently ignored, the authors of DSM-IV-TR also indicate that the inclusion of a diagnosis in the manual "does not imply that the condition meets legal or other nonmedical criteria for what constitutes mental disease, mental disorder, or mental disability" (American Psychiatric Association, 2000, p. xxvii).

Despite the disclaimer, diagnoses are both utilized and accepted in court cases involving personal injuries and workers' compensation. Plaintiffs' attorneys particularly like the diagnosis of PTSD, because it requires the occurrence of a specific traumatic event, which may be alleged to have been the proximate cause of an individual's disability. Many other diagnoses are potentially relevant to litigants in personal injury or workers' compensation cases, however. The forensic evaluator must consider each potentially accurate diagnosis and either rule it in or out on the basis of the evidence accumulated in the course of the comprehensive evaluation of the plaintiff. To facilitate transparency, we recommend that each relevant potential or alleged alternative DSM-IV-TR diagnosis be identified in the expert's report, with specification as to which criteria the plaintiff met and which he or she did not meet (See also Greenberg, Shuman and Meyer, 2004).

Some people who exhibit many of the characteristics of PTSD do not meet the requirement of DSM-IV-TR's Criterion A that "the person experienced, witnessed, or was confronted with an event or events that involved actual or threatened death or serious injury, or a threat to the physical integrity of self or others." It is also required that "the person's response involved intense fear, helplessness, or horror." For children, "this may be expressed instead by disorganized or agitated behavior" (pp. 427–428). Victims of sexual abuse by therapists, physicians, clergy, and other professionals, for example, may exhibit many of the characteristics of PTSD and would meet the requisite criteria for that diagnosis *except for* Criterion A, because they were never threatened with "death or serious injury, or a threat to the physical integrity of self or others." They may also have never felt "intense fear, helplessness, or horror." For these individuals, we recommend reference to posttraumatic symptoms that resemble PTSD in every way except for Criterion A.

For forensic assessment purposes, under DSM-IV-TR, PTSD is virtually unique among diagnoses in that it requires the examiner to render a factual determination about whether or not the event in question actually occurred—a determination that is supposed to be left to the trier of fact. This is especially problematic in cases of alleged sexual abuse, including sexual misconduct by a therapist, where the only two parties with direct knowledge of the event typically contradict each other. In such cases, the authors recommend consideration of a conditional diagnosis, where the examiner describes the reported symptoms and any diagnoses consistent with those symptoms but leaves the factual determination of the allegedly traumatic event to the trier of fact.

It should be noted that the definition of Posttraumatic Stress Disorder in ICD-10 is more like the definition in DSM-III-R than that in DSM-IV-TR, particularly the initial criterion:

> **F43.1 Post-traumatic stress disorder** Arises as a delayed or protracted response to a stressful event or situation (of either brief or long duration) of an exceptionally threatening or catastrophic nature, which is likely to cause pervasive distress in almost anyone. Predisposing factors, such as personality traits (e.g. compulsive, asthenic) or previous history of neurotic illness, may lower the threshold for the development of the syndrome or aggravate its course, but they are neither necessary nor sufficient to explain its occurrence. Typical features include episodes

of repeated reliving of the trauma in intrusive memories ("flash-backs"), dreams or nightmares, occurring against the persisting background of a sense of "numbness" and emotional blunting, detachment from other people, unresponsiveness to surround-ings, anhedonia, and avoidance of activities and situations remi-niscent of the trauma. There is usually a state of autonomic hyperarousal with hypervigilance, an enhanced startle reaction, and insomnia. Anxiety and depression are commonly associated with the above symptoms and signs, and suicidal ideation is not infrequent. The onset follows the trauma with a latency period that may range from a few weeks to months. The course is fluc-tuating but recovery can be expected in the majority of cases. In a small proportion of cases the condition may follow a chronic course over many years, with eventual transition to an enduring personality change (F62.0). Traumatic neurosis [World Health Organization, 1992, retrieved October 28, 2009 from http:// apps.who.int/classifications/apps/icd/icd10online/]

Thus, some people experiencing symptoms that would not qualify for a PTSD diagnosis in DSM-IV-TR would likely qualify for that diagnosis in ICD-10.

Although some think of PTSD as a purely psychological condi-tion, Wilson (2004) suggests that "PTSD is a normal, biologically hardwired pattern of reactivity to extremely stressful situations" (p. 15). He notes that "[re]experiencing phenomena involves cogni-tive processing, information storage, and retrieval from memory" (p. 19), and may involve 16 different forms of reliving a traumatic experience consciously or unconsciously, changed state of awareness, sensory or perceptual changes, and bodily reactions related to hyper-arousal. People try to protect themselves from the severe residue of the trauma via up to seven symptoms associated with avoidance, and exhibit hyperarousal that may take different forms, including "sleep cycle disturbance..., anger, irritability, and hostility..., impairment in cognitive processing of information..., hypervigilance..., [and/or] hyperarousal and self-monitoring difficulties" (pp. 27–28).

PTSD is not a unitary phenomenon. A specific individual may show evidence of various diagnostic criteria at different times, and two people may accurately be diagnosed with PTSD without sharing many, if any, specific symptoms.

PTSD is also recognized to be very persistent over time in many people. Zatzick, Jurkovich, Rivara, Wang, Dan, Joesch, Salkever, and Mackenzie (2008) found that, of 2,707 injured patients who sought care from one of 69 hospitals across the country, 20.7% had PTSD and 6.6% had depression one year post-injury. Each disorder was independently associated with functional impairment in activities of daily living, health, and ability to work or do other normal activities. Patients with one of the disorders were one-third as likely to be working after a year, and patients with both disorders one-fifth to one-sixth as likely to be working.

Compensation Neurosis

The term *compensation neurosis* was coined by C.T.J. Rigler in 1879 with regard to the increased reports of disability following railroad accidents (Mendelson, 1992). The great weight of the research, however, indicates that most plaintiffs do not become free of symptoms soon after the litigation ends, nor do they quickly return to work (Ackerman & Kane, 1998; Binder & Rolling, 1996; Binder & Willis, 1991; Binder, Trimble, & McNeil, 1991; Bryant & Harvey, 2003; Butcher & Miller, 2006; Call, 2003; Eisendrath and McNiel, 2002; Hyler, Williams & Spitzer, 1988; Nicholson & Martelli, 2007b; Resnick, 1997; Ryan & Warden, 2003; Samra & Koch, 2002; Shuman, 2000a, 2000b; Walfish, 2006; Wilson & Moran, 2004).

Research on "compensation neurosis" has found that (1) speed of recovery and psychological responses to accidents do not differ between countries that have laws allowing compensation for pain and suffering and those that do not; (2) few people indicate a significant reduction in symptoms upon resolution of litigation (except to the degree that litigation-related stress ends) (3) 50–75% of people injured in compensable accidents remain unable to work for two or more years post-litigation, and treatment time does not differ significantly for people who litigate and those who do not (Resnick, 1997); (4) there is normally improvement in PTSD symptoms and general functioning with time, with or without litigation (Blanchard, Hickling, Taylor, Buckley, Loos & Walsh, 1998); (5) people with real disability and suffering due to minor head traumas are relatively likely to litigate, and relatively unlikely to be discouraged or deterred by the effort and time necessary to fight in court (Heilbronner, 1993); (6) "patients with *less* severe injuries, as measured by posttraumatic neurological data, are *more* likely to seek monetary compensation" (Binder & Rohling, 1996, p. 9); (7) "patients not involved in litigation also report posttraumatic symptomatology following mild head injury" (Fordyce, 1991, p. 194).

Malingering

The *Diagnostic and Statistical Manual of Mental Disorders, Fourth Edition, Text Revision* (*DSM-IV-TR*, 2000, p. 739) defines malingering as "the intentional production of false or grossly exaggerated physical or psychological symptoms, motivated by external incentives such as avoiding military duty, avoiding work, obtaining financial compensation, evading criminal prosecution, or obtaining drugs." While that definition is acceptable, the listed criteria for suspecting that malingering is present are problematic: whether the person being evaluated was referred by an attorney; objective findings differing markedly from the level of stress or disability claimed by the patient; the patient's failing to cooperate with diagnosis and treatment processes; and/or, evidence of an Antisocial Personality Disorder. The first three criteria are of minimal value. Referrals to forensic mental health experts are common when a plaintiff is alleging emotional or psychological injuries, whether those injuries are real or feigned. A discrepancy between alleged stress or disability and objective findings is common in personal injury cases, especially those involving PTSD, and for good reason: it is the unique experience of the trauma by the plaintiff, not objective findings, that leads to the degree of disability identified. Patients with chronic pain very frequently lack objective medical findings to identify the source or degree of pain, yet the pain continues even without any evidence of false or exaggerated symptoms, and in the absence of any identifiable economic or personal gain. People with PTSD also commonly fail to cooperate with diagnosis and/or treatment, as do some people with serious brain damage who, lacking awareness of the severity of the damage, refuse to cooperate. Therefore, none of the first three *DSM-IV*-TR criteria is especially helpful in diagnosing malingering. That leaves only the fourth criterion, a diagnosis of an Antisocial Personality Disorder, as a potentially helpful clue to the possibility of malingering. With three of the four criteria being of questionable applicability in personal injury cases, use of the *DSM-IV-TR* criteria is not recommended, as it is "poorly conceptualized and lacking empirical support" (Otto, 2008, p. 367; see also Nicholson & Martelli, 2007a, and Vitacco, 2008).

Although concerns about "compensation neuroses" have been thoroughly debunked, there remains concern that, in individual cases, a plaintiff will have sufficient financial or other incentive to either consciously exaggerate symptoms or to report symptoms that are not present. However, experts must show great caution in calling someone a malingerer. There is substantial stigma associated with that label, and it may prevent an individual from getting appropriate care. It can also directly cause psychological trauma to the individual, and could lead to the person losing disability income or employment benefits (Drob, Meehan & Waxman, 2009).

Rogers (2008a) defines feigning as "the deliberate fabrication or gross exaggeration of psychological or physical symptoms without any assumptions about its goals" (p. 6), noting that psychological tests are able to demonstrate feigning, but not malingering. Rogers recommends using *feigning* to describe exaggeration or apparent fabrication until and unless there is unequivocal evidence of malingering. This is yet another reason for the requirement that the evaluator conduct a comprehensive evaluation that considers the characteristics of the individual, the environment, and clear evidence of a reason for the individual to malinger (Ackerman

BEWARE
The DSM criteria for malingering are of little use. Do not rely on the criteria to determine if an individual is fabricating or exaggerating symptoms.

& Kane, 1998; Walfish, 2006; Young & Kane, 2007). It must also be kept in mind that plaintiffs who display feigning or even substantial evidence of malingering may, in addition, have real, demonstrable psychological disorders. The evaluator has a responsibility to diagnose any disorders that are present (Ackerman & Kane, 1998; Drob, Meehan & Waxman, 2009; Kane, 2007a; Rogers, 2008a).

Shuman (2005) wrote that malingering is "the voluntary falsification or fabrication of physical or psychological symptoms.... The MMPI has been found to be the most helpful psychological test in identifying exaggeration and minimization of symptoms, although it will not identify all malingering...." (p. 14-9). However, claims of specific disability may be made in the course of a clinical interview, claims that can sometimes be refuted with direct credible evidence that the person is successfully using the skill or function that he or she claims to lack.

Scrignar (1996) indicated that the incidence of malingering in personal injury suits is unknown. However, it is important to note that "[p]ersonal injury litigants are carefully screened by plaintiff and defense attorneys, private investigators, physicians, and mental health professionals (p. 208)." While the degree is not known, this "intense scrutiny identifies at least some of the pretenders and likely forces some malingerers out of the civil courts." (p. 208).

One must also consider the psychological meaning of compensation. Some people seek money as compensation, but many people have additional or different motivations. Some look for "justice" as compensation for perceived or concrete harm caused by a defendant (Kane, 2007b; Resnick, 1997; Rogers, 2008d). Some wish to prevent injury to someone else, especially in cases involving sexual misconduct by professionals, driving while intoxicated, or sexual harassment. Some wish to ensure that there is recognition of the meaning and importance of the traumatic event(s) for the victim. Victims commonly need assurance that their suffering is understood by others, even if their level of suffering has diminished by the time of the evaluation (Resnick, 1997). In our experience, malingering is much more likely among those seeking only money than it is among those with the other goals, for whom injunctive relief, simply winning the case, and especially the opportunity to be fairly heard (Tyler, 1984) may be ample reward.

Another factor in the presentation of the plaintiff is the fact that plaintiffs' attorneys continually ask questions that encourage people with injuries to think about their injuries, potentially leading to the plaintiff seeing himself or herself as significantly – and possibly permanently—disabled. Family members, physicians, and other people may reinforce this attitude, particularly if they don't insist that the plaintiff functions as well as he or she is able. In addition, "Physical injury and pain often produce a regression, characterized by a breakdown of the more mature coping mechanisms. Injured patients may become totally dependent on their families, physicians, and attorneys, even though they were formerly quite autonomous" (Resnick, 1988, p. 93).

Much of the data on the nature and extent of an individual's injuries and disability come from the plaintiff, raising concern about the potential for malingering or exaggeration of symptoms. Evaluators must use caution in labeling someone as a malingerer, which can have a significant adverse affect on the person's lawsuit, employment benefits, and/or disability benefits (Drob, Meehan & Waxman, 2009). To assess the possibility of malingering appropriately, the evaluator must conduct a comprehensive evaluation that addresses the alleged trauma, the individual's status pre- and post-trauma, the social and physical environments, and evidence of significant exaggeration or malingering.

Malingering must be conscious and intentional. In contrast, exaggeration may be caused by naiveté, an unconscious desire for emotional support, or other factors (Rogers, 2008a; Sella, 1997). Feigning does not imply malingering, Rogers indicates. He also notes that malingering does not imply the absence of legitimate disorders. Any disorders present should be identified by the evaluator (Ackerman & Kane, 1998; Drob, Meehan & Waxman, 2009; Kane, 2007a; Rogers, 2008a).

Exaggeration may also relate to the questions attorneys continually ask their clients about their injuries and status, promoting the client's perspective involving being permanently injured.

Unethical attorneys may try to foster this perception deliberately (Lees-Haley, 1997; Youngjohn, 1995). Family members, physicians, and others may also reinforce such behavior if they don't insist that the person function as well as he or she is able. Malingering must also be distinguished from a Factitious Disorder, which involves conscious fabrication or production of psychological or physical symptoms or signs to permit taking on the sick role (DSM-IV-TR, American Psychiatric Association, 2000; Vitacco, 2008). The clinician who suspects or has evidence of feigning should explore the reasons for it with the individual—that is, why he or she appears to have a significant need to be viewed as suffering and sick (Vitacco). People with Factitious Disorders are generally not aware of their motivation (Nicholson & Martelli, 2007a). They are not malingering, since their motivation is unconscious.

Worley, Feldman and Hamilton (2009) suggest that the *DSM* criteria "make it virtually impossible to diagnose a case as anything other than a somatoform disorder when intentionality cannot be proved with traditional forensic evidence. There are no psychological tests of consciousness, and even strong evidence of a relationship between the occurrence of inauthentic illness behavior and tangible benefits would not suffice to overrule a somatoform diagnosis" (retrieved November 5, 2009 from www.psychiatrictimes.com/print/article/10168/1482349?verif).

DSM-IV-TR uses the following criteria for a diagnosis of Factitious Disorder:

A. Intentional production or feigning of physical or psychological signs or symptoms.

B. The motivation for the behavior is to assume the sick role.

C. External incentives for the behavior (such as economic gain, avoiding legal responsibility, or improving physical well-being, as in Malingering) are absent.

Code based on type:

300.16 With Predominantly Psychological Signs and Symptoms: if psychological signs and symptoms predominate in the clinical presentation

300.19 With Predominantly Physical Signs and Symptoms: if physical signs and symptoms predominate in the clinical presentation

300.19 With Combined Psychological and Physical Signs and Symptoms: if both psychological and physical signs and symptoms are present but neither predominates in the clinical presentation [DSM-IV-TR, p. 517]

Rogers and Shuman (2005) indicate that we have no method to accurately ascertain the conscious or unconscious motivations of an individual in describing more serious physical or psychological difficulties than are actually present. They therefore recommend using the term "feigning," to indicate "deliberate fabrication or gross exaggeration of psychological or physical symptoms" (p. 24), rather than trying to discriminate between Factitious Disorder and malingering. Rogers and Shuman also suggest avoidance of imprecise terms such as "overreporting," "secondary gain," or "suboptimal effort," because these pejorative terms may suggest motivation that cannot be known or measured with any degree of certainty.

The American Academy of Clinical Neuropsychology (2009) developed a consensus statement regarding assessment of effort, response bias, and malingering. They noted that feigners use one of two strategies: they "intentionally diminish or reduce capability and intentionally exaggerate symptom complaints" (p. 1096). This may involve providing the evaluator with a history that is false and/or incomplete. They caution that some instances of insufficient effort do not indicate malingering, particularly if insufficient effort is found on only one of several tests administered. They indicate that significant evidence of possible malingering includes "gross (1) disparity between real-world observations and either test performance or self-report, (2) inconsistency between type or severity of injury and test performances, (3) inconsistency between an individual's behavior when he or she is aware of being evaluated versus when not aware of being evaluated, and (4) inconsistency across serial testings that cannot be explained by an underlying neurological process or known psychiatric condition" (p. 1103). They urge that records and other collateral information be obtained, and emphasize that it is the totality of the individual's behavior (tests, questionnaires, interviews, observations) that must be the basis for considering a diagnosis of malingering.

See Chapters 5 and 6 for a more detailed discussion of the assessment of malingering.

Limits of the Evaluation Process

No assessment will answer all of the possible questions that may be relevant to a given personal injury case. The goal, therefore, is to conduct a comprehensive assessment using a biopsychosocial approach. The best assessment instruments available to address the referral question(s) should be utilized, to ensure that the results of the evaluation will be as accurate as possible. When further assessment appears to have diminishing returns, it is appropriate to end the assessment process. That does not preclude additional follow-up if questions occur during the writing of the report. However, one cannot count on having access to the plaintiff once the basic evaluation is completed, especially if one was retained by the defense in the case.

Unfortunately, it is not uncommon for some referral questions to go beyond the evaluator's ability or the current state of psychological science. In these instances, the evaluator will not know or be able to obtain an accurate answer. It is imperative that evaluators resist the temptation to try to know everything. Going beyond one's data on any question will detract from the credibility of the entire report, and will violate ethical and legal mandates to tell "nothing but the truth" (Dvoskin & Guy, 2008).

Iatrogenic Factors and the Power of Apology

Court cases can have a major negative affect on the life of the litigants. Obtaining information about the amount and type(s) of harm to the plaintiff, attending numerous meetings with the attorney(s), undergoing evaluations and depositions, filing the complaint, and, in a small percentage of cases, going through a court trial—all of these can be time-consuming and expensive. Litigants with significant psychological or emotional complaints, in particular, and especially those who lack resilience, may be significantly traumatized by the litigation process (Wayte et al., 2002).

For people with PTSD, the healing process is slowed by reliving the trauma and experiencing the psychological and (if present) physical impairments caused by the traumatic event. Tort cases require plaintiffs to repeatedly recall the trauma, as they discuss it with their attorney(s), evaluators for the plaintiff and defense, and at depositions, making resolution of the PTSD more protracted (Samra & Connolly, 2004; Samra & Koch, 2002; Scrignar, 1996; Simon & Wettstein, 1997). The plaintiff discusses the traumatic event and its aftermath with the attorney until there is a cogent statement about the trauma and its consequences that includes all of the essential facts. The plaintiff is reminded, both directly and by impli-cation, that nothing important is to be forgotten, since the jury may eventually need to hear all the essential details. Treatment bills, and unpaid bills for various expenses, become conditioned stimuli that bring out reminders of the traumatic event. The plain-tiff's suffering increases as the stress of the litigation process is added to the stress of the traumatic event, making it more difficult for psychotherapy to reduce symptoms (Strasburger, 1999; Wayte et al., 2002). The potential for a quick resolution of PTSD dimin-ishes, and the likelihood of a chronic PTSD becomes increasingly probable.

Research indicates that the shorter the interval between the trauma and a settlement in a tort case, the less psychological impair-ment is likely (Binder, Trimble & McNeil, 1991). The reason for this, apparently, is not that a settlement causes remission. Rather, the settlement removes the anxiety and stress associated with the litigation process, permitting healing to progress as a substantial portion of the plaintiff's stress is reduced.

3
chapter

According to Shuman (2000a), "[d]elay has significant negative effects on claimants (even 'successful claimants' who eventually prevail) and society" (p. 882). The person who is already suffering from one anxiety and/or depressive disorder will likely feel more stress from new stressors than he or she would without the preexisting condition. Even positive sources of stress, such as a marriage or getting a new job, may have a significant adverse affect. By the time the settlement conference or trial occurs, the plaintiff may have much more severe symptoms of PTSD and/or other psychological problems than he or she had at the start of the case. A case that is unnecessarily drawn out is likely to exacerbate the plaintiff's symptoms, potentially prompting a tort claim itself, or a claim for punitive damages (Ackerman & Kane, 1998). In addition,

> [d]elay exacerbates both the acute and chronic loss that the claimant experiences, and the cost to the injurer and society which they must ultimately pay either directly through tort judgments and disability program payments by means of taxes and insurance premiums, or indirectly because of decreased productivity…. [U]nnecessary delay…may also exacerbate harm to defendants for whom allegations of fault become the dominant-disturbing focus of their lives [Shuman, 2000a, pp. 882–883].

Further, for many plaintiffs a traumatic stress case is about factors other than money. Many plaintiffs fight for their perception of justice. Plaintiffs may also feel vindicated by a verdict that the defendant was responsible, as well as a perception that the litigation may prevent the defendant from hurting someone else (Ackerman & Kane, 1998; Shuman, 1994b, 2000a, Shuman & Daley, 1996).

Thousands of articles document the negative impact of stress on physical illness and injuries, the greater likelihood that injuries will happen when an individual is stressed, and the lessened productivity of people who feel significant stress, among other effects (see, e.g., Groer, Meagher & Kendall-Tackett, 2007; Miller, 2007. Simply being party to a lawsuit may cause the plaintiff to suffer increased physical, emotional, and work-related problems.

For all of these reasons, the plaintiff is likely to suffer less impairment and disability if the legal case is settled relatively quickly. The expert witness can contribute to an early settlement by doing a good job of providing impartial evidence of the nature and extent of the plaintiff's psychological injuries and a balanced assessment of the strengths and weaknesses of each party's position. In addition to providing a thorough and impartial evaluation, the expert can also provide information about the positive role that apologies can play in fostering settlements.

A number of authors have observed that apologies facilitate settlements in tort cases, and plaintiffs commonly indicate that a sincere apology might even have prevented the lawsuit from being filed (Geier, 2006; Gutheil, 2006; Lowes, 2009; MacDonald & Attaran, 2009; McDonnell & Guenther, 2008; Shuman, 1994b, 2000a, 2000b; Wayte et al., 2002). A 2008 survey of 700 medical professionals by the Medical Protection Society found that over 90% believed that patients who receive an apology and explanation are less likely to sue (retrieved November 6, 2009 from http://www.medicalprotection.org/uk/press-release/Patients-are-less-likely-to-sue-if-they-receive-an-apology). Everyone involved in tort cases should become aware of the positive affect of apologies, to foster early settlements and decrease the likelihood that plaintiffs will suffer substantial impairment and disability as a result of protracted litigation.

Conclusion

Having explained these broad concepts of psychological evidence, in Chapter 4 we turn toward the practical, and offer step-by-step professional and ethical guidance to psychological experts as they begin working with attorneys on a case.

3
chapter

INFO

The litigation process is likely to place extra stress on claimants, sometimes prolonging their emotional and physical injuries. A thorough and impartial evaluation can contribute to a swift resolution, lessening the likelihood that the claimant will suffer further impairment.

APPLICATION

Preparation for the Evaluation   4

Maintaining one's efficacy and ethics often depends upon decisions that are made in the very first moments of contact between an attorney and a potential forensic mental health expert, and deal only with the structure of the professional relationship. A lack of clarity regarding the professional relationship can result in bitter disputes about fees, confidentiality, and a host of other serious issues. Perhaps most importantly, this chapter sets forth a series of concrete steps that each expert can take to clarify his or her role and the specific questions that are likely to be asked at trial, and to counteract the legion of obvious sources of potential bias that threaten the expert's objectivity and credibility. By attending to and preparing the structure of the professional relationship, experts create a sound and credible infrastructure for the evaluation and opinions that emerge.

Although this book is intended for all forensic mental health experts, we will focus on ethical requirements for psychologists. Similar requirements will be found in ethics codes for psychiatrists and social workers.

The Initial Call from the Attorney

Most cases begin with a call from an attorney inquiring whether the forensic mental health expert would consider doing an evaluation of an individual who has allegedly been injured, and who indicates that part or all of the injury involves psychological factors. In this initial phone call, one wants to learn what role the attorney wants the expert to play, the basic description of the circumstances of the alleged injury, the names of other attorneys involved in the case, and the timetable for the case, particularly when the report would have to be available. If there is not sufficient time for the expert to do a high-quality review of the case and, if relevant, an assessment of the plaintiff, the attorney must be asked to seek a continuance so that a quality evaluation can be conducted (Melton et al., 2007). If no problems arise with the above information, the expert should ask the attorney to provide the names of the plaintiff and defendant, to ensure that one does not have any conflicts prior to tentatively accepting the case.

At this point, one does **not** want to receive any privileged information–for example regarding the attorney's theory of the case, since that information is appropriately obtained only if one agrees to accept the case. Some attorneys will offer too much detail to the expert in the initial call, with the intent of putting the expert in a position of having to refuse to be retained by the other side in the case if the expert's participation is requested by opposing counsel. Until and unless one is retained by the attorney who initially calls, it is essential to keep one's options open.

Once the forensic expert has been retained and learns the attorney's theory of the case, one could be accused by the opposing counsel of being biased because the expert was privy to the attorney's case theory prior to conducting the evaluation. All that is required to counteract this form of bias is to be aware of it and to think about alternative explanations for the facts asserted by the retaining attorney. The expert should also be aware of the possibility that the retaining attorney has left other facts out of his or her rendition of the case. Although the best attorneys, in our experience, tell the expert all of the essential facts, pro and con, many attorneys do not. The forensic expert must, therefore, always be looking for other facts that are relevant to the forensic evaluation.

Fees should be discussed in the initial call as well. The plaintiff's attorney will want to know the expert's hourly rate, and the typical amount of time spent evaluating a plaintiff in a personal injury case. A defense attorney may, at least initially, need to know only the hourly rate, since the attorney may not be seeking an evaluation of the plaintiff. Both plaintiff and defense attorneys will seek to have the expert review medical and other records. Without knowing more about the amount and nature of such records, however, it is not possible to estimate the cost of this review. On the basis of the expert's experience with records reviews, however, together with the other tasks the attorney wants the expert to address, the expert should specify the amount of the retainer needed in order to start work on the case. We recommend that the retainer requested be realistic, but liberal, since it is far easier to return unspent money than to receive additional payment if the case requires more work than anticipated. It should also be made clear to the retaining attorney that the expert will request an additional retainer if you find that the initial retainer is not sufficient. One good method when there is likely to be ongoing consultation is for the expert to require a retainer equal to 10 hours in advance, and to bill monthly for hours spent during the previous month.

4
chapter

Record Keeping

The initial record in the case is the expert's notes to him- or herself about the initial conversation with the attorney (Hess, 2006). Keeping in mind that this record is discoverable, like all others if the expert is to testify in the case, the expert should note the basic information learned in the conversation and the topics covered. Similar records should be kept of every substantive conversation with the retaining attorney or anyone else involved in the case, including the plaintiff. Substantive conversations include any discussions of facts or opinions related to the instant case.

It is also recommended that the expert stamp every document received with the date of receipt, as well as noting the start- and end-times of phone calls and meetings. Between the notes the expert takes and the date stamps, it will be possible for the expert to respond to any questions regarding when he or she became aware of specific information (Hess, 2006).

Psychologists should also be familiar with the American Psychological Association's *Record Keeping Guidelines* (2007). These guidelines include recommendations that the psychologist be responsible "for the maintenance and retention of their records" (p. 995), that they strive "to maintain accurate, current, and pertinent records of professional services…" (p. 995), that records be maintained in a manner that ensures "their accuracy and to facilitate their use by the psychologist and others with legitimate access to them" (p. 997), that records be protected "from unauthorized access, damage, and destruction" (p. 998), that the "psychologist strives to be attentive to the situational context in which records are created and how that context may influence the content of those records" (p. 999), among other provisions. For further discussion of the *Guidelines*, see Drogin, Connell, Foote and Sturm (2010).

The Referral Question(s)

The referral questions involve the information that the attorney wants to acquire from the assessment of the plaintiff, review of records, and related tasks. The referral questions should generally predict the specific questions that the attorney expects to ask on direct examination. There are several basic questions: (a) Was the plaintiff injured by the alleged behavior of the defendant? (b) If so, in what way(s), and to what degree(s)? (c) What are the consequences of the alleged injury(ies)? (d) What has the plaintiff done, or could the plaintiff do, to mitigate the negative effect(s) of the injury(ies)? (e) What factors in the plaintiff's history, if any, may have contributed to the injury(ies)? (f) If some factors may have contributed, what are those factors, and how may they have contributed? (g) Was the behavior or negligence of the defendant the proximate cause of the injury or injuries sustained by the plaintiff? The attorney may have a variety of additional questions as well. If the attorney has difficulty fully articulating the referral questions, the attorney might be asked, "What are the questions that you think you might want to ask me on direct examination?"

While the expert may acquire a wide variety of information in the evaluation process, his or her responsibility is to focus on the referral question(s). Information not specifically relevant to the legal issues should not be included in the expert's report.

BEST PRACTICE

Clarify or confirm the specific referral question(s) with the referring party whenever possible and feasible.

Evaluator Competence to Conduct the Evaluation

If the expert has adequate education or training in conducting assessments for the purpose of responding to referral questions like those just noted, and the specific case requirements also fall within the expert's areas of competence, then the expert should feel free to accept the case and proceed to identify relevant forensic issues (Heilbrun, 2001; Heilbrun et al., 2009; Melton et al., 2007). In some cases, however, the expert will have the education, training and experience to conduct evaluations but lack specific knowledge about a pivotal aspect of the case. For example, if there may be a traumatic brain injury, in most cases the assessment should be done by a neuropsychologist. If there are allegations of sexual misconduct by a therapist, the assessment should be done by someone who has substantial experience in dealing with therapist sexual misconduct issues. If the plaintiff is a child, the assessment should be probably be done by a child psychologist. In each of these instances, the psychologist who lacks specific education, training, and/or knowledge may have an ethical obligation to either refer the case to a psychologist with the requisite knowledge or, at the least, to retain as a consultant a psychologist or other professional with that essential knowledge. If the expert knows another psychologist who is fully competent to do the assessment, we recommend referring the case to that psychologist, to try to ensure that no essential part of the case is missed. On the other hand, if the expert knows no psychologist who could take on the entire case, but does know of someone who could provide the necessary

consultation (e.g., a neuropsychologist who does not accept forensic referrals), this could be discussed with the retaining attorney. If he or she accepts that alternative, then the expert could proceed with the case, bringing in the consultant to the degree and in the manner necessary to ensure that the forensic mental health assessment is properly conducted.

Of course, everyone must have a "first case" for any forensic issue. However, prior to taking on a new type of case, forensic psychologists should seek the appropriate education and training to prepare them for this type of case. One should also seek the consultation of an experienced colleague, which should be documented and freely discussed in the report and testimony.

Complex Cases and Relationships with Other Professionals

In complicated cases, including but not limited to class actions or other mass tort cases, each party will likely engage numerous experts to address various aspects of the case. Some of these experts will be mental health professionals, such as psychiatrists, psychiatric nurses, or social workers, who may offer discipline-specific testimony on the standard of care. Others (e.g., forensic accountants, forensic dentists, and forensic pathologists) may work in fields almost completely removed from mental health. We suggest several steps by which forensic mental health experts can maximize their effectiveness and value to the legal process:

- Prior to accepting the case, seek clarity regarding the questions that are likely to be asked of each expert for reports, at deposition, or at trial. Which questions are for the psychologist or psychiatrist alone, and which will be addressed by more than one expert?

- Make sure that the forensic mental health expert's expertise is appropriate for each referral question that will be posed to the expert

- Ask whether the attorney wants the experts to interact with one another, or to refrain from interacting, as the case progresses.

- If the attorney allows the various experts to share observations and opinions, remember that all such discussions among testifying experts are likely to be discoverable. It is thus best to refrain from speculation about the case, and only share opinions that are likely to be offered at trial and that can be defended with evidence and logic.

- To the extent that other experts' opinions will be relied upon, it is best to be an informed consumer, and critically assess the credibility of the other experts before deciding to rely on their findings.

- Avoid guildism and other forms of arrogance. When other expert opinions differ from your own (including those of the opposing party), consider the possibility that the other expert is correct.

- Above all, be respectful of professionals from other disciplines who are working as experts on the case.

Relationship with the Attorney

Because an attorney has an ethical duty to zealously advocate for his or her client, it is often difficult for that attorney to understand that the forensic mental health expert's responsibility is to be *impartial* – that is, to advocate for his or her data, but not for either side in a case (Bank & Packer, 2007). The *Specialty Guidelines for Forensic Psychologists* (Committee on Ethical guidelines for Forensic Psychologists, 1991, p. 665) indicate that a psychologist's "essential role [is] to the court... to assist the trier of fact to understand the evidence or to determine a fact in issue." A first task for the psychologist is to ensure that the attorney understands the psychologist's ethical obligation for impartiality. This may be accomplished via a discussion in which the psychologist informs the attorney that he or she will let the attorney know, as the assessment progresses, whether the data support the attorney's theory of the case, with the attorney having an opportunity to stop the assessment if the data do not support his or her theory.

To maintain impartiality, the psychologist should avoid investment in any specific case outcome, should establish firm boundaries between the expert and the attorney, and should avoid going beyond the data in either a report or testimony (Greenberg, 2003; Heilbrun, 2001; Heilbrun, Marczyk & DeMatteo, 2002; McCartney-Filgate & Snow, 2004; Melton et al., 2007; see also Guidelines VII.B, C. and D of the *Specialty Guidelines for Forensic Psychologists*, 1991). If for any reason the forensic expert does not believe he or she can remain impartial, the case should be declined (Heilbrun et al., 2009). Further, because of the inherent difficulty in withdrawing from a case already in progress, psychologists must monitor their objectivity and zealously avoid "slipping" into the role of advocate or teammate during the pendency of the case.

The American Bar Association has indicated that expert witnesses should be independent rather than advocating for the theory of the expert's client, the attorney. According to Murphy (2000), the ABA "has stated that, unlike attorneys, expert witnesses do not owe a duty of loyalty to their clients. An expert must remain independent from his or her 'client' and not become the client's advocate. In essence, an expert must analyze, explain, and offer an accurate opinion of the relevant issue before the court, not strive to advocate and persuade the fact-finder of a certain point of view. The expert's main duty to provide truthful and accurate information comes from the court and the ethical guidelines of his professional organization, if any."

BEST PRACTICE

Always remain impartial and establish firm boundaries between yourself and the referring attorney. If you feel you cannot be impartial, it is best to decline the referral.

In addition to the role of consulting or testifying expert, a psychologist or psychiatrist may also be called as a fact witness (usually reserved for the therapist for the plaintiff). The forensic mental health expert must be very clear as to which role he or she is to play, and the limits of each role. The testifying expert should be aware that everything he or she does is likely subject to disclosure except for the case theory of the retaining attorney. The consultant is working under the attorney's privilege, not his or her own professional ethics code, and everything about the case is privileged unless he or she is permitted by the attorney or ordered by the court to divulge it. There is also an exception to privilege if the consulting expert has some information that cannot be obtained any other way, but this is rarely an issue. As a fact witness, a therapist would not normally be asked to render opinions, though some courts will permit a therapist, testifying as a fact witness, to opine about some aspects of the plaintiff's condition (e.g., diagnosis, treatment progress and related matters). The therapist, not having done an impartial, complete evaluation of the case, must not testify as if he or she were a forensic expert (Heilbrun et al., 2009).

Although most attorneys have some knowledge of what a psychologist or psychiatrist does in an evaluation and the value of a psychologist's or psychiatrist's expertise, few attorneys are familiar with the details of the evaluation process. They understand that an expert can use tests and interviews to establish whether their clients had psychological damage from a traumatic event, and whether there is a causal nexus between the trauma and the client's symptoms, but not how the expert evaluates those issues. The less knowledgeable the attorney, the more important it is for the expert to educate the attorney regarding the evaluation process by discussing what the expert will do if retained to assess the attorney's client, and what the expert has done by the end of the evaluation to identify whether there is proximate cause (Saks & Lanyon, 2007). If the

INFO

The existence of a consulting (non-testifying) expert usually need not be disclosed by the retaining attorney.

expert is retained by the plaintiff's attorney, the question of whether the case goes forward will depend upon the conclusions of both the expert and the attorney that there is a causal nexus between the psychological damage suffered by the attorney's client and the traumatic event (Gutheil & Bursztajn, 2003). Any influences that might keep the expert from conducting a thorough, impartial, and credible evaluation should also be addressed at this stage. If the expert has any skeletons in his or her closet (e.g., licensing complaints and/or malpractice suits, even if the expert was never found culpable in any way), they must be discussed with the attorney. Similarly, if there is even a remote chance of a conflict of interest (real or apparent), it is imperative for the expert to discuss this with the attorney, so that he or she may make an informed decision about whether or not to engage the expert. It is essential that neither the expert nor the attorney be surprised by anything that comes up as the case progresses.

As noted, the expert must establish financial arrangements with the retaining attorney (Heilbrun, 2001; Melton et al., 2007). There should be a written "statement of understanding" that spells out what the expert requires, including:

- hourly and daily fees
- what happens if an appointment is not kept or a deposition or trial is postponed or cancelled at the last minute
- a clear statement that the attorney is the expert's client, and that all payments to the expert are to come from the attorney (or the insurance company, if a defense expert).
- the size of the retainer (sufficient to cover the basic assessment), and that no forensic work be done until the retainer is paid.
- that the retainer is "evergreen," i.e., that additional amounts will be required as the initial retainer is used up
- that expenses will be charged for as part of the retainer

- that there are minimum fees associated with the expert's booking time for the evaluation, for a deposition, and for court
- that a report will not be furnished until all fees have been paid in full
- the expert's policy regarding refunds for time reserved but canceled well in advance
- that health insurance cannot ethically be billed for a forensic evaluation
- that the attorney will provide all necessary information to the expert
- that the plaintiff will be asked to sign an informed consent/assent statement, including acknowledging that the expert may contact the authorities if the plaintiff is believed to engage in child abuse or is otherwise a danger to self or others
- that a re-evaluation may be necessary if the period of time between the evaluation and a deposition or court trial is substantial (e.g., more than six months)
- that the expert will accept a subpoena by fax or mail and will acknowledge receipt by either means

A sample, detailed "forensic services contract" will be found in Appendix A. The psychologist must never work on a contingency basis, which would create an obvious and unacceptable conflict of interest (Heilbrun et al., 2009; *Specialty Guidelines, 1991,* Guideline IV.B.).

BEWARE Do not agree to financial compensation contingent upon the outcome of the case.

Ethical Standards 3.05 and 3.06 of the *Ethical Principles of Psychologists and Code of Conduct* (2002) require that the psychologist avoid multiple relationships and conflicts of interest that may impair a psychologist's objectivity, competence, or effectiveness.

A sample statement of understanding can be found in Appendix B.

BEWARE It is unethical to enter into conflicting multiple relationships. Do not take on more than one role at a time.

Authorization to Proceed

In addition to the "statement of understanding," the retaining attorney should send the expert a letter specifying that he or she is being retained for the purpose of providing an assessment for the specified case, and itemizing the referral questions that the expert is to address (Melton et al., 2007).

Ethical Issues

Because ethical issues are discussed at length in the first book in this series, they will only briefly be addressed here. Two primary documents address ethics issues for forensic psychologists: the *Ethical Principles of Psychologists and Code of Conduct (EPPCC)* (American Psychological Association, 2002) and the *Specialty Guidelines for Forensic Psychologists* (Committee on Ethical Guidelines for Forensic Psychologists, 1991). The ethics code for forensic psychiatrists is the *Ethics Guidelines for the Practice of Forensic Psychiatry* (American Academy of Psychiatry and Law, 2005). The ethics code for psychiatrists is the *Principles of Medical Ethics with Annotations Especially Applicable to Psychiatry* (American Psychiatric Association, 2009). The ethics code for social workers is the *Code of Ethics* (National Association of Social Workers, 2008). Since this book is primarily addressed to psychologists, only the two documents addressing psychologists' ethics will be discussed here.

As previously discussed, Ethical Standard 2 addresses "competence." Psychologists are required to practice within the boundaries of their "competence, based on their education, training, supervised experience, consultation, study, or professional experience" (2.01). As noted, providing expert testimony for the first time on a particular issue requires great caution; seeking the consultation of an experienced colleague is an excellent way to make up for a lack of case-related experience. Psychologists must base their work

BEST PRACTICE

If providing expert testimony for the first time, be sure to consult at length with an experienced colleague who can guide you and give you advice.

upon "established scientific and professional knowledge of the discipline" (2.04).

Psychologists "take reasonable steps to avoid harming... [those] with whom they work...." (3.04). Psychologists avoid multiple relationships "if the multiple relationship could reasonably be expected to impair the psychologist's objectivity, competence, or effectiveness in performing his or her functions as a psychologist... (3.05). Psychologists avoid conflicts of interest (3.06). Psychologists clarify relevant issues when services are requested by a third party (e.g., an attorney requesting an evaluation of a plaintiff) (3.07). Psychologists obtain informed consent (or assent) (3.10) (see the discussion of informed consent, below).

Psychologists discuss the limits of confidentiality (4.02). If any audio- or videorecording is done, psychologists get the permission of all parties, including the person recorded or his or her legal representative (4.03). If the recording is court ordered, psychologists must make sure that the subject is aware that the interview will be recorded. Psychologists do not include in reports information not "germane to the purpose for which the communication is made" (4.04), especially when information is of questionable relevance or would unduly prejudice the subject of the report. "Psychologists base the opinions contained in their recommendations, reports, and diagnostic or evaluative statements, including forensic testimony, on information and techniques sufficient to substantiate their findings" (9.01a). "Except as noted in 9.01c, psychologists provide opinions of the psychological characteristics of individuals only after they have conducted an examination of the individuals adequate to support their statements or conclusions. When, despite reasonable efforts, such an examination is not practical [or possible, e.g., when the subject refuses to be examined], psychologists document the efforts they made and the result of those efforts, clarify the probable impact of their limited information on the reliability and validity of their opinions, and appropriately limit the nature and extent of their conclusions or recommendations" (9.01b). "When psychologists conduct a record review or provide consultation or supervision and an individual examination is not warranted or necessary for the opinion, psychologists explain this and the sources of information on which they based their conclusions and recommendations" (**9.01c**). "Psychologists administer, adapt, score, interpret, or use assessment techniques, interviews, tests, or instruments in a manner and for purposes that are appropriate in light of the research on or evidence of the usefulness and proper application of the techniques" (**9.02a**). "Psychologists use assessment instruments whose validity and reliability have been established for use with members of the population tested. When such validity or reliability has not been established, psychologists describe the strengths and limitations of test results and interpretation" (**9.02b**). Psychologists get informed consent for assessments or evaluations except in a few circumstances (**9.03a**), using language appropriate for the individual (**9.03b**).

Release of test data is often a point of contention in forensic cases. It is briefly discussed in Ethical Standard 9.04, but will be discussed at length below.

Psychologists carefully interpret the results of their assessments, taking a number of factors into consideration (**9.06**). "Psychologists do not base their assessment or intervention decisions or recommendations on data or test results that are outdated for the current purpose" (**9.08a**). This includes having assessment data at the time of a deposition or trial that is recent enough for the psychologist to testify that it is likely to accurately represent the current status of the plaintiff. There is no formally accepted period of time, but we recommend that the plaintiff be re-assessed if more than six months have passed since the assessment about which testimony is to be given. It is not helpful to the Court, and may not be considered relevant, to testify as to the status of the plaintiff substantially more than six months earlier, while being able to say little or nothing about the plaintiff's condition as of the trial date. The exception to this rule is when previous test results are being used for comparison to the subject's current test results.

Ethical Standard 9.11 addresses the maintenance of test security. It is discussed in the next section, together with Ethical Standard 9.04.

Test Materials and Release of Test Data

Attorneys generally want to obtain all information a psychologist utilized or relied upon in forming his or her opinions, while psychologists have an ethical duty to protect test materials and to prevent the misuse of data from psychological tests. Groth-Marnat (2009a) indicates, "If test materials were widely available, it would be easy for persons to review the tests, learn the answers, and respond according to the impression they would like to make. Thus, the materials would lose their validity" (p. 50). There is evidence that some attorneys coach their clients regarding how to respond to psychological tests (Cato et al., 2002; Elhai, Gold, Sellers, & Dorfman, 2001; Hall & Porier, 2001; Lees-Haley, 1997; Wetter & Corrigan, 1995; Youngjohn, 1995).

Ethical Standard 9.04(a) indicates, "[T]*est data* refers to raw and scaled scores, client/patient responses to test questions or stimuli, and psychologists' notes and recordings concerning client/patient statements and behavior during an examination. Those portions of test materials that include client/patient responses are included in the definition of *test data*.... Psychologists **may refrain from releasing test data to protect a client/patient or others from substantial harm or misuse or misrepresentation of the data of the test...**" (Ethical Standard 9.04(a), emphasis added; see also Committee on Psychological Tests and Assessment (2007b)). The section in boldface is generally taken to mean that the raw test data may be released only to a person who is capable of interpreting it and ethically bound to respect and observe this ethical standard–generally another licensed or certified psychologist–in order to prevent harm from misinterpretation or misrepresentation of the test data.

Further, Ethical Standard 9.11, addresses "maintaining test security" as follows: "The term *test materials* refers to manuals, instruments, protocols, and test questions or stimuli, which do not include test data as defined in Standard 9.04, Release of Test Data. Psychologists make reasonable efforts to maintain the integrity and security of test materials and other assessment techniques consistent with law and contractual obligations, and in a manner that permits adherence to this Ethics Code." Barnett (2009, p. 10) emphasizes that "all efforts should be made to maintain appropriate test security so that assessment results can be used as intended," with "a reasonable level of confidence in the validity of the test results." Taking Ethical Standards 9.04 and 9.11 together, psychologists *may* give test data to attorneys, so long as the client/patient has provided written informed consent for that release. However, if the psychologist believes that release of the raw tests data may cause substantial harm to the patient/client or someone else, or if the psychologist believes that releasing the test data is very likely to lead to inappropriate release or promulgation, misuse or misrepresentation of the information, the test data may not be released. "Raw testing data (e.g., actual test stimuli and questions, test manuals, the examinee's answers, and test scores) may be misused by non-psychologists" (Heilbrun et al., 2009, p. 71; see also Committee on Psychological Tests and Assessment (2007b)). Releasing test data to an individual who is not trained to interpret it may exacerbate the potential for the misunderstanding, misrepresentation, or misuse of the information.

Further, psychologists must follow statutory and case law related to release of information. If case law or statute prohibits releasing information under the circumstances that exist in a particular case, the law would take precedence, and the psychologist would refuse to release the test data. The outcome would be similar if the psychologist believed that release of the test data would violate the requirements of the Health Insurance Portability and Accountability Act of 1996 (HIPAA). It should also be noted that "HIPAA does not require release of [records] in situations in which information is compiled in reasonable anticipation of, or for use in, civil, criminal, or administrative actions or proceedings" (Fisher, 2003, p. 195).

It is important to note that waivers of confidentiality, under HIPAA, are case-specific. Thus, psychologists must be careful to avoid inadvertent violations of HIPAA when asked about prior cases in which they have testified. Even when information is divulged in deposition or trial testimony, it is not necessarily a matter of public record. A person's rights under HIPAA are not forfeited when a person files a lawsuit. Further, in some cases, the prior plaintiff may not be the person who actually received health care, and thus has no right to waive the privacy and confidentiality right of a third party. Even in cases in which the plaintiff was the person who received health care, signed releases are litigation-specific and time-limited; HIPAA specifically prevents re-disclosure of identifiable health information. In relevant cases, the expert may request that the court order release of the records under a protective order that protects the confidentiality rights of third parties.

The psychologist must also determine who the client is. If the assessment is requested by someone other than the evaluatee, e.g., an attorney or employer, it is that individual or entity, not the evaluatee, who is the psychologist's client. A written release from the evaluatee in that circumstance is not sufficient to permit release of test data. The release must come from the client, whether the attorney or someone else (Committee on Psychological Tests and Assessment (2007b)).

If the patient/client has not signed a written informed consent for release form, the psychologist may not release the test data absent an explicit court order or statutory authority. A subpoena from an attorney does not provide a sufficient basis for releasing test data, except possibly in jurisdictions in which a subpoena has the authority of a court order.

Attorneys do not have the training to evaluate or understand most of the raw data from an evaluation. Consequently, they will be unable to validly present or use the test data unless assisted by a psychologist retained for that purpose. Further, unlike judges, opposing counsel may have little interest in preserving or protecting the rights of third parties, such as test publishers, that may be harmed by the release of raw test data. Prohaska and Martin (2007) wrote about neuropsychological raw data in The *Alabama Lawyer,* but their argument is equally valid for all psychological raw test data. They indicated that it is

> unreasonable for attorneys or decision-makers to assume that individuals with improper training or no training may be able to utilize raw neuropsychological test data in a proper manner.... The neuropsychologist does not want to see the data misused or abused and the attorney, likewise, has ethical concerns over the falsification of evidence through compromised test materials. Production of raw test data directly to an attorney who is not a

trained neuropsychologist or to other untrained professionals falls short of the protection relevant to the verification or cross-examination process. The best course of action is for the production of the raw test data to take place between neuropsychologists [p. 223].

A psychologist releasing test data without either a signed informed consent statement or a court order is in danger of violating Ethical Standard 9.04 of the EPPCC, as well as statutes and/or administrative code in many jurisdictions. It should be noted that many psychology licensing board have adopted the APA Ethical Principles of Psychologists and Code of Conduct (EPPCC) as part of their administrative code. Finally, if the court orders release of otherwise protected information, psychologists should consider consulting an attorney for the purpose of requesting a protective order, limiting use of the information.

Psychologists have an affirmative duty to avoid releasing test materials because of the need to maintain the integrity and security of the test materials, contractual agreements between the test publisher and the psychologist, the need to prevent entry of test materials into the public domain (*EPPCC*, Ethical Standard 9.04; *Specialty Guidelines*, Guideline VII.a.2.a.; Heilbrun et al., 2009), and in some cases, copyright protections and rights. Test publishers generally consider their tests to be trade secrets. According to one major test publisher, Pearson Assessments:

> We continue to advise our customers that the test instruments covered by these Legal Policies are trade secrets and their usefulness and value would be compromised if they were generally available to the public. This position has been consistently taken in correspondence, court cases, news articles and on the website for these assessments for many years. This position is consistent with the longstanding practice of requiring that all purchasers have the appropriate qualifications to administer and interpret the instruments being purchased and that such purchasers agree to maintain the confidentiality of the instruments.

Richard Campanelli, Director of the Office of Civil Rights at the U.S. Department of Health and Human Services, has indicated that HIPAA's requirements for disclosure "do not supersede Trade Secrets law" (Morel, 2009, p. 641). In addition, the *Code of Conduct* of the Association of State and Provincial Psychology Boards (ASPPB) indicates that a "psychologist shall not reproduce or describe in popular publications, lectures, or public presentations psychological tests or other assessment devices in ways that might invalidate them" (III. I. 4).

Kaufmann (2005) notes that attorneys and their clients could manipulate the results of tests if they were given information regarding test construction, items on tests, and specific responses to test questions, "'thereby undermining the conclusions and expert opinions based on those results.' Additionally, since the value of psychological tests would be reduced if this information were released, the court's search for truth may be impeded." "The primary rationale for the psychologist nondisclosure privilege is to promote justice" (p. 100). "Court appointed independent evaluators, who protect the objectivity, fairness, and integrity of the testing process, perform a valuable truth-seeking function for the court" (p. 118). "Limiting access to psychological test materials improves the early detection of exaggerated or frivolous claims.… Seeking truth in courtrooms is a vital interest that outweighs the overly zealous need to discover information in a single case. Justice for all outweighs the needs of a single case.… Handing test answers to test takers or their attorneys violates the court's rational means of ascertaining the truth" (pp. 125–126). "Reason, experience, and past practice require limiting administration and scoring of psychometric tests to licensed psychologists or those under direct supervision by licensed psychologists" (p. 127). Kaufmann proposes that both case law and statutes affirm a privilege that shields psychological test data and materials from public disclosure. "Recognizing a psychologist privilege not to disclose psychological test materials promotes the truth-seeking function of the judiciary and serves public policy" (p. 131).

Kaufmann (2009) offers two legal arguments against disclosing test materials. The psychologist could assert a psychologist privilege to avoid disclosure on the basis of state and federal law or case law, including a reference to *Detroit Edison v. NLRB* (1979). Alternatively, the psychologist could assert an intellectual property restriction and contractual requirements, including noting that the test is copyrighted, trademarked, and is a trade secret of its publisher, and the psychologist's contract with the publisher requires the psychologist to keep secret the contents of the test. Finally, the psychologist might notify the test publisher, whose rights are in jeopardy from disclosure, to allow the publisher to advocate in court against such disclosures.

To protect test materials and raw data, the psychologist may also move for a protective order, either including an explanation or resulting in a hearing that would permit the psychologist to explain the need to maintain the integrity of the test(s) to the judge. The psychologist could also request that the judge review the test materials *in camera* to permit the psychologist to explain the good public policy of maintaining test security. The protective order, if issued, would protect the test materials and raw test data from becoming part of the public record. The protective order should include sealing of the records and transcript related to raw test data, and destruction of any test materials or raw test data in the hands of any attorney at the conclusion of the trial.

Kaufmann (2009) recommends several techniques to persuade the judge of the importance of test security. First, judges and attorneys understand the need to maintain the security of the Law School Admissions Test (LSAT) and of the Bar Examination. Just as public access to the LSAT and Bar Examination would destroy the validity, reliability, and worth of these examinations, the same may be said for psychological tests. Second, keeping psychological tests secure will prevent cheating by examinees and coaching by attorneys, eroding the value of the tests and justice in court. Third, attorneys have a responsibility to be zealous, but to temper that zealousness with candor. The *ABA Model Rules of Professional Conduct* indicate that:

> Rule 3.3 Candor Toward The Tribunal
> (a) A lawyer shall not knowingly:
> > (1) make a false statement of fact or law to a tribunal or fail to correct a false statement of material fact or law previously made to the tribunal by the lawyer;

(2) fail to disclose to the tribunal legal authority in the controlling jurisdiction known to the lawyer to be directly adverse to the position of the client and not disclosed by opposing counsel; or

(3) offer evidence that the lawyer knows to be false....

Note that if taken seriously, this obligation should preclude an attorney from coaching a client on how to take psychological tests, if doing so would result in purposely misleading results. In any event, citing this obligation notifies attorneys that any attempt to mislead the court will not be acceptable. Fourth, the psychologist's attorney could request that a special master be appointed – someone who is an expert in the area who will help the judge address issues of law and facts.

In summary, Kaufmann (2009) has provided forensic psychologists with the rationale for the need to protect psychological tests, substantial arguments supporting the protection of tests, and methods for trying to achieve protection of test materials and raw test data. It is incumbent on psychologists to try to protect test materials and raw test data to the degree possible, to preserve the viability of the methods for conducting assessments.

Number and Duration of Assessment Sessions

While it is common for defense experts to be allowed only a single meeting of limited duration with the plaintiff, that is rarely sufficient for a complete evaluation (Ackerman & Kane, 1998; Wilson & Moran, 2004). Plaintiff's experts, in contrast, often conduct evaluations of two or more parts and of substantial length. Evaluations by experts for the plaintiff and the defense should both be permitted to conduct evaluations of sufficient length to address the essential issues in a case, and of sufficient number to get an adequate sample of the plaintiff's behavior and functioning. Few plaintiffs can fully tell their stories in less than several hours of interviewing (Wilson & Moran), in addition to the time spent responding to tests and questionnaires. Although a single eight-hour day may be sufficient, fatigue is likely to play a significant role for both the plaintiff and evaluator. Two half-day sessions will often be sufficient, however, although a third may be necessary.

Between the two sessions the evaluator can score any psychological tests administered, review information received from the plaintiff, and/or call any collaterals who should be interviewed. Sufficiently detailed evaluations are necessary to provide relevant and accurate evidence to the trier of fact, thereby promoting informed decision-making. Special circumstances may also call for even more extensive evaluations. At the University of Toronto Hospital, for example, pain patients are sometimes brought into the hospital for several days so that staff can adequately assess both behavioral and psychological aspects of the plaintiff's condition (Nicholson, personal communication, January 31, 2006).

If the plaintiff or his or her attorney does not allow an evaluation of sufficient length, the evaluator must discuss with the retaining attorney whether an adequate evaluation can be conducted – and, if so, what could be left out without severely reducing the validity of the evaluation. If it does not appear that a sufficient evaluation can be accomplished in the time allotted, it may be necessary to request a court order that the plaintiff be made available for two or three sessions lasting up to four hours each so that a complete evaluation may be conducted. If the court refuses to so order, and the forensic mental health expert does not believe that an adequate evaluation can be done in the time allowed, he or she may have an ethical duty to withdraw from the case, since it may not be possible to testify to a reasonable degree of certainty whether and to what degree the plaintiff is disabled. Alternatively, the expert might choose to present a set of findings and opinions that can be supported by less-than-complete access to the plaintiff; however, these limitations and their consequences must be fully described in the report and testimony to avoid misleading the court.

BEST PRACTICE

Make sure there is enough time to conduct a thorough evaluation. You will likely need to meet with the plaintiff more than once in order to obtain all the necessary data and information. If the plaintiff or referring attorney does not agree to more than one meeting, and you do not believe that is enough time to conduct a thorough evaluation, you may be ethically obligated to decline the referral.

Informed Consent re: Lack of Confidentiality and *Tarasoff* Duty

In any case in which an individual's mental status is at issue, the results of his or her psychological evaluation will typically not be confidential. The person must be informed about this, and may need to be reminded about it periodically during the evaluation to ensure that the consent given remains informed, especially if the evaluation takes place over two or more days.

A thorny issue that has been discussed in the professional literature is whether a psychologist (or other mental health professional) who is retained by an attorney to evaluate the attorney's client may have a duty to report potentially dangerous behavior by the attorney's client. According to numerous sources (e.g., Anderson, Barenberg & Trembley, 2007), a psychologist or other mental health professional who is not going to testify will generally fall under the attorney-client/work product privilege; however, there are exceptions. Examples include the "crime-fraud" provision of the attorney-client privilege, or under various mandated reporting statutes regarding child abuse that exist in every state, or under the case law associated with the state's requirement that mental health professionals are potentially liable if they do not report a belief that the attorney's client is a danger to himself or herself or someone else (Child Welfare Information Gateway, 2008; Hansen, 2004; Morgan, 2004; Shuman, 1995b).

This last duty, to report a danger to a third party, is often referred to as a "Tarasoff" duty, after the California case that initiated such cases throughout the country, or "the duty to warn or protect." It should be noted that, if the psychologist is going to testify, information previously acquired under the attorney-client privilege is no longer privileged, and the psychologist will have to testify regarding it if asked (Niland, 2004; Shuman, 1995b). Note that these duties to warn and/or protect have been codified by legislation or case law in all 50 states, and that there is significant variation from state to state – including a few states that have explicitly rejected such a duty via case law. For example, while the *Tarasoff* line of cases began with a duty to warn, they eventually established a duty to take reasonable steps designed to protect a (usually identifiable) third party. Thus, forensic psychologists should learn their exact duties and rights in the state(s) in which they practice. Although this book solely addresses civil law, some guidance may come from the American Bar Association's *Criminal Justice Mental Health Standards* (1989). Standard 7-3.2(b) addresses

> Duty of evaluator to disclose information concerning defendant's present mental condition that was not the subject of the evaluation. If in the course of any evaluation, the mental health or mental retardation professional concludes that defendant... presents imminent risk of serious danger to another person, is imminently suicidal, or otherwise needs emergency intervention, the evaluator should notify defendant's attorney. If the evaluation was initiated by the court or prosecution, the evaluator should also notify the court.

Thus, the ABA recognizes that there are situations in which even a criminal defendant may be so imminently dangerous to himself or herself or others that a report should be made at least to the retaining attorney, and, if the expert was appointed by the court or retained by the prosecution, notice should go to the court. This, of course, leaves out the responsibility of the psychologist to adhere to the requirements of his or her state law or licensing board, and the potential for a civil lawsuit for failure to report under statute or case law in a given jurisdiction.

Kapoor and Zonana (2010) discuss the pros and cons of reporting of child abuse by psychiatrists retained to do evaluations. They indicate that 18 states require "all people" to report child abuse, and that four additional states require that attorneys report. The authors indicate that "those who fail to report when mandated to do so are typically treated harshly. The criminal penalty for failing to report is usually a misdemeanor punishable by a fine, but most states also allow a civil action to be brought by representatives of the abused child against mandatory reporters who fail in their duty. The result is a system that is heavily weighted toward protection of children." (p.50). The psychiatrist "may also note the potentially catastrophic consequences to herself it were ever

discovered that she did not fulfill her mandated reporting obligation: a licensing board investigation or malpractice suit" (p. 51).
They indicate that most states have no legislation or case law indicating whether psychiatrists retained by attorneys are covered by
the attorney-client privilege. "In the absence of clear case law or
legislation stating that attorney-client privilege outweighs the psychiatrist's mandated reporting obligation, she would conclude that
she must report" (p. 52). On the other side of the balance scale,
Kapoor and Zonana indicate that the medical ethic to "first, do no
harm" may be an argument against reporting a suspicion of child
abuse, since reporting would harm the individual being evaluated.
They also note that reporting would be expected to lead to the
retaining attorney becoming upset, and that the psychiatrist's
forensic practice could be hurt as a result of reporting. They also
indicate that a psychiatrist may conclude that statements made by
the evaluatee fall under the attorney-client privilege, and that if the
attorney is not mandated to report in that jurisdiction the psychiatrist
would not be either. They note that only Maryland has indicated, via
an Attorney General's opinion, that psychiatrists retained by the
defense in criminal cases are exempt from mandated reporting.

In contrast, Gutheil and Brodsky (2010) discuss the duty to
warn or protect during forensic independent medical examinations. They conclude that

> In essence, the essential protective role of clinician may be
> impossible to set aside, even for forensic purposes. That is, the
> role of licensed health care provider acting within a professional
> capacity may give rise to a duty (whether conceived in ethical or
> legal terms) to avert harm.... Moreover, the protection of society
> or of the general public may be a broad requirement that cuts
> across various role functions and triggers in each a duty to take
> action. Failure to act may be seen (in practice, if not with a clear
> legal basis) as turning the examiner into an accomplice of the
> examinee" (p. 58).

They specify the "statutory command" of "child abuse" as an
exception to the obligation of the expert to the retaining attorney
(p. 58).

BEWARE ⚠
The state-specific information regarding the duty to report child abuse presented on pages 102–103 is not consistent among sources, and both statutes and case law may change at any time. You must ascertain the specific and current requirements in any state in which you are practicing.

Most of the publications on this issue address the statutory requirement in all 50 states and the District of Columbia that mental health professionals, among others, must report suspected child abuse. According to Niland (2004, p. 10), laws fall into four categories: "(a) those that require reporting by some people, but exclude lawyers, (b) those that require some people, including attorneys[,] to report, (c) those that require *everyone*, including attorneys[,] to report, and (d) those that require everyone to report, but exclude attorneys by recognizing the attorney/client privilege." Further, the "crime/fraud" exception to the attorney-client privilege indicates that information from a client is not protected if it involves a plan by the client to engage in any future crime. Niland indicates that the Wisconsin State Bar Committee on Professional Ethics has stated that an attorney may report under the child abuse reporting statute if he or she reasonably believes that the client will perpetrate child abuse in the future.

Two states, Mississippi and Nevada, specifically include attorneys among the list of people who must report child abuse (Morgan, 2004). Several states require any person, including attorneys, to report suspected child abuse: Delaware, Florida, Idaho, Indiana, Kentucky, Maryland, Mississippi, Nebraska, New Hampshire, New Mexico, North Carolina, Oklahoma, Pennsylvania, Texas and Utah (Anderson, Barenberg & Tremblay, 2007; Child Welfare Information Gateway, 2008). States that specifically exclude attorneys from having to report include New Jersey, Ohio, Oregon, Rhode Island, Tennessee and Wyoming (Morgan). Morgan reports that some courts have held that attorneys must report based on the "crime/fraud" confidentiality exception, while other courts have disagreed. Anderson et al. indicate that nine states require that lawyers reveal information if it may prevent a client from causing death or substantial bodily harm: Arizona, Connecticut, Florida, Illinois, Nevada, North Dakota, Texas, Virginia and Wisconsin. The American Bar Association (2009) has a table indicating whether lawyers are mandatory reporters and the language regarding privilege at http://www.abanet.org/domviol/pdfs/mandatory_reporting_statutory_summary_chart.pdf.

Hansen (2004) indicates that Rule 1.6 of the ABA Model Rules of Conduct was revised in 2003, changing the language for when an attorney may breach confidentiality from "to prevent the client from committing a criminal act that the lawyer believes is likely to result in **imminent** death or substantial bodily harm" to "**reasonably certain** death or bodily harm," to facilitate the reporting of child abuse by attorneys (emphasis in Hansen's article). Further, Hansen indicates, the American Academy of Matrimonial Lawyers (AAML)'s Bounds of Advocacy, Standards of Conduct 2.26, indicates, "An attorney should disclose evidence of a substantial risk of physical or sexual abuse of a child by the attorney's client."

A summary of state laws on mandatory reporting of child abuse is available at http://www.childwelfare.gov/systemwide/laws_policies/state/index.cfm?event=stateStatutes.processSearch (retrieved October 8, 2009). Not all of the information is consistent with the previous statements. For example, the entry for Nevada states that attorneys are mandated reporters "unless they have acquired the knowledge of the abuse or neglect from clients who are, or may be, accused of the abuse or neglect." Oregon lists attorneys as mandated reporters, but also indicates, "An attorney is not required to make a report of information communicated to the attorney in the course of representing a client, if disclosure of the information would be detrimental to the client," according to this web site. Hansen (2004) indicates that eight states mandate reporting by "any person" but exempt attorneys. Hansen also notes that "it is unclear whether an attorney has a duty to report suspected child abuse, [and] it is even murkier as to whether an attorney has a duty to warn a third party" (p. 76). It may be relevant that a mental health professional retained by an attorney has the attorney as his or her client, not the attorney's client.

Mental health professionals who violate mandatory reporting laws are subject to both statutory and licensing punishments – though they may also be sanctioned or sued for violating confidentiality or privilege under some circumstances. Attorneys who violate reporting laws could face statutory punishments or sanctions under the Rules of Professional Conduct. Anderson et al. indicate that they have "found a considerable number of cases involving tort damage claims against mandated reporters or their employers for failure to report suspected abuse or neglect adequately" (p.44), some of which have been successful. (It is unclear whether any of these mandated reporters learned of the suspected abuse or neglect in the course of forensic evaluations.) The bottom line is that it is essential that both attorneys and mental health professionals retained by attorneys check the requirements in the relevant jurisdiction, to determine whether mandated reporting laws are applicable to forensic assessment—and, if so, to ensure that they are followed. In cases involving duties that are unclear or contradictory, it is recommended that the psychologist seek the advice of an attorney in the same state who is well acquainted with these matters before deciding how to proceed.

In summary, it is likely that experts in jurisdictions in which attorneys are mandated reporters must report child abuse, and other behavior (e.g., elder abuse) specified under mandatory reporting statutes. In those jurisdictions in which attorneys are not mandated reporters, an expert retained as a consultant is likely to be prohibited from reporting due to attorney-client privilege. This should be investigated carefully with an attorney knowledgeable about statutes and administrative code for experts in his or her jurisdiction. A psychologist or psychiatrist retained as an expert witness is likely to have to report abuse or other actual or potential danger he or she learns about in the course of doing an evaluation in some jurisdictions; consultation with a knowledgeable attorney is very important to clarify this. We recommend that a forensic expert include in his or her statement of understanding with the retaining attorney that the expert will have to report information addressed in mandatory reporting requirements that the expert learns while working on the case—at least in jurisdictions in which such situations are not specifically exempted from reporting under attorney-client privilege. As indicated in the "Statement of Understanding" (see chapter 5) given to and discussed with the examinee, the individual being evaluated should also be advised of this possibility.

Rural versus Urban Settings

It is generally accepted that psychologists practicing in rural areas may be called upon to perform some tasks that could be ethically problematic if there were additional resources and choices. One example might involve a therapist for an individual in a personal injury case who is one of a very few psychologists in the geographic area. The general ethical prohibition against a therapist serving as a forensic expert for his or her client/patient may need to be waived if the patient/client cannot reasonably obtain an evaluation from and testimony by an independent psychologist. The psychologist in this dilemma should consult with knowledgeable colleagues, consult with the plaintiff's attorney, review the professional literature regarding conflicts of interest and multiple relationships, and decide how far he or she can go in this situation.

In the event that the psychologist's decision results in an allegation of unethical conduct or a lawsuit, in our experience there is no more helpful piece of evidence than a documented consultation with an attorney or a generally respected colleague. While such a consultation is not "insurance" against an adverse finding, it is the clearest evidence possible that the psychologist carefully considered different alternatives in making the decision about acting in a legally and ethically defensible manner.

Biases

Everyone has biases that may interfere with a truly impartial evaluation of an individual in a personal injury case. These pre-existing values, which may or may not be beyond our awareness, create different beliefs about social justice, personal responsibility, and the exculpatory effects of poverty, youth, or mental illness; each of these can affect our opinions on forensic questions (Dvoskin, 2007). It is ethically incumbent on the evaluator to consider his or her biases and to try to limit their influence in the given case.

One potential source of bias is money. Forensic evaluators are paid for their time. Most people are influenced by money; there is no reason to believe that psychologists are exceptions. In addition, psychologists also share the human wish be praised by judges and by the lawyers who hired them. Skillful lawyers, when first discussing a case with a potential expert, may present the facts of the case in a manner intended to sway the psychologist's opinions toward the interests of the attorney's client. Finally, many psychologists are competitive, making it difficult to refrain from wanting to "win" the case.

These barriers to objectivity may become especially problematic in expert testimony. However, we do not advocate refraining from expert testimony; indeed, courts generally want and value the help of psychological experts.

Dvoskin (2007) suggested a number of affirmative steps to confront and clarify sources of potential bias. Perhaps foremost among these is transparency; expert witnesses should always show their work, thereby allowing opposing parties to scrutinize their evidence and logic, and triers of fact to decide if the opinion is credible. It is equally important to take seriously the "whole truth" part of the oath that each expert witness takes. When there is mixed evidence, experts should be sure to cite both supportive and opposing information.

Specialty Guidelines for Forensic Psychologists

The *Specialty Guidelines* were adopted by the American Psychology-Law Society in 1991 to provide a model for the behavior of psychologists involved with the legal system. The *Specialty Guidelines* are aspirational in most jurisdictions, although some state licensing boards have adopted them as either models or requirements for psychologists who indicate that they practice forensic psychology. The *Specialty Guidelines* define the nature of forensic psychology, indicate the responsibilities of forensic psychologists, define what forensic psychologists should be competent to do, describe various aspects of relationships with the legal system and clients, discuss confidentiality and privilege, and address public and professional communications. The Guidelines emphasize that "forensic psychologists are aware that their essential role as expert to the court is to assist the trier of fact to understand the evidence or to determine a fact in issue" (Specialty Guideline VII.F., p. 665). See pages 64–75 of the first book in this series, as well as elsewhere in this book, for a more extensive discussion of the *Specialty Guidelines*. The *Specialty Guidelines* are presently undergoing revision. They are being reviewed by several American Psychological Association committees as this book is being written. It is anticipated that a final draft will be ready in 2011. The sixth revision of the draft *Specialty Guidelines* was issued on March 18, 2011. Final approval is anticipated to be no later than early 2012 (Personal communication from Randy Otto, April 12, 2011).

Need for Incremental Validity

Virtually any evaluation can accumulate a large amount of data, but at some point obtaining additional information will no longer provide much that is new or different. The expert's goal should be to acquire data until reaching the point at which such additional data do not appear likely to add to the information needed by the expert to make judgments and draw conclusions relevant to the instant case. In other words, data gathering should generally cease when new data does not appear to add incremental validity to the data already obtained.

Expert opinions are almost always inferential in nature. Ideally, experts should explicitly describe the evidentiary and logical basis for each opinion. As incremental validity is achieved, the size of the "inferential leap" will shrink. Each new piece of data, if it is probative, will reduce the size of the inferential leap. Thus, the strongest and most influential opinions will be those with the most parsimonious inferences. Ideally, only one opinion would account for all the data, a goal that is not always achieved. Short of that standard, the expert should be prepared to explain why one possible explanation for the data is more likely than others.

The expert's goal, then, is to explore all of the important and relevant issues to the degree required to identify and test hypotheses and draw conclusions, and then stop. Only if the expert has reason to believe that a new source has a significant probability of adding data that will increase the validity of the data should the investigation continue (Faust, 2003; Groth-Marnat, 2009a; Hunsley, 2003; Hunsley & Meyer, 2003). At the same time, the expert cannot know what data will be produced by a specific test, review of records, or interview until the procedure has been conducted. However, if a substantial amount of data has been accumulated, the data have a clear direction, and there are little or no contradictory data, in general the expert should stop the data collection process.

Garb (2003) observes that personality inventories (e.g., the MMPI-2; Butcher et al., 1989), interviews, and brief self-rating instruments often add incremental validity related to diagnosis and assessment of psychopathology and personality. Groth-Marnat (2009a) indicates that the "addition of an MMPI to background data has consistently led to increases in validity although the increases were quite small when the MMPI was added to extensive data" (p. 22). Projective tests may not add predictive validity, but may provide a rich source of hypotheses that may be considered in the evaluation (Ackerman & Kane, 1998).

In certain cases, it will become quite clear at some point that the expert's opinion is very unlikely to be consistent with the retaining attorney's theory of the case or the interests of the attorney's client. As soon as an expert becomes aware of the likelihood that his or her opinion will not be useful, it is honorable and appropriate to let the attorney know, so that wasteful expenditure on the case can be avoided. This allows the attorney time to negotiate a settlement or seek a different expert. In the short run, this may appear contrary to the expert's fiscal interests. However, in addition to demonstrating integrity, it has been our experience that this practice also enhances the expert's reputation and credibility, thus adding long-term value to the expert's practice.

BEST PRACTICE

If your opinion is unlikely to be useful or is not consistent with the referring attorney's theory of the case, we recommend that you alert the referring attorney and possibly to withdraw from the evaluation.

Thin Skulls, Crumbling Skulls

The law of torts indicates that the tortfeasor takes the victim as he or she is. Whether the defendant caused an injury in an otherwise healthy person or worsened a preexisting condition, the defendant is responsible for any impairments and disabilities that resulted. In many cases, there will be a combination of the two: both a direct traumatic injury and an acute exacerbation of any existing psychological or emotional problems. The U.S. Department of Health and Human Services' 1999 "Mental Health: A Report of the Surgeon General," indicated that, in any year, 28% of the population has a diagnosable substance abuse or mental health problem. The Population and Public Health Branch (PPHB) of Health Canada estimates the annual prevalence of mental health and substance abuse disorders in Canada to be 20% (Health Canada, 2004). The lifetime prevalence of mental and substance abuse disorders is much higher than these numbers. Thus, the probability based on these estimates that an individual has a diagnosable mental health or substance abuse disorder is 20–28%, while the probability he or she has had such a disorder at some point in his or her life is much greater.

The fact that a given plaintiff may have a current or prior diagnosable mental disorder led to discussion of such concepts as a "thin-skulled man" or someone with an "eggshell personality," or a similar term that reflects the fact that some people react more extremely to a given trauma. For example, Breslau, Chilcoat, Kessler and Davis (1999) found that previous exposure to trauma is associated with a greater risk of PTSD from subsequent trauma. Similarly, elderly individuals often have pre-trauma symptoms similar to those of PTSD, including cognitive impairment, sleep difficulty, and/or mood disorders. They are also

INFO

The thin skull principle says that you take your victim as you find him. It holds a defendant liable for all consequences resulting from his or her activities leading to an injury to another person, even if the victim suffers an unusually high level of damage (e.g., due to a pre-existing vulnerability or medical condition).

relatively likely to have had a significant trauma at some earlier date in their lives that may resurface as a result of a current trauma.

The task for the evaluator is to assess the status of the plaintiff prior to the current trauma the additional problems engendered by the trauma, and the impact of the new trauma on the ability of the individual to function. This is more difficult with an elderly individual than for someone much younger because the elderly person is relatively likely to have various psychological or emotional symptoms, a lower activity level, and other age-related deficits. Since many elderly individuals do not work, lost income may not be an issue. However, quality of life and treatment issues may be substantial, including the possible need for long-term rehabilitation and nursing home care (Miller, 2001).

Further complicating the issue is that a given traumatic event will have differing impacts on different people, based on an individual's history of traumatic experiences and other factors. The critical factor is not the nature of the traumatic event itself, but *how the plaintiff reacted to the event* and *what the event meant to the plaintiff* that will determine the actual affect on the individual. Resilient individuals will tend to show a milder reaction to trauma than will those with less resilience. The response of an individual should ultimately depend on the combination of the severity of the actual traumatic experience, his or her interpretation of the event(s), history of traumatic experience, degree of resilience, and personality and temperament (Levy & Rosenberg, 2003). For an especially resilient individual, the traumatic event may lead to no loss of functional ability and may turn from a traumatic event to a chance for personal growth (Linley & Joseph, 2005; Maddi, 2005).

The 9/11/2001 attack on the World Trade Center in Manhattan offers some examples. Franz, Glass, Arnkoff, and Dutton (2009) found that the effect of the destruction of the Twin Towers was greater for individuals with a history of mental health treatment than for those without such histories. Another estimate indicated that 52% of 250 participants in the World Trade Center Worker & Volunteer Medical Screening Program in New York City who were interviewed 10-12 months following 9/11 reported mental health symptoms that required further evaluation, and 20% reported symptoms consistent with PTSD (Warner, 2003).

The Supreme Court of Canada discussed the concept of a "crumbling skull" in *Athey v. Leonati* (1996). An individual was in two motor vehicle accidents in 1991, one in February and the second in April. That autumn, his physician permitted him to resume a regular exercise routine, and he herniated a disk. The Supreme Court indicated that

> [t]he so-called "crumbling skull" rule simply recognizes that the pre-existing condition was inherent in the plaintiff's "original position." The defendant need not put the plaintiff in a position *better* than his or her original position. The defendant is liable for the injuries caused, even if they are extreme, but need not compensate the plaintiff for any debilitating effects of the pre-existing condition *which the plaintiff would have experienced anyway.* The defendant is liable for the additional damage but not the pre-existing damage [citations omitted]. Likewise, if there is a measurable risk that the pre-existing condition would have detrimentally affected the plaintiff in the future, regardless of the defendant's negligence, then this can be taken into account in reducing the overall award [citations omitted]. This is consistent with the general rule that the plaintiff must be returned to the position he would have been in, with all of its attendant risks and shortcomings, and not a better position [paragraph 35; emphasis added].

Under this analysis, a preexisting condition in a crumbling skull case would lead to a decision that the tortfeasor would need to return the plaintiff to his or her pre-trauma condition, but not into better condition, than prior to the tortious event. In *Athey*, the Supreme Court of Canada ruled that the herniated disk would not have occurred but for the second accident, requiring treatment of that condition and related conditions.

No U.S. cases using the "crumbling skull" concept were identified in searches of Loislaw and Findlaw in November, 2009. A Louisiana case, however, cited the same principle. In *Miramon v. Bradley* (1997), a woman had been in motor vehicle accidents in

1988 and 1990. She was still being treated for the effects of the first accident at the time of the second. "All of her treating physicians and therapists agreed that the second accident exacerbated Ms. Miramon's problems" (p. 477). The trial court denied Ms. Miramon any recovery because none of the experts could identify a single, specific cause of the exacerbation. The court of appeals reversed, ordering that both medical expenses and compensation for pain and suffering be given to Ms. Miramon on the basis that "if a defendant's tortuous conduct aggravates a pre-existing condition, the defendant is liable to the extent of the aggravation…. This is true even though the tortuous conduct is not the sole factor in the aggravation, but is a significant contributing factor" (p. 478).

Conclusion

Having described the important practical details of accepting work on a case, Chapter 5 explains in detail the various ways of collecting reliable and valid data, including psychological interviews, sources of collateral information, and especially the strengths and weaknesses of various psychological instruments commonly used to assess psychological harms.

Data Collection | **5**

There is a substantial amount of information the expert must review as part of conducting an assessment of the plaintiff. It must be kept in mind that the goal of the assessment is to ascertain whether, and if so to what extent, the traumatic event caused a psychological injury to the plaintiff, and how different the plaintiff is now from before this event. The traumatic event may have been the sole cause of the apparent psychological injury, the major but not sole cause, a significant contributing factor, a minor influence, or no influence at all. The data to address these issues are found in relevant records, interviews with credible collateral informants, and through a forensic evaluation of the plaintiff that includes psychological testing and interviews. There is no standardized format for the conducting of the evaluation; each expert must design an assessment that comprehensively addresses all of the relevant issues, including the legal questions. The expert needs to obtain a thorough picture of relevant information regarding the plaintiff and the case, to strive for accuracy and completeness (Saks & Lanyon, 2007). In the following section, we describe steps that are consistent with best practices, although experts will use flexibility in determining how each is used in a specific case.

Obtaining Records

The expert's task in most cases is to advise the retaining attorney of the records that are needed for review (both records already in the attorney's possession and additional records that have not yet been obtained). In most cases, this will include records that describe the individual's functioning prior to the trauma, in order

BEST PRACTICE

Be sure to obtain the following records if possible (to the degree relevant) prior to conducting the evaluation

● Medical records

● Mental health records

● School records

● Arrest records

● Employment records

● Military records

to create a baseline against which post-trauma functioning can be assessed. Such records may include medical, psychotherapy, school, arrest, employment, military, and any other records relevant to the individual's functioning prior to and after the traumatic event. Reports or interviews with credible collateral informants, such as former employers and neighbors, can also provide a good basis for comparisons.

These records should go back far enough so the evaluator can assess with reasonable certainty how the plaintiff was functioning prior to the allegedly traumatic event. In most cases, three to five years prior to that event will suffice. An important exception, however, concerns any major potentially traumatic events that occurred earlier in the plaintiff's life. Was the plaintiff ever involved in any significant accidents? Was the plaintiff physically or sexually abused as a child or assaulted as an adult? Were there other major traumas reported by the plaintiff or a significant other earlier in the plaintiff's life? If so, medical, work, school or other relevant records around the time of earlier traumas should be sought as well.

In what ways has the individual's lifestyle changed since the events reported as part of the current tort action? What does the individual say he or she can no longer do–or do as well? Check registers, credit card statements, and the activities they imply may provide significant information in this respect (Greenberg, 2003).

Medication records—both before and following the allegedly traumatic incident—will shed light on the assessment by a physician of the plaintiff's status, as well as providing data on the direct and side effects of the medication. In addition, it is important to inquire about non-prescribed drugs, both illegal and over-the-counter.

While assessing the plaintiff, the expert can also gauge how the medication appears to be affecting the individual's behavior and capacities. Note that the role of the non-medical expert is not to render an opinion on the appropriateness of the medication or dosage, but to assess the individual's level of functioning before and after the trauma, and before and after specific treatments were rendered.

According to Sageman (2003),

> It is of the utmost importance to gather the most comprehensive information on the litigant, including past medical and mental health records, previous neuropsychological testing, occupational history, depositions, all legal testimonies, diaries (if available), and contemporary pictures and/or videos. The standard for a mental health expert is to review all the [reasonably] available evidence before seeing the subject of a forensic examination, especially if retained by the opposite side.... The more thorough the review of the evidence, the greater is the credibility of the expert.... (p. 324)

It will be difficult, if not impossible, for the expert to testify to a "reasonable degree of certainty" regarding changes in the plaintiff as a result of the allegedly traumatic incident if the expert has not conducted a review of records sufficient to support the expert's conclusions. Such a failure to review available, relevant records may be considered to be below the standard of practice (Ackerman & Kane, 1998; Heilbrun, 2001). This opens the door to possible sanctions from a licensing board. In *Deatherage v. Washington Examining Board of Psychology* (1997), the Washington Supreme Court ruled that a psychologist was not immune to discipline from the state psychology licensing board for his failure to qualify statements in child custody evaluations, mischaracterization of information, failure to verify information, and misinterpretation of test data (Cohen, 2004; Ewing, 2003). In addition, despite witness and/or quasi-judicial immunity under most circumstances, courts have begun to allow civil lawsuits against experts by litigants who have retained those experts and who allege that the expert practiced below the minimum standard for his or her profession or was

5
chapter

negligent (Cohen; Ewing). To our knowledge, however, successful board discipline and lawsuits of this type have been rare, and associated with relatively extreme departures from these standards. The records review is likely to yield many questions and hypotheses that can be addressed during the testing and interviewing portions of the evaluation, including helping with decisions regarding what tests and other data collection instruments to utilize. This is yet another reason for ensuring that the records reviewed are as thorough and complete as possible. It should also be considered that the interview of the plaintiff may yield information regarding potentially important additional third party sources (whether records or people to interview) (Heilbrun, personal communication, February 11, 2010).

Timeline

Even if the relevant records go back only three to five years prior to the allegedly traumatic incident, it is usually very helpful to create a timeline for the major life events in the plaintiff's life. If the plaintiff experienced potentially traumatic major life events significantly prior to the allegedly tortious event, creation of a timeline may be essential to the understanding of the course of events in the plaintiff's life. If the plaintiff alleges that he or she previously had no difficulty obtaining medical or dental care, but has not been able to obtain such care following an alleged medical malpractice, then medical records going back a number of years may be essential. We recommend that the timeline include direct quotations from significant records, providing a chronological summary of the major events in the plaintiff's life. Relevant records include the plaintiff's deposition(s), if available. A good timeline is also valuable in deposition or court testimony, particularly if there are a great many records that were reviewed for the case. The source of each piece of data should be specified (Heilbrun, 2001). Little or no attempt should be made to resolve contradictions between sources in the timeline, which should include all potentially relevant data regarding the plaintiff's major life events. The timeline provides the attorneys with a basis for understanding what data the psychologist considered in formulating his or her opinions. Finally, in large and/or complex cases, often with dozens of depositions and thousands of pages

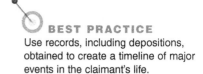

BEST PRACTICE
Use records, including depositions, obtained to create a timeline of major events in the claimant's life.

of records, a chronology of the case can be essential in helping the expert to keep the facts straight for deposition or trial testimony.

The Assessment Setting

The evaluation should be conducted in an environment that facilitates the assessment process. It should have good lighting, privacy, quiet, and minimal distractions or interruptions. The evaluatee should not be asked to complete forms in a waiting room or other public setting. The setting should maximize the ability of the plaintiff to concentrate. If the setting is inconsistent with any of these conditions in a way that could potentially affect the results of the evaluation, the expert must take those factors into account when interpreting tests and interviews, and it must be noted in the report of the evaluation (Pope & Vasquez, 2007).

Informed Consent

A key portion of the assessment process is obtaining the informed consent of the plaintiff, unless the evaluation is court-ordered or the plaintiff is too young or cognitively disabled to be able to give informed consent (Ethical Standard 9.03, *Ethical Principles of Psychologists and Code of Conduct*, 2002). Even in those latter situations, however, we recommend attempting to thoroughly inform the plaintiff, and gaining the plaintiff's assent. This includes informing the plaintiff, preferably in writing:

- of the nature and purpose of the assessment (including who retained the expert)

BEST PRACTICE
Conduct the evaluation in a private location, free of distractions and interruptions, to the degree possible. Noisy, crowded, or otherwise inappropriate environments can adversely affect the results and credibility of the evaluation.

5
chapter

- that the assessment is not confidential (although only a small number of people may have access to the information)
- to whom the results will be furnished (*Specialty Guidelines*, Guideline IV.E.)
- that there is no "doctor-patient" relationship between the expert and the plaintiff
- that the expert depends on the plaintiff being open and honest
- that the plaintiff is not required to answer every question, and does not have to tell the expert anything said by his or her attorney
- that the expert may disclose any information from the plaintiff necessary to protect the public safety, including child abuse or a plan to hurt himself or herself or others
- that the plaintiff is entitled to some feedback, but not to a copy of the raw data or of the expert's report
- that information given to the expert after the formal evaluation must be in writing
- that the plaintiff promises to do his or her best on each of the tests and other instruments
- that audio or video taping of tests and other instruments will not be permitted
- that some parts of the evaluation may have to be repeated if the period of time between the evaluation and a deposition or trial exceeds six to twelve months
- that the interview may need to be updated shortly before a deposition or trial regardless of how much time has passed
- that a cell phone may only be used during breaks
- that the plaintiff may consult his or her attorney regarding legal rights or what he or she should sign or do.

If the evaluator is not certain that the plaintiff has understood the explanation, the plaintiff should be questioned in sufficient detail to determine the level of understanding, generally including asking the plaintiff to paraphrase what he or she has been told. If the plaintiff does not understand

BEST PRACTICE

Always obtain informed consent prior to the evaluation, unless consent is not required. Be sure to inform the claimant of the nature and purpose of the evaluation, that the evaluation is not confidential, and that the results will be reviewed by other parties (e.g., attorneys)

the written document, the expert should discuss each item in plain language, trying to ensure understanding, and should document any questions regarding the adequacy of the plaintiff's understanding. If the plaintiff will not sign the document, but verbally agrees to proceed, the expert should document both the refusal and the verbal agreement to proceed. If the plaintiff will not proceed, the expert should stop the evaluation and consult with the retaining attorney.

A sample informed consent statement can be found in Appendix B.

If the above language appears to be too difficult for some plaintiffs, it might be necessary to rephrase each item in simpler language, followed by a request that the subject paraphrase the statement that has just been articulated. If the plaintiff does not appear to be able to give informed consent, or assent, that should be discussed with the retaining attorney. If this attorney does not represent the plaintiff, then the retaining attorney should discuss this situation with the plaintiff's attorney prior to proceeding. If the evaluation has been ordered by the court at the request of the defense, the attorneys may need to discuss the situation with the court. The expert's report should note the questionable understanding, discuss the apparent cause of that problem, and indicate any affect on the results of the assessment (Heilbrun, 2001).

Barnett (2009) recommends that evaluatees be asked at the beginning of an assessment whether they have been evaluated by a forensic mental health expert in the past, and whether they have ever taken any psychological tests for any reason. For those evaluatees who have, the expert may wish to use tests or other instruments

5
chapter

that differ from those previously used to assess the plaintiff—or may want to obtain the previous test results to compare with the present results using the same test(s).

Requirements for Correct Administration of Psychological Instruments

As discussed in Chapter 2, there is much controversy in the field about the presence of third party observers (TPO) or audio or video recording of evaluations, specifically as applied to neuropsychological tests, personality tests, specialized forensic instruments, and forensic interviews. The decision about whether to allow TPO or recording devices for each of these sources of data must be made carefully and in full consideration of the various studies, positions, influences, and considerations discussed in detail in Chapter 2.

Psychological Testing

According to the Standards for Educational and Psychological Testing,

> [a] test is an evaluative device or procedure in which a sample of an examinee's behavior in a specified domain is obtained and subsequently evaluated and scored using a standardized process. While the label *test* is ordinarily reserved for instruments on which responses are evaluated for their correctness or quality and the terms *scale* or *inventory* are used for measures of attitudes, interest, and dispositions, the *Standards* uses the single term *test* to refer to all such evaluative devices (American Educational Research Association, 1999, p. 3).

Although there are numerous tests and other instruments that are relevant to personal injury evaluations, there are no forensic assessment instruments that were designed and validated specifically for personal injury evaluations. It is, therefore, necessary for the evaluator to choose tests and other instruments that were designed for other purposes but that have been validated for use in personal injury evaluations, or that may be used in such evaluations by virtue of the relevance of the test or instrument to the questions that must be addressed in the personal injury evaluation. If a psychological test is reliable and has been validated for assessing the kind of psychopathology found in personal injury litigation, that is likely to be sufficient to meet the reliability requirement of the "relevance/reliability" evidentiary legal criteria (Heilbrun, 2010, personal communication).

Experts may accurately portray an individual's psychological, motivational, emotional, intellectual, social, and other characteristics using psychological tests and other instruments. Empirical research connects information of these types with past, current, and future behavior and consequences. This process yields behavioral theories.

As discussed in Chapter 3, over-reliance on computer-based **interpretations** of psychological tests should generally be avoided in forensic cases (Otto, 2002). There are a number of tests for which the computer program will produce a report interpreting the test data. Although the printout usually specifies that the statements should be treated as hypotheses that must be verified with other data, some psychologists treat the software-generated interpretation as if it were dispositive and their own product, even incorporating (verbatim) some statements from the printout in their own reports. Only the author of the interpretive statements knows the algorithm utilized to create the interpretive program, or the empirical research upon which it is based, and the interpretation suggested is likely to be based on a common interpretation of the highest test scales rather than on all scales that may provide important information. Psychologists have an ethical responsibility to know how to interpret the tests they utilize (*EPPCC* Ethical Standards 2.01, 9.02).

5
chapter

Response Style

The individual's response style, or test-taking attitude, is a key consideration in an assessment. According to Heilbrun (2001),

> Response style has been defined to include four particular styles: (1) reliable/honest (a genuine attempt is made to be accurate;

factual inaccuracies result from poor understanding or misperception), (2) malingering (conscious fabrication or gross exaggeration of psychological and/or physical symptoms, understandable in light of the individual's circumstances and not attributable merely to the desire to assume the patient role, as in Factitious Disorder), (3) defensive (conscious denial or gross minimization of psychological and/or physical symptoms, as distinguished from ego defenses, which involve intrapsychic processes that distort perception), and (4) irrelevant (failure to become engaged in the evaluation; responses are not necessarily relevant to questions and may be random).... (pp. 165–166)

(See also Rogers & Bender, 2003; Rogers, 2008).

Heilbrun, Warren, and Picarello (2003, p. 71) add two additional categories:

"uncooperative, in which the individual responds minimally or not at all to assessment questions;" and "impaired: it involves experiencing communication deficits resulting from young age, thought and speech disorganization, intellectual deficits, and/or memory problems."

Psychological tests to evaluate response style must be both valid and reliable. The test that is almost universally utilized by forensic psychologists for assessing adults in personal injury cases is the Minnesota Multiphasic Personality Inventory, Second Edition (MMPI-2). The MMPI-2 is one of the few instruments for which there is significant data regarding both response style and the nature and extent of any psychopathology (Boccaccini & Brodsky, 1999; Greenberg et al., 2003; Lees-Haley, 1992; Otto, 2002; Posthuma, Podrouzek, & Crisp, 2002; Rabin, Barr, & Burton, 2005; Shuman, 1994, 2002 supplement). When used properly, the MMPI-2 should have no difficulty passing the requirements of the Federal Rules of Evidence or their equivalent state rules of evidence, including requirements for reliability, relevance, falsifiability, general acceptance within the scientific community, and peer review and publication. Otto (2002) identified 19 cases in which there was a challenge to the admissibility of the MMPI/MMPI-2. No appellate cases were identified in which

MMPI/MMPI-2-based testimony was excluded on the basis any of the standards in *Daubert v. Merrill Dow Pharmaceuticals* (1993). However, when using the MMPI-2 or any other psychological test, the evaluator must understand the

BEST PRACTICE
Always use valid and reliable psychological tests to evaluate the claimant's response style. The most scientifically validated measure for this purpose is the MMPI-2.

basis of the major underlying empirical research upon which various interpretations are based. This includes the nature of such studies, similarities and differences between the subject and the study population, error rates, and the overall quality and scientific rigor of the study.

Malingering and Feigning

The evaluator should choose tests that have demonstrated significant sensitivity and specificity in the assessment of feigning, and that also add incremental validity to the data that are obtained. The number of tests and other instruments should be sufficient to accomplish the task, yet few enough to be administered in a reasonable time without excessive fatigue (Kane, 2007c). This is particularly true for defense experts, whose time with the plaintiff may be limited, while plaintiff's experts often have substantially more time to evaluate the plaintiff. If the expert does not believe that he or she will have enough time with the plaintiff to conduct an evaluation sufficient to address the essential issues in the case, the expert should decline the case, or attempt to get the retaining attorney to arrange for more time, or seek a court order permitting more time.

Melton et al. (2007) indicate that "'[s]ensitivity' reflects a test's capacity to select many or most of the individuals who possess the trait or exhibit the behavior that the test is designed to measure. 'Specificity' is an index of the degree to which the test selects <u>only</u> those individuals possessing the trait or expressing the behavior that the test is designed to detect" (p. 738). A sensitive test will have few false negative results, and a test with high specificity will yield few false positive results. The best tests, in context,

5
chapter

will accurately identify people who are feigning, as well as individuals who are not feigning. No test is ideal for doing so, but many tests provide useful evidence of an individual's attempt to feign. The evaluator needs to try to keep both false positive and false negatives to a minimum (Gouvier, Hayes & Smiroldo, 2003). A factor in the assessment of feigning/malingering is the assessment of secondary cost. While some individuals may be willing to accept substantial limitations on their functioning in order to achieve a relatively small financial gain (for example, a few thousand dollars), the smaller the potential gain from a lawsuit the less likely it is that an individual is consciously or unconsciously feigning (Miller, 2003).

Minnesota Multiphasic Personality Inventory, Second Edition (MMPI-2)

The Minnesota Multiphasic Personality Inventory, Second Edition (Butcher et al., 1989) is the most-widely researched and utilized objective personality and psychopathology test (Butcher & Miller, 2006; Greene, 2008; Kane, 2007b). The validity scales of the MMPI-2 are especially well-suited for addressing whether an individual is failing to respond to the test items in an open and forthright manner, including the possibility of feigning or malingering—although the results may be ambiguous, and interpretations should be carefully made (Bender, 2008; Bianchini, Greve & Glynn, 2005; Boccaccini & Brodsky, 1999; Butcher & Miller, 2006; Fishbain, Cutler, Rosomoff & Rosomoff, 2003; Greene, 2008; Greenberg, Otto & Long, 2003; Kane, 2007b; Lees-Haley, 1992; Melton et al., 2007; Nicholson & Martelli, 2007e; Otto, 2002; Pope, Butcher & Seelen, 2006; Polusny & Arbisi, 2006; Posthuma, Podrouzek, & Crisp, 2002; Rabin, Barr, & Burton, 2005; Resnick et al., 2008; Rogers, 2003; Rogers, 2008a; Rogers, Sewell, Martin, & Vitacco, 2003; Rogers & Shuman, 2005; Shuman, 1994, 2002 supplement). Nicholson and Martelli (2007f) note that the MMPI-2's validity scales are not usually elevated in cases of traumatic brain injury, so elevations are particularly suspect. Assessing the individual's response style with the validity scales of the

MMPI-2 permits the evaluator to identify whether, and to what degree, the plaintiff was defensive, consistent, exaggerated symptoms, attempted to appear virtuous, and so forth. The individual's response to the validity scale items can generally be extended, with caution, to the entire evaluation. An individual who provides a valid MMPI-2 protocol is generally likely to respond validly to other tests, instruments and interviews during the evaluation (Boccaccini & Brodsky, 1999; Graham, 2006; Pope, personal communication, May 14, 2006; Pope, Butcher, & Seelen, 2000; Rubenzer, 2009). Because of its great popularity in assessing response validity (and specifically the likelihood of malingering), the MMPI-2 will be discussed at some length. The scales will be briefly described here, but for the meaning of specific scores, experts should refer to the manual and associated research.

The initial validity measure is the "Cannot Say" or "?" Scale, the number of items to which there was no response, or for which "true" and "false" were both marked. Samuel, DeGirolamo, Michaels and O'Brien (1995) found that people involved in personal injury suits, as a group, left significantly more blanks than did people not involved in litigation. They also found that the closer the evaluation is to the date of the alleged trauma, the greater the likelihood that the person will leave more than 30 blank items, producing a profile that is questionable or invalid. This may be addressed by requesting the plaintiff to respond to the blank items, either reading from the test booklet or by having the items read to him or her. This variation in the standardized test administration should be noted in the test report, but is not likely to have an adverse affect on the validity of the test.

Second, two scales address the consistency of responses. The Variable Response Inconsistency Scale (VRIN) consists of 67 paired items, with the items in each pair being either opposite or similar in meaning. The True Response Inconsistency Scale (TRIN) is made up exclusively of items that are opposite in content. Someone who responds too inconsistently (higher than a T Score of 79) has an invalid test protocol. Both VRIN and TRIN should be examined before concluding that the individual is responding with excessive inconsistency, typically either random responding or a fixed response set. Either response set suggests responding without regard to the content of the item, thereby invalidating the test (Butcher et al., 2001). These scales are also useful in interpreting elevations of the F Scale. Elevations on VRIN, TRIN, and F suggest responding without attention to the meaning of the items. Elevation on F without elevations on VRIN or TRIN suggest a deliberate attempt to "fake bad" or a "cry for help" (Heilbrun, personal communication, February 11, 2010).

The L Scale addresses the individual's tendency to try to appear especially virtuous or perfect, or otherwise to portray oneself in an unrealistically positive light. T Scores of 65–69 suggest the person was accentuating the positive. T Scores of 70 or greater suggest extreme exaggeration of positive qualities (Pope et al., 2006). L Scale T scores of 80 or more invalidate the test protocol (Butcher et al., 2001).

The F (Infrequency) Scale is made up of items that were endorsed by 10% or fewer of the people in the original normative population among the initial 361 items on the MMPI-2. T Scores of 79 or fewer generally indicate a valid test. T Scores from 80 to 89 suggest that exaggerating is likely. Scores of 90 or more suggest that a test protocol may not be valid. (Butcher et al., 2001). T Scores of 100 or greater indicate a profile that is not interpretable because the responses are so extreme (Pope et al., 2006). Possible causes of an invalid F Scale include exaggeration of problems (which may be a call for help), malingering, great defensiveness, random responses, and/or substantial psychopathology (Groth-Marnat, 2009a). It is important to note that research has found that high F Scale scores significantly correlate with histories of trauma, PTSD, dissociation, depression, and environmental trauma in the person's family of origin (Elhai et al., 2004). People who feel stigmatized or rejected as a result of posttraumatic changes may respond to test items in a manner that emphasizes the injuries and pain they feel, to try to make certain that their problems and psychological pain are noticed (Briere, 2004). The F Scale is, therefore, less useful in the assessment of trauma victims than in assessing other populations.

The Fb (F Back) Scale contains items numbered 281 or greater, addressing items like those on the F Scale that are in the second half of the MMPI-2. In addition to the factors cited for the F Scale, a high score may be due to fatigue. The same cutoff scores as for the F Scale should be used (Butcher et al, 2001; Pope et al., 2006). However, a meta-analysis by Rogers et al. (2003) suggested using a cutoff score for Fb that is 12 points greater than the cutoff score for the F Scale, to try to reduce the number of false-positives.

The K Scale addresses defensiveness, in a manner more subtle than the L Scale. A high score is generally not an indication of psychopathology. T Scores of 65–74 imply "faking good," presentation of an unrealistically positive portrait of oneself or of life due to either unconscious or conscious exaggeration. A high score on the K Scale is likely to markedly reduce the scale elevations of the clinical scales on the test. Although special consideration had to be given to interpretation of high scores on the original MMPI when the individual was of a high socioeconomic status or had advanced education, the MMPI-2's K Scale was normed on a more educated population, making this differential interpretation unnecessary. However, people who have less than a high school education may produce a lower K Scale, potentially indicating too little defensiveness, with a consequent increase in the level of the clinical scales (Graham, 2006; Pope et al., 2006).

The S (Superlative Self-Presentation) Scale also addresses defensiveness, but is made up of items from throughout the test rather than only the first 370 from which the K Scale is drawn. High scores on this scale are obtained by people who claim various positive qualities, such as believing in human goodness, feeling serene, feeling content, denying negative feelings, and/or denying moral flaws. A valid test protocol is suggested by scores of 69 or fewer. Moderate defensiveness is suggested by scores from 70–74, and a score of 75 or greater may indicate invalidity of the test due to "faking good," presenting an unrealistically positive image of oneself or of life either unconsciously or consciously. The five subscales of the S Scale may be interpreted if the scale T score is 65 or greater (Butcher et al., 2001; Pope et al., 2006).

Because people who feel stigmatized or traumatized may produce high scores on F and/or Fb Scales, researchers have attempted to produce additional scales that take this into consideration. The most successful effort to date is the Fp (Infrequency-Psychopathology) Scale, which consists of items answered in the scored direction by at most 20% of the normative sample or a psychiatric patient sample. If the F Scale is elevated, and VRIN and TRIN indicate that random responding is unlikely, a T Score of 100 or greater on Fp suggests exaggeration of psychopathology, or "faking bad," unconsciously or consciously. When Fp is under 70, it is likely that any psychopathology indicated by the individual is real. T Scores falling between 70 and 99 may indicate a "cry for help" or another reason for exaggeration (Butcher et al., 2001; Nichols, 2001). Graham (2006) indicates that scores of 100 or more strongly suggest malingering, as does the MMPI-2 manual (Butcher et al., 2001). The Fp scale is the most sensitive and specific indicator of exaggeration on the MMPI-2 (Nichols, 2001; Polusny & Arbisi, 2006; Pope et al, 2000; Resnick et al., 2008). Rogers et al. (2003) indicate that "Fp appears to be the most effective scale in the assessment of feigning," in part because "these cut scores appear to be effective across disorders and even moderately useful with the problematic diagnosis of PTSD" (p. 173). Rogers, Payne, Berry and Granacher (2009) found that Fp cutting scores do well at discriminating between legitimate and feigned patients in clinical settings, yet produce few false-positives among people with PTSD. Briere (2004) and Elhai et al. (2004) indicate that Fp is more sensitive than the F Scale at determining the validity the responses of an individual with PTSD. Greene (2008) suggests that a raw score of six or seven on Fp indicates either inconsistent responding or malingering.

The F – K (F minus K) Index, also called the Dissimulation Index, implies "faking bad" if the *raw* score for the K Scale is 15 or more points lower than the *raw* score for the F Scale (Butcher et al., 2001). Scores of 25 or greater strongly suggest exaggerated psychopathology (Nichols, 2001; Rogers, Sewell & Salekin, 1994). Greene (2008) indicates that high cutoff scores should be used in order to minimize false-positives. According to Rogers et al.

(1994), if F – K equals or is less than –8, feigning is very unlikely. The F – K Index is particularly good at identifying "motivated faking" according to Briere (2004).

The ODecp (Other Deception) Scale (Nichols & Green, 1997) was developed to try to identify extremely defensive people. With a cutoff score of 20, the false positive rate was 5%. The MMPI contained a nearly identical scale, the Positive Malingering (MP) Scale.

The Gough Dissimulation Scale (Ds on the MMPI, Dsr on the MMPI-2) addresses psychopathology, but uses items that psychiatric patients do not usually endorse (Graham, 2006). Rogers et al. (2003) found it to be nearly as effective as the F and Fp Scales at indicating malingering. Based on their meta-analysis of 65 feigning and 11 diagnostic studies, Rogers et al. recommended utilizing Fp plus either F or Dsr. Rogers et al. (2009) found that false positives are seldom produced by Ds cutting scores of 35 or more. Greene (2008) recommends utilizing a cutoff score of at least 38 in order to minimize false-positives.

It is essential to remember that an invalid test protocol means exactly that. It does not justify, absent other information, an inference that the person was lying, malingering, or behaving dishonorably. Indeed, there are often many possible explanations for invalid test scores. Further, one does not interpret clinical scales if one determines that the test protocol is not valid. A clinical interview should be done and collateral information sought to ascertain why the individual responded as he or she did, but neither individual scales nor codetypes can be interpreted (Greene, 2000.

Fake Bad Scale (FBS)

The Fake Bad Scale (FBS, Lees-Haley, English & Glenn, 1991) is derived from the MMPI-2, but requires separate discussion because of the substantial controversy regarding its use. Prominent authors and researchers are found on both sides of the issue. The arguments have markedly increased since Pearson Assessments added the FBS to the scored validity scales on the MMPI-2, calling it the "FBS (Symptom Validity) Scale" (Butcher, Gass, Cumella,

Kally & Williams, 2008). The FBS includes 43 items from the MMPI-2.

Butcher et al. (2008) questioned the validity of the FBS. Their criticisms include (a) actual physical problems cause high FBS scores, (b) stress related to litigation may cause elevated scores, (c) women's scores tend to be about two points higher than men's, (d) people who have been through severe trauma generally have higher scores, (e) there are too many false-positives, and (f) there is no consensus regarding the cutoff point for "probable malingering." They cite a study of women with eating disorders, eight percent of whom would be called malingerers even using a very conservative cutoff score of 30. Using the recommended cutoff score of 29+, 11% would be classified as malingers. Butcher et al. observe that the "FBS appears to be a measure of general maladjustment and somatic complaints, as opposed to malingering" (p. 197). They also point out that the FBS does not include any evidence of the conscious intent to malinger that is required if malingering is to be diagnosed. Further, people with somatoform disorders, who unconsciously present psychological symptoms via physical symptoms, have a tendency to score high on the FBS. They also point out that there is no manual for the FBS, making it difficult for psychologists to understand the basis for the scale. They cite three Florida trial court cases (*Williams v. CSX Transportation, Inc.*, 2007; *Vandergracht v. Progressive Express et al.*, 2005; *Davidson v. Strawberry Petroleum et al.*, 2007) in which the FBS was excluded because it was not generally accepted in the psychological community (*Frye v. United States*, 1923).

Ben-Porath, Greve, Bianchini and Kaufmann (2009a) replied to Butcher et al. (2008). They first indicated that malingering should not be diagnosed based on any single scale or test, and that "a formal diagnosis of malingering should be based on the integration of diverse sources of information" (p. 63). They also indicate that malingering should not be diagnosed without specifying an external reward. They point out that the recommended cutoff score has changed on the basis of research, consistent with the scientific method. To address the issue of false positives, they cite Greiffenstein, Fox and Lees-Haley (2007), who indicated that only

1.2% of respondents among 1,052 medical and psychiatric patients without an evident incentive to exaggerate exceeded the cutoff of 29+, making them false positives. Other research cited indicated false positive rates from 0 to 2.9%. With regard to patients with mild traumatic brain injuries (mTBI) or chronic pain, they wrote that "[n]one of the no-incentive mild TBI patients and only 1.5% of the no-incentive pain patients score 29 or higher. In contrast, 28.9% of the mild TBI patients with incentive and 27.5% of the chronic pain patients with incentive scored higher than 29" (p. 72). They noted that no test offers an unequivocal gauge of intent, but that scoring above a specified level may provide an indication that malingering is likely. Further, they indicate, somatization and other disorders may also be present, but "[o]nly at the higher levels will the score be specific to intentional exaggeration" (p. 75). Regarding gender bias, they admit that women tend to get scores two points higher than men, but note that research indicates that "women who were diagnosed as malingering independent of their FBS scores were more likely to elevate FBS than similarly diagnosed men" (p.76), and that "the gender effects disappear at levels of FBS that indicate the possibility of malingering" (p. 77). They also note that the FBS has been accepted in many court cases, even if excluded by some courts.

Williams, Butcher, Gass, Cumella and Kally (2009) responded to Ben-Porath et al. (2009) by noting that the FBS was added to the MMPI-2 Extended Score Report without offering guidance to psychologists on how to avoid misuse of the scale. They again criticized the lack of a manual or manual supplement comprehensively discussing the scale. They again indicated concern about gender bias and the validity of using a cutoff score of 29+. They concurred with Ben-Porath et al. that an elevated score is not, alone, sufficient to diagnose malingering—but wrote that web-based guidelines for the FBS do not offer that advice. They note concern that Ben-Porath et al. advocate using the FBS in any situation in which the MMPI-2 is used, rather than limiting use to those situations in which there is clearly an external incentive. They note continued concern that "the FBS is highly correlated with empirically validated scales measuring somatoform disorders and somatic problems" (p. 190), and that there remains a lack of consensus regarding the correct cutoff score for a presumption of malingering. They cite research that found that people with TBIs or somatization disorders may score above standard cutoffs. They conclude by suggesting that "[o]ne can view the FBS only in a highly favorable light by ignoring the methodological problems in the studies underlying its development or by disregarding a significant body of empirical research that casts doubt on the accuracy of the FBS, even as an adjunct to diagnosing malingering" (p. 196).

Ben-Porath, Greve, Bianchini and Kaufmann (2009b) responded to Williams et al. by indicating that Williams et al.'s example demonstrated misuse of the scale, not appropriate use. They reiterated that neither "faking bad" nor malingering would reasonably be diagnosed on the basis of any single scale. They indicated that the FBS has been admitted over objections in some Florida court cases, as well as in other states. They state that the research supporting their position adhered more closely to scientific standards than did those studies cited by Williams et al. They closed by writing that "the expert using the MMPI-2 along with other techniques will continue to be able to rely routinely on the FBS in assisting triers of fact" (p. 4 of 4).

Resnick et al. (2008) indicated that the FBS did not differentiate between malingered and real PTSD in their research. "This finding may be due to the relatively high average elevations noted on the FBS Scale by genuine PTSD patients (M = 82.00)" (p. 119).

Greene (2008) identified the cut scores related to differing degrees of false positives. He found that a cut score of 28 yields a 10% false positive rate; 31 yields a 5% rate, 34 yields a 2% rate, and 35 yields a 1% false positive rate.

Rubenzer (2009) noted the great disparity in published studies, some indicating that the FBS is the best MMPI-2 validity scale for addressing feigning by people with psychological disabilities or injuries related to nonpsychotic disorders, while other research found the FBS to be essentially ineffective. Rubenzer indicated that a positive indicator is that the FBS highly correlates with results of cognitive Symptom Validity Testing. He found that recent reports on the FBS in compensation cases are favorable toward its use. However, he wrote, "[w]idely different cutoff scores are maximally effective across studies, and two groups appear prone to elevated scores: females with a prior psychiatric history and patients with severe objectively manifested physical distress, such as drug withdrawal" (p. 119). In addition, the FBS has been reported to have an excessive false positive rate—but, Rubenzer indicates, "scores above 28 were rarely found (false-positive rates from .01–.03) in nonlitigating cases" (p. 120). Since *litigating* cases are the context in which test results are crucial, however, the false positive rate remains a concern.

Nelson, Hoelzle, Sweet, Arbisi and Demakis (2010) did a meta-analysis of 32 studies on the FBS that met inclusion criteria, out of 83 FBS studies identified. Their pooled samples included 2,218 individuals who were judged to have over-reported, and 3,123 who did not over-report. The authors excluded studies that did not involve a forensic context. However, they included criminal forensic samples rather than limiting their analysis to personal injury cases. They also included simulating groups. The over-reporting sample included those subjects found to have shown exaggerated cognitive symptoms and/or insufficient effort on symptom validity tests, who were considered to be "known" feigners. It was found that the "FBS demonstrated greater effect sizes when effort was known to be insufficient (d = 1.16) and when traumatic brain injury was the condition associated with over-reporting of symptoms (d = 1.28)" (pp. 714–715). In the seven studies of posttraumatic stress and Posttraumatic Stress Disorder, FBS showed a large effect size (.86) but the F Scale and its variations (Fb, Fp, etc.) showed even larger effect sizes (.91–1.23). The authors concluded that the FBS is an appropriate validity measure in forensic neuropsychology work, particularly when there is evidence of a TBI. While the present authors consider this study to add to the "pro-FBS" side of the balance scale, we have concern about the inclusion of criminal forensic samples, and about the assumption that feigning is "known" if there is cognitive exaggeration or diminished effort on symptom validity tests.

BEWARE
There is much controversy surrounding the use of the Fake Bad Scale (FBS). Use caution when interpreting the results and do not rely on it as the sole indication of malingering.

The results also indicate that the F family of MMPI-2 scales have larger effect sizes than FBS when posttraumatic stress is found, as is frequently the case in personal injury actions.

Until there is a substantial body of research, preferably by researchers who lack a pre-existing position on the FBS, indicating the best cutoff score for significance, and with a very small false positive rate, caution must be used in interpreting the Fake Bad Scale. Like all psychological tests, it should be considered to suggest malingering only in the context of substantial additional evidence supporting that diagnosis. If a plaintiff has a raw score of 29 or more, the psychologist should carefully review other evidence supporting or contradicting a diagnosis of malingering, including identification of a significant incentive to malinger. Confirmation bias must be avoided. If there is not both evidence of a significant incentive and other data suggesting malingering, one should not conclude that malingering is occurring. Psychologists should also review new research on the FBS as it gets published, to ascertain whether the scale should be used and to decide whether its use can be defended in court.

MMPI-2 RF

The Minnesota Multiphasic Personality Inventory-2-Restructured Form contains 338 items from the MMPI-2. In our opinion, this instrument has significant promise, and appears likely to improve on the MMPI-2 in some ways, especially because it includes more of the research basis for various interpretations. However, at the present time, we don't believe that the quantity of published peer-reviewed research by psychologists independent of the publisher, Pearson Assessments, is yet sufficient for this test to be utilized in forensic assessments. While research on the MMPI-2 has indicated that it can draw on the thousands of published studies on the MMPI for interpretation, one cannot yet say that the MMPI-RF can draw on the thousands of published studies on the MMPI and MMPI-2 for interpretation. The database of information regarding codetypes with the MMPI-2 is substantial, including decades of empirical studies. Use of the RF alone prevents the psychologist from taking advantage of the very substantial database of information regarding MMPI-2 codetypes (Greene, 2011). As the research base for the RF expands, forensic psychologists may find the most relevant and probative studies in either database. Therefore, our recommendation for the foreseeable future is to administer the full MMPI-2, so as to take advantage of as much research as possible.

Personality Assessment Inventory (PAI)

The Personality Assessment Inventory (Morey, 1991) offers the advantages of a lower required reading level than the MMPI-2 (fourth grade versus sixth grade), non-overlapping scales, four rather than two options per item, and shorter overall length (344 vs. 567 items) and testing time. Research has found that it can distinguish real and simulated psychiatric patients, but it also has a high false positive rate regarding feigning, as almost 20% of genuine patients were classified as feigners (Bender, 2008). Bender indicates that there is no evidence yet that it can distinguish individuals describing traumatic brain injury and other neurocognitive deficits accurately, versus simulating such deficits.

Resnick et al. (2008) described the three PAI scales for detecting malingering: Negative Impression (NIM), Malingering Index (MAL), and Rogers Discriminant Function Index (RDF). NIM addresses rare symptoms, whereas MAL and RDF address spurious psychopathological patterns. The authors indicate that NIM is able to differentiate between real and feigned civilian PTSD, but also note a 35% false positive rate with combat veterans. MAL and RDF have not performed well in differentiating real from feigned PTSD. Resnick et al. recommend that the MMPI-2, rather than the PAI, be utilized when addressing feigned PTSD.

Sellbom and Bagby (2008) reviewed research on the PAI's ability to address malingering. They note that the PAI is effective in screening *out* malingering, but that there are too many false positives to permit the PAI to be used to screen *in* malingering, particularly in forensic evaluations. Iverson and Lange (2006)

INFO

The PAI is effective at screening **out** malingering, but less effective for screening **in** malingering.

wrote that the "literature to date suggests that PTSD can be successfully faked on the PAI" (p. 88). Rogers (2008d), in contrast, concluded that the PAI effectively addresses malingering. Rubenzer (2009) summarized "the evidence for the PAI validity indicators (as) mixed, even in better-designed studies...(of) actual PTSD patients... likely to produce elevations on them.... The primary advantage of the PAI is that the [malingering index] (and potentially the RDF) adds a detection strategy not found on other instruments" (p. 123). According to Morey (2003), the MAL is comprised of scores on PAI scales or combinations of scales "that tend to be observed much more frequently in the profiles of persons simulating mental disorder (particularly severe mental disorders) than in actual clinical patients" (p. 52). The RDF consists of "weighted combinations of 20 different PAI scores.... The formula yields a discriminant function score that has a cutting score of roughly 0.... [S]cores greater than 0 suggest malingering, whereas scores less than 0 suggest that no effort at negative distortion was made...." This formula works for both clinical and community samples, for both of which the mean score is "roughly –1.00 (with a standard deviation of approximately 1.0" (p. 55).

Mullen and Edens (2008) investigated the legal cases in which the PAI has been utilized by reviewing appellate cases between 1991 and 2006. They found 125 published cases, about half of which were from the United States. Canadian cases comprised 89 percent of the international cases, with 9.5 percent from Australia and 1.5 percent from the United Kingdom. Personal injury cases comprised 22 percent of the total. There were no cases in which the PAI was excluded for any reason. Since appellate cases only deal with limited issues, however, this does not indicate how consistently the PAI was accepted at the trial court level.

Trauma Symptom Inventory (TSI)

The Trauma Symptom Inventory (Briere, 1995) includes three validity scales, with its Atypical Response Scale (ATR) in particular addressing possible malingering. With a cut score of T >

90, the false positive rate is 5%. Resnick et al. (2008) found the TSI's validity scales to be only somewhat successful at detecting malingering. Sellbom and Bagby (2008) did a literature review of the TSI, concluding that its validity scales were insufficient to separate malingers from legitimate patients. We therefore recommend at this time that psychologists not rely on the validity scales of the TSI.

Millon Clinical Multiaxial Inventory, Third Edition (MCMI-III)

The Millon Clinical Multiaxial Inventory, Third Edition (Millon et al., 1997) was normed only on clinical populations, with no normal control group. It has been found to exaggerate psychopathology, making "normal" individuals appear to have significant disorders (Ackerman & Kane, 2005; Craig, 1999; Groth-Marnat, 2009a; Hess, 1998; Hynan, 2004; Rogers, Salekin, & Sewell, 1999, 2000; Schutte, 2000). Melton et al. (2007) indicate that the response style scales of the MCMI-II and III "have not been subjected to much research, and the research that has been conducted has been discouraging" (p.60). Sellbom and Bagby (2008) concluded, "Under no circumstances should practitioners use this measure in forensic evaluation to determine response styles" (p. 205).

5
chapter

Structured Interview of Reported Symptoms (SIRS)

The Structured Interview of Reported Symptoms (Rogers, 1992) is often considered the best test of malingering (Melton et al., 2007; Rogers & Bender, 2003). The 172-item structured interview is designed to assess response styles, including feigning. It has been established as an accurate assessment for differentiating malingerers from clinical groups (Resnick et al., 2008; Rogers, 2008c). It has eight primary scales that address a specified strategy to detect feigning:

> [D]etection strategies are organized into two general categories: *unlikely* (i.e., the mere reporting of these test items is indicative of feigning) and *amplified* (i.e., higher-than-expected frequency or intensity of reported symptoms is considered indicative of feigning). Primary scales in the unlikely category include rare symptoms (RS), symptom combinations (SC), improbable and absurd symptoms (IA), and reported versus observed symptoms (RO). Those in the amplified category consist of blatant symptoms (BL), subtle symptoms (SU), selectivity of symptoms (SEL), and severity of symptoms (SEV).... In addition, a defensiveness scale (DS) evaluates defensiveness via the denial of common psychological problems. (Rogers, Payne, Berry & Granacher, 2009, p. 216)

Rogers et al. (2009) analyzed data from 569 people who had forensic neuropsychiatric evaluations involving workers' compensation, disability determinations, or personal injuries. They were able to divide the individuals into three groups: those with feigned mental disorders (FMD), those with feigned cognitive impairment (FCI), and those with genuine cognitive and/or mental disorders (GEN-Both). Three hundred eighty of the 569 individuals were part of compensation cases. Referral sources included both defendants (63.4%) and plaintiffs (35.1%).

Rogers et al. (2009) established criterion validity by comparison with the MMPI-2, and a number of Symptom Validity Tests, including the Victoria Symptom Validity Test (VSVT; Slick, Hopp, Strauss & Thompson, 1997); the Test of Memory Malingering (TOMM; Tombaugh, 1996); and the Letter Memory Test (LMT; Inman, Vickery, Berry, Lamb, Edwards, & Smith, 1998). Several intelligence tests were also administered. The SIRS correlated very well with the validity scales of the MMPI-2. As indicated by the test manual, the SIRS did not do well at specifying feigned cognitive impairment (FCI). They found that people with IQs below 80 appeared similar to people feigning cognitive impairment despite their having real pathology, so the SIRS should not be used with people with low IQs. Traumatic brain injuries did not produce significant SIRS profiles. There was no significant difference between patients referred by defense vs. plaintiff attorneys.

Rogers et al. (2009) also noted that the National Comorbidity Survey indicated that about two-thirds of people with PTSD diagnoses also had at least two other psychiatric diagnoses, making comorbidity the norm. It was also found that about half of the people diagnosed with PTSD showed some psychotic symptoms. Rogers et al. indicated that only patients with a Major Depression had only one Axis I diagnosis. Rogers et al. ended by concluding, "the SIRS is a highly reliable measure of FMD [feigned mental disorders].... The current investigation establishes its effectiveness for compensation and disability cases with common trauma-related diagnoses (PTSD and major depression)" (p. 223).

Heilbrun (2001, pp. 182-183) wrote that the SIRS works well to differentiate legitimate from malingering individuals, but does not work as well for a "'partial malingerer'—the individual who experiences genuine symptoms, but who also selectively reports, exaggerates, or fabricates some symptoms depending on the circumstances." The SIRS has a false-positive rate of 2–3% (Rogers & Shuman, 2005).

The SIRS-2 (Rogers, Sewell & Gillard) was published in February, 2010. The publisher indicates that the SIRS-2 has additional scales and indexes for evaluation of responses. We do not recommend that the SIRS-2 be used in forensic evaluations until sufficient independent research has established the validity and reliability of the test.

Structured Inventory of Malingered Symptomatology (SIMS)

The Structured Inventory of Malingered Symptomatology (Widows & Smith, 2005) is a screening test that addresses both psychological and neuropsychological problems. Only a fifth-grade reading level is required. It has been demonstrated to be effective as a screening instrument, but should not be used with people who are severely impaired, who may produce false-positive patterns (Smith, 2008). If the SIMS indicates that the individual may be malingering, a more definitive test should be administered, e.g., the SIRS or the MMPI-2. If time permits, we recommend using the SIRS and/or MMPI-2 rather than the SIMS.

Symptom Validity Testing (SVT)

Symptom Validity Testing (SVT) usually refers to cognitive rather than emotional or behavioral symptoms. It is designed "'to detect poor effort or intentional failure' using a variety of strategies… Failure on a performance-based validity test can corroborate feigning in a modality distinct from self-report, in a mode that probably requires intentionally poor performance (consciously not attending to the task, purposely answering incorrectly), and weighs against interpreting elevations on self-report validity scales as benign over-reporting" (Rubenzer, 2009, p. 127). Rubenzer (2009) indicates that SVTs primarily use scoring below chance as the primary means of identifying feigners, but that research suggests that this method identifies at most 10% of possible malingerers. Headaches, emotional distress, a psychiatric disorder, or any other cause of difficulty with attention or information processing may interfere with appropriate responding (Nicholson & Martelli, 2007c). Research indicates that malingerers do not tend to perform significantly below chance on these instruments (Nicholson & Martelli). Rogers (2008b) estimated the percentage as 25% or fewer. The cutting scores on SVTs are usually set at a point at which both clinical and nonclinical groups score well (Nicholson & Martelli). Rogers (2008d) noted that "SVT is the only [psychological testing] detection strategy that can provide definite evidence of cognitive feigning. However, most feigners do not perform substantially below chance, thereby limiting SVT to demonstrating the presence, but not the absence, of feigned cognitive impairment" (p. 394).

A common type of SVT is a forced-choice method involving "presentation of some sensory, cognitive, or other stimuli/test material whereupon the person is subsequently asked to provide a response. Possible responses are limited, usually to an either-or decision, with one response being correct and one wrong. If the person chooses more wrong responses than could be expected on the basis of chance responding, it may be concluded that he or she was intentionally performing below his or her true capacity or deliberately choosing wrong responses in an effort to appear more impaired than he or she actually is" (Nicholson & Martelli, 2007c, p. 429). Rogers (2008b) wrote that it is a strength that "failures significantly below chance provide definitive evidence of feigning" (p. 25), but that malingerers seldom fail such tests. The American Academy of Clinical Neuropsychology consensus statement (Heilbronner et al., 2009) concurs that below chance failures provide significant evidence of feigning, and that the greater the number of instruments on which the individual has a below chance performance, the greater the likelihood that he or she is malingering.

The most common cognitive SVT involves having the person memorize something simple, though the task may appear difficult and has been demonstrated to be performed well by both healthy and clinical populations (Nicholson & Martelli, 2007c). Rubenzer (2009) recommends the Word Memory Test (WMT, Green, 2005; Green et al., 1996), which he indicates may be the best of the SVTs because it has close to 100% sensitivity, among the very best of the SVTs. However, he notes, it may have a greater false-positive rate than some other SVTs. Rubenzer also suggests using "the age-corrected [WAIS] Digit Span scale score, the difference of the Vocabulary and Digit Span age-corrected scale scores…, and Reliable Digit Span (the number of digits repeated forward and backward, correct for both trials, summed)" (p. 128). Bender (2008) indicates that by definition "only 5% of the normative sample (both healthy and clinical samples) score below the 5th percentile on the Digit Span subtest of the WAIS-III," suggesting that it may be useful in assessing effort. However, both Digit Span and Reliable Digit Span may be inappropriate for people with borderline or lower IQs. Rubenzer notes that the Test of Memory Malingering (TOMM, Tombaugh, 1996) docs well at identifying feigned cognitive impairments, except when there is a cognitive

5
chapter

impairment from dementia or a similar non-traumatic condition. Rubenzer also recommends that evaluators include the Memory Complaints Inventory (MCI, Green, 2003) to ensure that memory and/or concentration problems are not missed.

Slick, Sherman and Iverson (1999) defined "malingered neurocognitive deficit" as "the volitional exaggeration or fabrication of cognitive dysfunction for the purpose of obtaining substantial material gain, or avoiding or escaping formal duty or responsibility" (p. 552). They proposed a set of criteria for assessing malingering that has become known as the "Slick criteria." If there is questionable performance on one or more neuropsychological or self-report tests, *and* an external reward, *and* questionable or inconsistent presentation, the person may be described as possibly, probably, or definitely malingering. "Definite" malingering involves (1) presence of a significant external incentive, (2) performance below a chance level on a forced-choice measure, and (3) inability to fully account for the below-chance responding based on developmental, psychiatric, or neurological factors. "Probable" malingering involves (1) presence of a significant external incentive, (2) that performance is not below chance, but that other neuropsychological testing strongly suggests feigning, and/or evidence of feigning from the individual's self-report, and (3) inability to fully account for the performance or information in #2 based on developmental, psychiatric or neurological factors. "Possible" malingering involves (1) the presence of a significant external incentive, (2) evidence of feigning from the individual's self-report, and (3) inability to fully account for the information in #2 based on developmental, psychiatric or neurological factors.

Neuropsychologists generally accept the Slick criteria. Rubenzer (2009) indicates that other authors suggest that failing two or three cognitive or psychiatric validity indicators should be considered evidence of malingering. Bender (2008) indicates that "possible" malingering is not helpful in a forensic evaluation.

Rubenzer (2009) wrote that Goldberg, Back-Madruga, and Boone (2007) used a literature survey to assess the affect of psychiatric disorders on SVTs. They determined that depression did not affect the outcome of any of 12 SVTs, but that there were insufficient data regarding Bipolar Disorder, personality disorders, or PTSD on SVTs. Rubenzer notes that PTSD should not adversely affect a cognitive SVT unless the person also has memory problems.

Bender (2008) identified signs of neurocognitive malingering:

1. The degree of cognitive impairment is beyond that expected given the severity of the injury.

2. The degree of impairment is inconsistent with the degree of functional disability.

3. Reported symptoms and/or cognitive profile(s) do not make neurological sense.

4. Test performance does not fit known cognitive profiles (e.g., better performance on free recall than on recognition).

5. Discrepant performance on tests of similar ability.

6. Frequent near misses.

7. Failing on easy items, and passing more difficult ones.

8. Quick to say, "I don't know" (p. 85).

Results of a SVT may be below recommended cutoffs for a number of reasons. The person may not read well, may evidence difficulty responding to the items, the SVT may be culturally inappropriate, the person may be actively resistant or disinterested, the person may have a headache, pain, medication side effects or other physical problem that reduces performance, the person may have a Factitious Disorder or other psychiatric or neurological disorder, and/or the evaluator may make an error (Nicholson & Martelli, 2007a; 2007f). In addition, "poor effort is neither necessary nor sufficient for a determination of malingering to be made in TBI cases" (Bender, 2008, p. 69). Evaluators need to know and understand the variety of possible causes for below-cutoff scoring on SVTs and consider them before labeling the behavior as malingering. However, there is general agreement among neuropsychologists that below-chance performance on symptom validity testing strongly suggests conscious feigning, and, possibly, malingering, especially if on more than one instrument (Nicholson & Martelli,

2007f; Rogers, 2008b; Rubenzer, 2009), though other possible causes need to be ruled out before coming to the conclusion that it *is* malingering.

Many SVTs have been recommended as having demonstrated success in the assessment of symptom validity, including (alphabetically):

Digit Memory Test (Nicholson & Martelli, 2007f; Sweet, Condit & Nelson, 2008)

Digit Span (from WAIS) (Berry & Schipper, 2008; Rubenzer, 2009; Sweet, Condit & Nelson, 2008)

Portland Digit Recognition Test (PDRT) (Nicholson & Martelli, 2007f; Sweet, Condit & Nelson, 2008)

Reliable Digit Span (from WAIS) (Nicholson & Martelli, 2007f; Rubenzer, 2009; Sweet, Condit & Nelson, 2008)

Rey Memory for 15 Item Test (Rey MFIT) (Rogers, 2008d; Sweet, Condit & Nelson, 2008)

Test of Memory Malingering (TOMM) (Melton et al., 2007; Nicholson & Martelli, 2007f; Rogers, 2008d; Rubenzer, 2009; Sweet, Condit & Nelson, 2008)

Validity Indicator Profile (VIP) (Melton et al., 2007; Rogers, 2008d)

Victoria Symptom Validity Test (VSVT) Nicholson & Martelli, 2007f; Sweet, Condit & Nelson, 2008)

Word Memory Test (WMT) (Melton et al., 2007; Nicholson & Martelli, 2007f l Rogers, 2008d; Rubenzer, 2009; Sweet, Condit & Nelson, 2008)

Malingering in Pain Patients

Some authors (e.g., Bianchini, Greve & Glynn, 2005; Fishbain, Cutler, Rosomoff & Rosomoff, 1999; Mendelson & Mendelson, 2004) suggest that it is particularly difficult to accurately diagnose malingering in pain patients. Pain may be considered chronic when its duration exceeds six months, and may be a reaction to peripheral pathology or to abnormalities in the nervous system (Nicholson & Martelli, 2007d). There is some evidence that actuarial analysis of questionnaires may permit evaluation of malingering in pain patients, but none that it can be detected via verbal statements (Nicholson & Martelli). The MMPI and MMPI-2 have been extensively utilized in research on chronic pain. Meyers, Millis and Volkert (2002) indicated that compensation-seeking patients scored higher on the validity scales, but there were too many false-positives when individual scales were addressed. They suggested a weighted index that included the F – K Index, F, Fp, Ds-r, Es, the total difference of the obvious—subtle T scores, and the FBS. Arbisi and Butcher (2004), in contrast, concluded that no validity scale profile accurately assessed compensation seeking by chronic pain patients. Finally, we add that it is also possible that people who have experienced the most psychological distress are more likely to seek compensation for it.

Bianchini, Greve, and Glynn (2005) posited that the problem with assessing malingering in pain patients was that there was no properly developed and calibrated instrument for that purpose. They defined "Malingered Pain-Related Disability (MPRD) as the intentional exaggeration or fabrication of cognitive, emotional, behavioral, or physical dysfunction attributed to pain for the purposes of obtaining financial gain, to avoid work, or to obtain drugs (incentive)" (p. 407). One of the factors they addressed is "inconsistency," on the basis that it is much more difficult to be consistent if someone is feigning symptoms than if one is exhibiting real symptoms. They considered inconsistencies to be "compelling" if the patient behaves substantially differently when being evaluated than how he or she behaves when unaware of being observed. They also indicated that "definitive" evidence of feigning is offered when an individual gets a below-chance score on at least one forced-choice symptom validity test. Patients who did not exhibit either of these extreme response patterns were considered "probable" feigners if it appeared that the patient was intentionally underperforming. They proposed that MPRD be diagnosed if (a) there is "evidence of significant external incentive;" (b) there is "evidence from physical evaluation;" (c) there is "evidence from cognitive/perceptual (neuropsychological) testing; (d) there is "evidence from self-report;" and (e) if "behavior meeting necessary criteria from groups B, C and D are not fully accounted for by psychiatric, neurologic, or developmental factors" (p. 412). They require at least two findings consistent with malingering in order to minimize false-positives.

Nicholson and Martelli (2007d) reviewed the Bianchini et al. criteria. They indicated that "there is considerable evidence that pain and related problems (e.g., psychoemotional distress, sleep disturbance) may produce interference effects resulting in poor performance and 'failure' on such measures, with false positive identification of malingering or poor effort" (p. 491). Nicholson and Martelli concurred with Bianchini et al. that below-chance responding on symptom validity testing make it likely that someone is feigning, but cautioned that such results should still be viewed cautiously because of the potential interference factors. However, they questioned many of the specific factors Bianchini et al. specified. For example, Bianchini et al. indicated that a marked difference in behavior when the patient does not know he or she is being observed is a significant factor. Nicholson and Martelli point out that there is great variability in the behavior of legitimate pain patients, and that they are often able to do things when relaxed or distracted that they are not able to do (or do well) when stressed. They also point out that many pain patients report being able to function less well than they are actual able. They also indicate that one must always consider that the patient has a Factitious Disorder rather than feigning, especially if there is not clearly an external incentive to feign. Nicholson and Martelli also note that patients with traumatic brain injuries, anxiety, distrust of the assessment situation, or other problems may perform less well during an evaluation than when feeling relatively well and engaging in some desired activity. They caution that assessment of feigning in pain patients must be done very cautiously and conservatively, since "fear or pain avoidance, undue concern about the significance of bodily sensations, hypersensitivity associated with neurobiological or psychosocial factors, or other central sensitization effects may result in self-report of pain and related disability disproportionate to expectation on the basis of known pathology" (Nicholson & Martelli, 2007e, p. 510).

In summary, there is no "state of the art" means of determining malingering in pain patients, short of an admission by the plaintiff. The evaluator needs to carefully weigh the evidence in the context of the above comments to draw at least a tentative conclusion. This should be combined with data from the MMPI-2 and/or SIRS, as well as records and other collateral data, to draw a firmer conclusion.

Other means of assessing malingering

Resnick, West and Payne (2008) observe that feigners claiming PTSD or a postconcussional syndrome often have an adequate grasp of the nature of those disorders, making statements of symptoms an inadequate basis for ruling malingering in or out. They recommend the following model for identifying malingered PTSD:

- Understandable motive to malinger PTSD
- At least two of the following criteria:
    Irregular employment or job dissatisfaction
    Prior claims for injuries
    Capacity for recreation, but not work
    No nightmares or, if nightmares, exact repetitions of the civilian trauma
    Antisocial personality traits (not applicable to criminal-forensic cases)
    Evasiveness or contradictions
    Noncooperation in the evaluation
- Confirmation of malingering by one of the following criteria:
    Confession of malingering
    Unambiguous psychometric evidence of malingering
    Strong corroborative evidence of malingering (e.g., videotape contraindicating alleged symptoms).

Wilson and Moran (2004) identified "critical cues to malingering":

- Noncooperation with psychological and medical assessment requests and procedures (e.g., psychological testing, medical evaluations, etc.).

5
chapter

- Evasiveness, vagueness, and inability to produce details about the trauma.
- Incorrect details of the stressors or providing improbable or implausible information about the trauma experience.
- Manifestation of behaviors inconsistent with known scientific/medical/clinical patterns of PTSD.
- A general tendency to focus blame for all problems on symptoms of the trauma.
- Falsification or alteration of documents, certificates, reports, or other forms of "evidence...."
- An overemphasis on PTSD-related "flashback" experiences relative to other PTSD symptom clusters.
- Psychometric testing shows a pattern of inconsistency, defensiveness, malingering..., or lying but *does not* indicate probable PTSD (e.g., low scores on measures of PTSD on MMPI, TSI..., etc.).
- A history of antisocial personality or behaviors or previous claims for compensation or lawsuits (i.e., litigation proneness) that preceded the traumatic event (p. 628).

Rogers (2008b, 2008c, 2008d) suggests a detection strategy for a feigned (not necessarily malingered) syndrome might include: (a) claiming rare symptoms, those reported by fewer than five percent of clinical populations; (b) quasi-rare symptoms, which may be found in clinical populations but remain unusual; (c) improbable symptoms, those with "a fantastic or preposterous quality" (p. 19); (d) combinations of symptoms that are seldom found in clinical populations; (e) indiscriminant endorsement of problems; (f) endorsing a great number of "unbearable" or "severe" symptoms; (g) obvious symptoms of mental disorders; (h) substantial discrepancies between reported and observed symptoms; and

(i) endorsement of inaccurate symptoms of a psychological disorder, possibly based on a stereotypical view of the disorder.

The malingering evaluation is essentially an evaluation of feigning, an attempt, conscious or unconscious, to present oneself in a manner that is not an accurate presentation of one's symptoms and status. A comprehensive evaluation is necessary, addressing all relevant aspects of the person's functioning. Multiple strategies are necessary for the detection of the ways in which an individual may feign (Rogers, 2008d).

Martelli, Nicholson, Zasler and Bender (2007) recommend that evaluations of feigning include the following elements:

1. Establish rapport and a basic working relationship with patients and examinees.... Valid data collection requires a collaborative effort. The possibility of dissimulation might be reduced given better rapport....

2. Ensure that emotional variables affecting motivation are adequately assessed during an interview that is conducted prior to the exam. Specifically, assess the impact of anger or blame and feelings of resentment or victimization, as well as the other variables shown in the literature to be associated with poor recovery and adaptation to impairment. Assess pain, fatigue or other factors that may actually interfere with optimal performance....

3. Make efforts to maximize validity of exam procedures. Where possible, utilize instruments with built-in symptom validity measures....

4. Employ shorter symptom validity tests in order to minimize possibility of negative reactions owing to the nature of protracted participation in easy, boring, or atypical tasks....

5. Remain aware that, in science and medicine, situations are rarely either-or, or clear-cut, or one-dimensional.... Cut-off scores, by their nature,

5
chapter

always entail judgment, inherently result in misclassification and impose an artificial dichotomy on essentially continuous variables....

6. Utilize and devise models that measure the degree of apparent motivation and effort, using multiple data sources, and estimate confidence levels of inferences, given consideration of the multiple factors that contribute to exam findings.... (p. 18)

A final point needs to be made. Research that indicates that "rare responses" are a significant indicator of probable malingering may not adequately take into consideration that, for any test or other instrument, the normal curve will assign some people to the ends. The farther from the mean, the greater the likelihood that someone *is* feigning—but even two full standard deviations leaves more than two percent of the population who, if called malingerers, may be false positives. The damage done by a false accusation of malingering can be very significant—loss of court cases, loss of disability benefits, stigma, and so forth. No single measure should be considered adequate to brand someone as a malingerer. At least two, and ideally more, should be necessary— and, even then, unless the person confesses, or is videotaped doing things he or she says cannot be done, or something equivalent, the evaluator needs to proceed with great caution. Is the person exaggerating in order to try to ensure that he or she gets help? Is a significant other indicating disbelief? Is the plaintiff primarily interested in pursuing justice, or preventing others from being harmed as he or she was harmed? Regardless of the indicator(s) of exaggeration or feigning, it is very important to try to understand *why* the plaintiff appears to be feigning or malingering, with the request for money damages being only one possibility, and sometimes not the primary purpose of the lawsuit.

Frequency of test use

One means of determining what test(s) to use is to consider what other forensic and clinical psychologists use in their evaluations. The clinical test most widely used in both contexts is the Minnesota Multiphasic Personality Inventory, Second Edition (MMPI-2).

Surveys indicate that test was used by 85–94% of evaluators (Boccaccini & Brodsky, 1999; Camara, Nathan, & Puente, 2000; Watkins, Campbell, Nieberding, & Hallmark, 1995;).

The second-most-frequently utilized test in forensic evaluations is the Wechsler Adult Intelligence Scale, currently in its fourth edition (WAIS-IV). Surveys indicated use by 50–94% of evaluators (Boccaccini & Brodsky, 1999; Camara et al., 2000; Watkins et al., 1995). The WAIS would generally be used if a detailed measure of intellectual ability is desired.

Third, according to research, is the Millon Clinical Multiaxial Inventory, Second or Third Edition (MCMI-II or III), used by 33–49% of forensic evaluators (Boccaccini & Brodsky, 1999; Camara et al., 2000; Watkins et al., 1995). This frequency of use is a matter for concern since, as indicated above, the MCMI has been shown to exaggerate psychopathology (Ackerman & Kane, 2005; Craig, 1999; Groth-Marnat, 2009a; Hess, 1998; Hynan, 2004; Rogers, Salekin, & Sewell, 1999, 2000; Schutte, 2000), potentially making a "normal" individual appear to have significant psychopathology. The MCMI should not, therefore, be used in forensic evaluations (Ackerman & Kane, 2005; Faust & Heard, 2003b; Sellbom and Bagby (2008).

Tests that are used less frequently by clinical or forensic psychologists include the Rorschach Inkblot Technique, with estimated frequency of use ranging from 28–82% (Boccaccini & Brodsky, 1999; Camara et al., 2000; Watkins et al., 1995); the Beck Depression Inventory (BDI): 18–71% (Boccaccini & Brodsky, 1999; Camara et al., 2000; Watkins et al., 1995); the Trauma Symptom Inventory (TSI): 15% (Boccaccini & Brodsky, 1999); Structured Inventory of Reported Symptoms (SIRS): 11% (Boccaccini & Brodsky, 1999); the Halstead Reitan battery: 7–29% (Boccaccini & Brodsky, 1999; Camara et al., 2000; Watkins et al., 1995); the Thematic Apperception Test (TAT): 3–82% (Boccaccini & Brodsky, 1999; Camara et al., 2000; Watkins et al., 1995); and the Symptom Check List 90-Revised (SCL-90-R): 14–26% (Boccaccini & Brodsky, 1999; Watkins et al., 1995).

The wide ranges of scores for some instruments very likely relate to the specific samples of respondents chosen by the authors.

5
chapter

Only Boccaccini and Brodsky (1999) exclusively sampled forensic psychologists, but their sample consisted of only 80 psychologists. The specific tests utilized in a given case will depend upon the type of case and the types of information needed.

Neuropsychologists most frequently use the Wechsler Adult Intelligence Scale, currently in its fourth edition (WAIS-IV), 76%; the Minnesota Multiphasic Personality Inventory, Second Edition (MMPI-2), 68%; and the Wechsler Memory Scale, currently in its fourth edition (WMS-IV), 51%. Other commonly used tests included the Beck Depression Inventory (25%), the Rorschach (14%), the MCMI (various forms) (9%), the TAT (6%), and the Symptom Checklist-90-R (5%) (Lees-Haley, Smith, Williams, & Dunn, 1995). A larger, more recent study indicates that the most frequently used neuropsychological assessment instruments are the WAIS-R or WAIS-III, 63.1%; the WMS-R or WMS-III, 42.7%; the Trail Making Test, 17.6%; California Verbal Learning Test (1st or 2nd edition), 17.3%; the Wechsler Intelligence Scale for Children (WISC-III), 15.9%; and the Halstead-Reitan Neuropsychological Battery (HRNB), 15.5% (Rabin et al, 2005). It should be noted that neuropsychologists depend heavily on databases associated with tests of ability and functioning, but that new versions of tests such as the WAIS-IV and WMS-IV will not have substantial, published research bases for years. It is therefore common for neuropsychologists to continue to use older versions in order to take advantage of the large published databases for those tests.

When assessing an individual's ability to return to work, neuropsychologists primarily use the MMPI-2 (39.9%), with other instruments utilized including the WAIS-R/WAISIII (15.9%), a driving evaluation (13.5%), the Beck Depression Inventory (BDI, first or second edition, 12.5%), a clinical interview (12%), and/or the Finger Tapping Test (10.3%). The percentages differed depending on whether the assessment was primarily addressing executive function, memory or attention (Rabin et al., 2005).

PTSD Assessment Instruments

A plaintiff alleging symptoms consistent with PTSD must be evaluated for the three primary components of PTSD: reexperiencing, avoidance, and hyperarousal (Briere, 2004). Several instruments address all three of these areas:

Trauma Symptom Inventory. The TSI addresses 10 types of responses to trauma, as well as having three validity scales (Briere, 2004; Briere, Elliott, Harris, & Cotman, 1995; Demare' & Briere, 1996; Edens, Otto, & Dwyer, 1998). Norris and Hamblin (2004) note that the TSI globally assesses the sequelae of trauma, not PTSD *per* se. Sellbom and Bagby (2008) indicate that the three validity scales should not be used to assess the possibility of malingering. We concur. Little weight should be placed on the validity scales of the TSI. Validity of the assessment should be addressed using the MMPI-2 and/or the SIRS.

Detailed Assessment of Posttraumatic Stress. The DAPS is especially useful for the expert who prefers a test with a documented correlation with the criteria for PTSD in *DSM-IV-TR* (Briere, 2001; McLearen et al., 2004; Greenberg et al., 2003). The DAPS also includes two validity scales and assesses comorbid conditions often found with PTSD: dissociation, substance abuse, and suicidality (Briere, 2004).

Clinician Administered PTSD Scale. The CAPS is a structured clinical interview that assesses all 17 criterion-related symptoms of PTSD and many of its associated features, and is frequently cited as the "gold standard" for evaluation of PTSD (Blake et al., 1995; Keane, Buckley, & Miller, 2003; Koch et al., 2005; Weathers, Keane, & Davidson, 2001). Interrater reliability is very good, as is diagnostic agreement (Koch et al., 2006).

Structured Clinical Interview for DSM-IV (First, Spitzer, Gibbon & Williams, 1997). The SCID has also been referred to as the "gold standard" for diagnosis of PTSD (Koch, Douglas, Nicholls & O'Neill, 2006, p. 63). However, it does not address dissociative disorders, disordered sleep, or factitious disorders. Test-retest reliability is moderate overall, but is excellent with victims of motor vehicle accidents (Koch et al.)

PTSD Checklist (Weathers, Huska, & Keane, 1991). The PCL is a 17-item self-report instrument derived by correlating its items with the CAPS. It has very good criterion validity, as well as good temporal stability (Koch et al., 2006).

Posttraumatic Stress Diagnostic Scale. The PDS is a self-report measure with good test-retest reliability, sensitivity and specificity (Foa et al., 1995; Koch et al., 2006).

Revised Mississippi Scale for PTSD (Civilian Version) (Norris & Perilla, 1996). The Mississippi Scale is a 35-item scale with five possible responses for each item. It addresses the primary PTSD symptoms. It has been found to address psychological distress well, but to address PTSD less well (Koch et al., 2006).

Questionnaires: Standardized and Nonstandardized

Questionnaires that permit a plaintiff to self-report information may provide important data regarding behavior, attitudes and beliefs (Heilbrun, 2001). Many of these questionnaires are commercially available, and clinicians often devise their own in order to conveniently gather information. The questionnaires are generally face valid–that is, the plaintiff can readily understand what is being asked. Most make no attempt to assess response style, although the latter can be addressed during a clinical interview, as well as through the use of the MMPI-2 validity scales, the SIRS, and other specialized measures of response style. All of these questionnaires may be considered as approaches to enhancing the structuring of information gathering through direct questions rather than psychological tests. Evaluators who make them a standard part of their assessments should have no difficulty having the questionnaires accepted as part of the information that forms the basis for the expert's opinions.

Some examples of questionnaires that may be useful:

Behavior Change Inventory (Hartlage, 1989). The inventory contains 68 adjectives, from "absentminded" to "worrisome," with one column for adjectives that describe the plaintiff "before" the traumatic event and a separate column for those that describe the plaintiff "now."

Posttraumatic Cognitions Inventory (PTCI, Foa, Ehlers, Clark, Tolin & Orsillo, 1999). The plaintiff is requested to rate 36 items on a seven-point scale ranging from "totally disagree" to "totally agree." The questions include such topics as "The event happened because of the way I acted," "I feel dead inside," and "My life has been destroyed by the trauma." The plaintiff's ratings may be

INFO

The following questionnaires may be helpful when conducting personal injury claim evaluations

● Behavior Change Inventory

● Posttraumatic Cognitions Inventory

● Personal history form

● Medical history form

● Major life events questionnaire

● "Differences" questionnaire

● PTSD diagnostic questionnaire

● Work history questionnaire

● Collateral information questionnaire

● Pain questionnaire

5 chapter

separated into "negative cognitions about self," "negative cognitions about the world," and "self-blame."

A personal history form will permit the evaluator to gather a great deal of information about the plaintiff's background, including personal and family history of psychological/psychiatric/substance abuse problems and treatment; work history and satisfaction; developmental history and problems; history of trauma experiences such as accidents, assaults, and victimization; history of problems with the law; current and past major stressors; and so forth. The evaluator can design the form to prompt particular questions, with clarifying follow-up in the interview when responses are not clear.

A medical history form that asks about the plaintiff's medical history to date and current status. This form is also a convenient place to ask the plaintiff to rate his or her levels of emotions and problem cognitions from 0 (none) to 10 (severe) in such areas as depression, anxiety, irritability, hopelessness, helplessness, suicidal thoughts, guilt, happiness, and difficulty concentrating. The plaintiff can also be asked to specify all legal and illegal drugs used, keeping in mind that many plaintiffs will self-medicate with alcohol or a variety of other substances.

A major life events questionnaire. The individual is asked to identify, for each five-year period of his or her life (with separate pages for 0–4, 5–9, etc.) what major life events occurred, whether positive (e.g., birth of a sibling, marriage, birth of a child, starting a job) or negative (e.g., divorce, a death in the family, sexual or physical abuse, getting fired from a job, being arrested). *This is the only form the individual should be permitted to take home,* since he or she may have a

limited memory of early life events and may need to
consult a parent or other older adult.

A "differences questionnaire" that addresses the
plaintiff's perception of how he or she has changed
as a result of the alleged traumatic incident. Because
this question is central to the personal injury lawsuit,
the answers may be pivotal in determining both the
severity of the traumatic incident and damages. The
form could be headed "*How are you different as a
result of the accident or incident.*" Additional
questions, explaining the heading on the form,
might include "how did you change..., what is the
current impact of those changes..., how does the
event or events affect your ability to function
normally... compare the way you were *before* the
event(s) with the way you are *now*." Two columns
are necessary, the first labeled "BEFORE" and the
second labeled "NOW." The person should be given
half a dozen pages with the "before" and "now"
columns labeled at the top, to emphasize that the
plaintiff should include as much information as
necessary to fully identify his or her perception of
how he or she has changed. Each "before" item
should be paired with a "now" item, so the evaluator
has a clear statement of how the plaintiff sees him-
or herself as having changed in direct response to the
alleged trauma.

A PTSD diagnostic questionnaire. The evaluator may use one
of the above standardized instruments and/or a form devised specifically to address how well the plaintiff meets the DSM-IV-TR
diagnostic criteria for PTSD. Because none of the standardized
instruments ask about *past* criteria in detail, the evaluator may want
to devise a form that asks both "Do you now have this symptom?"
and "Did you have this symptom in the past but do not now?" If
the plaintiff indicated that the symptom was present but stopped,
ask when that occurred and any other questions necessary to

5
chapter

understand the plaintiff's response. This may be particularly important if the evaluation is conducted a year or more after the alleged traumatic event. For example, a set of questions regarding PTSD criterion B(1) might read:

(a) "I have repeated memories of the event that often intrude upon my day, including images, thoughts, or perceptions": True False

(b) "I USED TO have repeated memories of the event that often intruded upon my day, including images, thoughts, or perceptions, <u>but do not any more</u>: True False

Following each pair of questions should be a few lines labeled "comments," to permit the plaintiff to provide more information about the response, and/or for the evaluator to note the plaintiff's answers to any questions regarding his or her response.

A work history questionnaire that addresses where the person currently works and the nature of the job. It should also include where the plaintiff worked (and the nature of the work) for at least five years prior to the allegedly traumatic event. The expert should seek a detailed description of each job (employer, duration, specific duties, reasons for no longer holding this job). This is an essential component of assessing the affect of the allegedly traumatic event on the plaintiff.

Collateral information questionnaire. If the plaintiff is accompanied by a knowledgeable individual (e.g., spouse/partner, parent, adult child) to the initial evaluation session, it is useful to ask that person to respond to a questionnaire that focuses on three important domains:

• What the plaintiff was like prior to the traumatic event;

• How the plaintiff changed following the traumatic event; and

• What the plaintiff is like now.

Like the "differences questionnaire" described earlier, the goal is to obtain specific, accurate observations regarding the plaintiff's behavior and any changes, beginning before the event and continuing to the present. Such changes may be negative (especially immediately after the event) or positive (if the person has overcome some of the initial deficits). It is important to administer this questionnaire during the first assessment session, if possible, so that the collateral interviewee cannot discuss this request with the plaintiff. This doesn't rule out the possibility that the plaintiff and the collateral have discussed this topic prior to the evaluation, but it should give a more accurate response than if it were not administered until some time after the initial evaluation session. As always, no one source of data should be presumed to be accurate and unbiased.

> *Pain questionnaires.* If significant pain is part of the pattern of reported symptoms, then the evaluator should administer one or more pain questionnaires. Again, the evaluator may use a standardized measure or one devised by the evaluator, or both. A form designed by the evaluator could address two key questions: (1) What does the plaintiff do in spite of the pain? and (2) What does the pain keep the plaintiff from doing at all? The goal is to learn how the pain has changed the plaintiff's life. The McGill Pain Questionnaire (MPQ, Melzack, 1975) is perhaps the most widely used pain assessment instrument. Other pain assessment instruments are also available (see, e.g., Gatchel & Kishino, 2006; Sherman & Orbach, 2006).

If dissociation is a significant consideration in the assessment, a useful tool is the Scale of Dissociative Activities (SODAS), developed by Mayer and Farmer (2003). The respondent is asked to rate each of 35 statements regarding various types of dissociative activities as "never," "rarely," "occasionally," "frequently," or "very frequently." The SODAS is offered for reproduction and use without permission as an appendix to the article.

There are numerous other instruments available for use in a personal injury evaluation. Psychological Assessment Resources (Odana, FL) offers a "Personal History Checklist" for adults and another for adolescents, a "Developmental History Checklist," a "Personal Problems Checklist" for adults or adolescents, and a "Health Problems Checklist." The Psychological Corporation (Pearson Assessments, San Antonio, TX) offers the Mooney Problem Check List (Gordon & Mooney, 1950). Norris and Hamblen (2004, pp. 66–98) describe numerous other instruments with various degrees of standardization that address symptoms that may be relevant to a forensic evaluation, including both trauma-related symptoms and general symptoms (for example, those addressed by the MMPI-2).

All of the instruments utilized, as well as the interviews conducted, are to address the central issues in the evaluation: How did the plaintiff change as a result of the allegedly traumatic event? What evidence is there that the changes are real and valid? To what degree has there been remission of symptoms since the allegedly traumatic event? The evaluator must keep in mind that a comprehensive evaluation requires the use of multiple measures of various types in order to address these questions.

Plaintiff Interviews

Both ethically and practically, an interview of the plaintiff is extremely important in an assessment for personal injury. The evaluator's goal must be to assess *the impact of the allegedly traumatic event on the plaintiff, how the plaintiff sees himself or herself having changed as a result of the trauma, how the plaintiff apportions responsibility for the trauma and its effects, and how the plaintiff's functioning has changed over the period of time since the traumatic event occurred.* Without a personal interview, there would be substantial limits to the conclusions that the evaluator could draw about the plaintiff and how he or she was affected by the traumatic event, even if the evaluator had access to substantial historical records and psychological testing (Greenberg, 2003; Heilbrun, 2001; O'Donnell, Creamer, Bryant, Schnyder & Shalev, 2006; Shuman, 1994, 2003 supplement). Groth-Marnat (2009a) observes that, "[w]ithout interview data, most psychological test results are meaningless" (p. 65). Groth-Marnat also notes that interviews facilitate rapport.

The *Specialty Guidelines for Forensic Psychologists* (1991) specify that forensic psychologists must try to have an "examination of the individual adequate to the scope of the statements, opinions, or conclusions to be issued.... When it is not possible or feasible to do so, they make clear the impact of such limitations on the reliability and validity of their professional products, evidence, or testimony" (Committee on Ethical Guidelines for Forensic Psychologists, 1991, p. 663).

Similarly, Ethical Standard 9.01(b) of the *Ethical Principles of Psychologists and Code of Conduct* (American Psychological Association, 2002), indicates that

> Except as noted in 9.01c, psychologists provide opinions of the psychological characteristics of individuals only after they have conducted an examination of the individuals adequate to support their statements or conclusions. When, despite reasonable efforts, such an examination is not practical, psychologists document the efforts they made and the result of those efforts, clarify the probable impact of their limited information on the reliability and validity of their opinions, and appropriately limit the nature and extent of their conclusions or recommendations.

The exception noted in Ethical Standard 9.01c indicates that an individual examination may not be warranted when the psychologist is solely conducting a records review or providing consultation. Under these circumstances, the psychologist must still indicate why an interview was not conducted and specify the basis for their conclusions and recommendations.

The psychologist is also required to have a personal interview by the *Code of Conduct* of the Association of State and Provincial Psychology Boards (ASPPB). The *Code* specifies that a "psychologist rendering a formal professional opinion about a person... shall not do so without direct and substantial professional contact with or a formal assessment of that person" (Section III.A.6, ASPPB, 2005).

BEST PRACTICE
You must make every effort to conduct a face-to-face interview with the claimant. You may not be able to form an opinion to a reasonable degree of psychological certainty without an interview as part of an assessment.

It is important to emphasize the need for the evaluator to make a good faith effort to conduct an interview. For example, if a plaintiff initially refuses an evaluation, a defense expert should probably inform the parties, in advance, of the limitations this will impose upon the evaluation. For example, this may provide the respective attorneys time and the information necessary to decide whether or not to convince the client or to seek or resist efforts to compel such an interview.

One exception to this rule involves provision of expert opinions that are not about the plaintiff. For example, an expert may be asked to testify about a particular study, without tying it to the individual plaintiff. As a rebuttal expert, a psychologist may be asked to comment upon the method of examination (e.g., leading questions) employed by an opposing expert, or on the state of the science in conducting personal injury evaluations, or on professional standards for conducting such evaluations. So long as one is not offering an expert opinion <u>about the plaintiff</u>, there is no ethical need to conduct an interview.

The interview provides a critical source of data regarding the connections among testing, third party, and other information and the legal questions in the case. Further, the interview must be sufficiently detailed and comprehensive in its coverage of essential issues. It must be private, so the plaintiff can speak freely.

Courts will generally admit testimony that is not based in part on an interview (Shuman, 1994, 2002 supplement). However, "standard psychiatric and psychological diagnostic techniques include an examination of the patient.... Thus, an in-court opinion not based on a personal examination of the patient, when it is possible to do so, violates accepted practice. This failure should bear on the weight given the resulting opinions" as well (Shuman, 1994, 2003 supplement, p. 9-7).

Structured interviews, such as the SCID, are favored by some interviewers, while other evaluators prefer formal and informal questionnaires and instruments like those discussed earlier to obtain information in the numerous areas that must be considered in a personal injury case, assessing how plaintiffs organize responses and exploring the unique aspects of the individual's history (Groth-Marnat, 2009a). Evaluators who prefer unstructured or partially-structured interviews may devote as much as several hours to asking the plaintiff about his or her experience and gathering more information related to questionnaire responses. It is also very important to attend to critical items on tests and other instruments, particularly if the individual has clinically significant scores on the MMPI-2 or other tests (Greenberg et al., 2003).

An essential goal of the evaluation is to understand *what the trauma means to the plaintiff*. No two people have identical responses to a traumatic event (Ackerman & Kane, 1998; Weiss & Ozer, 2006; Wilson & Moran, 2004). If three people who experience the same traumatic event were assessed, it would not be surprising to find that one of them has essentially recovered within a few weeks and the second within a few months, while the third continues to show evidence of serious traumatization a year or more after the traumatic event. The evaluator must understand what the stressor/trauma means to the plaintiff, why his or her response to the trauma was at the observed magnitude and for the reported duration. Without this understanding, the evaluator will have difficulty testifying to a reasonable degree of psychological/scientific certainty regarding the nature and extent of the plaintiff's psychological injuries.

There is also a need to assess whether the plaintiff has a psychological need to identify a physiological or other traumatic basis for his or her symptoms. The person with such a psychological need is not malingering–he or she feels real pain and suffering. This is part of the explanation for the substantial comorbidity between psychological disorders and disorders such as chronic pain, traumatic brain injuries, and others. The evaluator also needs to assess the social support available to the plaintiff, since social support following traumatic events is associated with a better prognosis (Briere, 2004). If the plaintiff's friends and family accept that psychological injuries are as real as physical injuries, this will strengthen the plaintiff's capacity to discuss his or her injuries forthrightly. Unfortunately, many have difficulty accepting psychological injuries as "real," with consequent attribution of the plaintiff's symptoms to malingering, secondary gain, or other illegitimate causes. When this occurs, the plaintiff may insist that the injuries are physical (e.g., soft tissue injury or traumatic brain injury, neither of which is readily detectible using formal diagnostic instruments such as MRI). These plaintiffs are often seeking acknowledgment of their injuries from their friends and families, as well as asking the jury to provide independent confirmation that the injuries are real and that the plaintiff is not responsible for what occurred (Miller, 2003).

Other non-financial motivations for exaggeration of symptoms may also need to be assessed in the interview. These include motivations seen in a genuine victim who exaggerates real symptoms in a search for "justice," to redress actual or perceived harm by an employer or by the person who caused the injury (Kane, 2007b; Resnick, 1997; Rogers, 2008d). Other plaintiffs have a goal of preventing injury to someone else, especially in cases such as sexual misconduct by professionals, sexual harassment, and "driving while intoxicated." Still others need assurance that people appreciate how badly they have suffered, even if they are no longer acutely traumatized and in fact are presently suffering less (Resnick, 1997). Malingering is far more likely if the person is motivated primarily by monetary gain. When other motivations are more prominent, simply winning the case is often reward enough. It should be noted that plaintiffs often overestimate the degree of satisfaction or vindication they will receive from a personal injury case, particularly when they seek something other than money from the lawsuit. In general, people are not very accurate when they estimate how satisfied they will be with the outcome of litigation (Blumenthal, 2005).

Collateral (Third Party) Information

Although the evaluator will have reviewed a variety of records (a form of collateral information), it is also important to interview people who know the plaintiff in a relevant context. However, if the psychologist has been retained as a consultant rather than a testifying expert, he or she should not contact any third party without the consent of the retaining attorney, since his or her participation in the case is not public knowledge (Otto, Slobogin & Greenberg, 2007). A testifying expert should notify the retaining attorney of whom he or she plans to interview, in case the attorney has any comments regarding that individual. Although some of the information obtained through third party interviews may be biased or inaccurate, such information can be invaluable, as it permits the evaluator to triangulate data to identify consistency or inconsistencies with the plaintiff's statements, and to form and test hypotheses (Heilbrun, Warren & Picarello, 2003). Melton et al. (2007) note that third-party information is especially useful in assessing response style, and may be valuable as a source of data with which the plaintiff may be confronted in interviews.

The informants of greatest value are usually those with the most contact with the plaintiff (Heilbrun et al., 2003). As discussed earlier, a spouse, relative, or significant other may be asked to complete one or more questionnaires about the plaintiff's history and behavior. Further interviewing of such collateral observers is sometimes beneficial, providing additional details regarding the plaintiff's functioning. Co-workers and work supervisors are also potentially significant groups to consider for collateral interviews, especially regarding a claim that the plaintiff became partially or completely disabled as a result of the event.

If the plaintiff is receiving individual psychotherapy, the therapist may be able to offer significant insights into the plaintiff's psychological injuries and his or her motivation for the lawsuit. Some of this information may come from the therapist's notes, but many therapists do not keep sufficiently detailed notes to permit the evaluator to learn a great deal about the nature and extent of the plaintiff's problems. Interviewing the therapist may close that gap.

Others who may provide information that significantly expands the written records include physical therapists, occupational therapists, physicians, and other professionals providing care to the plaintiff.

Like the psychotherapist, they may be able to provide a substantial amount of information that is not reflected in their notes. Because some of the people referenced above have a privileged relationship with the plaintiff, it will be necessary for the evaluator to ask the plaintiff to sign a HIPAA-compliant release of information form, specifically including each collateral informant, in order to obtain this information unless one has a court order specifying that medical and other privileged information is to be available to the evaluator. This form must be compliant with both HIPAA and any state laws regarding confidentiality and privilege as applied to medical records.

In addition, the evaluator should have the plaintiff sign an "authorization for collateral interviews" form that identifies people who might be interviewed, provides phone numbers for those individuals, and details the relationship to the plaintiff (including how long the plaintiff has known the person and in what context, and any specific information the plaintiff expects the collateral to be able to address). It is not necessary for the plaintiff to sign any kind of release for talking with friends, family, co-workers, and others, but it often helps to have the plaintiff tell the person he/ she may be called and to ask the individual to be open and honest with the interviewer. A sample Request for Collateral Interviews form can be found in Appendix C.

Heilbrun, Warren and Picarello (2003) and Otto, Slobogin and Greenberg (2007) recommend giving individuals who are considering participating in a collateral interview such information as the names of the expert and the plaintiff's attorney, the voluntary nature of the collateral's participation, the legal purpose of the evaluation, how the information may be used, and that information obtained from a given person will be attributed to that individual in a report and in testimony. The expert should also offer to answer any questions from the collateral interviewee prior to any decision about proceeding. The collateral may then make an informed choice regarding participation. They also recommend indicating whether information from each collateral source was "consistent" or "inconsistent" with the plaintiff's statements, rather than using such terms as "verifies" or "confirms." Otto et al. offer a model for third party interviews.

Use of Consultants by the Expert

On occasion there will be one or more questions that require more specific expertise than the expert can provide. One common example involves the possibility of mild traumatic brain injury (mTBI), when the expert is not a neuropsychologist. The expert may be able to do one or more screening tests, but adequately answering the essential questions may require a neuropsychologist (Goldstein, 2007). Either the psychologist or the attorney may retain a neuropsychologist for that purpose. The senior author of this book prefers to retain the consulting expert, whose report will then be incorporated into his comprehensive report. The neuropsychologist's report will also be included at the end of the forensic report as an appendix. The fee of this consulting expert is paid from the retainer of the primary expert. If the questions are exclusively neuropsychological, of course, then the case should be referred to the more appropriately qualified expert. However, in many cases, the combination of forensic and neuropsychological expertise cannot be found in one person, resulting in the need for two experts.

Ecological Validity

"Ecological validity" refers to the extent to which a procedure or instrument provides information applicable to an individual's real-world functioning. Two people with seemingly similar injuries may function very differently, with one confined to a bed and the other going about daily life, including work and socializing. It should also be noted that an individual whose psychological or neuropsychological test results are in the normal range may still have a legitimate problem and a significant inability to function in certain ways (Miller, 2003).

One means of assessing ecological validity is to interview people who are familiar with the plaintiff's daily functioning. The

5
chapter

plaintiff and each collateral informant could be asked to detail what the plaintiff does in the course of each day, how difficult it is (or appears to be) for the plaintiff to function normally, what complaints the plaintiff has, and so forth. Does the plaintiff who complains about (and/or tests as having) motor deficits, poor coordination, poor reaction time, and attentional difficulties nonetheless drive a motor vehicle or use equipment that could prove dangerous (a lawnmower, snowblower, or manufacturing equipment) (Faust & Heard, 2003a; Koch, O'Neill & Douglas, 2005)? Does the plaintiff indicate difficulty moving around without pain, but play with his or her children without evidence of disability?

Collateral information increases the *face validity* of the evaluation—the appearance of accuracy regarding the evaluation and its conclusion about the plaintiff's degree of disability (Heilbrun, 2001; Heilbrun, Marczyk & DeMatteo, 2002). The collateral information may be obtained with telephone calls, since research indicates that telephone interviews are equivalent in the quality of information obtained to interviews that are face-to-face (Heilbrun, 2001).

The evaluator wants the collateral to report what was *observed*, rather than offer any conclusions that may have been drawn. Since at least some of the collaterals are likely to be family members or friends, each with his or her own agenda, it is essential to use multiple sources of data—a number of collateral observers, various records, psychological testing, and interview information, looking for convergence of data. Any unique data suggested by a given collateral can be assessed with additional interviews, psychological tests, or other means.

To avoid having the collateral respond as he or she thinks the evaluator wants, and to avoid suggestibility in general, it is essential that the evaluator use broad, non-leading questions. As the interview continues, the questions may become more specific, to seek a detailed understanding without first risking "leading" the interviewee. Problems with recall or memory may be addressed through these more specific questions, using some details provided by the plaintiff (Greenberg, 2003; Heilbrun, 2001).

Incremental Validity

Each piece of information adds to the data collected. But at some point it is very likely that the information received will be neither new nor useful. At that point, the evaluator must decide whether more data are likely to mean better data, or whether the point of diminishing returns has been reached. The additional cost of more information is also a consideration. Unless the retaining attorney specifically requests additional case research, or the evaluator knows of an area that seems likely to produce significant new data, the cost of acquiring additional data may exceed the potential contribution of that data to the evaluator's database.

The ultimate goal, then, is for the evaluator to address all of the important, relevant issues to the degree required to formulate and test hypotheses and draw well-supported conclusions—and then stop (Hunsley, 2003; Hunsley & Meyer, 2003; Faust, 2003). Although an evaluator cannot know the result of an additional interview, test, or procedure until it has been attempted, the data collection should stop when the likelihood of significant new data appears small.

When assessing adults, personality inventories (e.g., the MMPI-2), interviews and brief self-rating instruments may add incremental validity for both diagnosis and the assessment of personality and psychopathology (Garb, 2003). There is considerable controversy about whether and how predictive validity may be added by projective tests, but it appears to be less than inventories, interviews, and self-rating instruments. For those experts who choose to rely on projective tests for forensic purposes, it is important to understand the criticisms of such tests, and the responses to them.

5
chapter

Limits on Evaluations

At the end of any evaluation, there are likely to be some questions that are not answered, or are only partly answered. Even so, in most cases the evaluation should be considered complete when all of the essential questions have been addressed, strong hypotheses formed, and substantial data accumulated. At that point, the evaluator should identify any potentially-important inconsistencies and gaps in the data and note them in the report, accompanied by a statement indicating how those factors may impact the validity of the report and its conclusions. In keeping with the oath to tell "the whole truth," experts also have an obligation to identify any significant findings that are not consistent with their conclusions (Heilbrun, 2001), or missing data that may have been significant. Finally, the expert must freely acknowledge any questions that the expert is simply not able to answer based on the available data.

Conclusion

The data having been gathered, we now turn to analyzing the data and forming the opinions themselves. In Chapter 6, we address the determination of diagnosis, how to describe impairment, and deciding and explaining the degree to which it has caused disability in the plaintiff.

Interpretation | 6

In light of the material described earlier in this book about assessing clinical and relevant functional questions, we will discuss in this chapter how to identify genuine mental and emotional disorders, and genuine and relevant deficits that are causally linked to the allegedly traumatic event(s). Potentially complicating factors will be considered, such as the plaintiff's response style, the mixed quality of information from records and collateral interviewees (e.g., bias, poor memory, and other complications noted by Heilbrun et al., 2003), limited information about some relevant factors, and inconsistency across sources.

Review of the Referral Questions and Psycholegal Issues

To ensure that the interpretation of the data is relevant to the instant case, the evaluator should review the referral questions and psycholegal issues to ensure that all essential data that can be collected have been collected, to ensure that they can be addressed in the interpretation. If they have, it confirms that it is time to move to the interpretation stage. If not, further work may need to be done to complete the assessment, although there will be cases where one or more of the referral questions simply cannot be answered.

Goal of the Interpretation

The goal of the interpretation is to identify trends in the data, and to resolve any inconsistencies identified. What significant, case-related information can be derived from the records, testing, interviewing of the plaintiff and collaterals, and any other sources? In what ways do the data converge? What information is consistent across all sources? What information is consistent across most sources? What information is not consistent with at least one other significant source? What do the data—their patterns and cross-source consistencies—mean? How might the inconsistencies best be resolved or explained? Significant inconsistencies that cannot be resolved should be clearly identified and discussed. One means of resolution is to indicate that, for example, of five collateral sources (records, co-workers interviewed), three said that the plaintiff could not work for more than an hour without taking at least a 30-minute break, while two said that the plaintiff consistently worked two or more hours without any breaks. What other data are there that might shed light on this apparent discrepancy regarding the plaintiff's ability to work for substantial periods of time? If the data taken as a whole suggest a conclusion, one should specify that data and the thinking that led to it. If the data are mixed, and the expert cannot draw a conclusion to a reasonable degree of certainty, it will be necessary to present the data in the report and indicate that a firm conclusion cannot be drawn. It must be kept in mind that the expert is to be impartial, presenting all relevant data, not just those data that support the retaining attorney's theory of the case or the expert's own conclusions (Bank & Packer, 2007; Goldstein, 2007; Heilbrun, 2001).

Given that every evaluation has limits, experts are not expected to testify to an absolute certainty, but usually only to a "reasonable degree" of psychological, medical, scientific, or professional certainty, as appropriate. See the discussion in Chapter 7 of "reasonable psychological/medical certainty" for a discussion of the meaning of this term.

Assessing Clinical Issues

Psychological tests may be used in forensic evaluations to help devise hypotheses that may be substantiated or contradicted by other sources of data, and/or to address the validity of hypotheses formulated on other bases. In both cases, the objective is to utilize hypotheses that can be confirmed or falsified in order to draw conclusions about people in litigation. Typically, opinions are based on inference, as the evidence rarely leads to one and only one possible conclusion. The expert's job is to evaluate the likelihood of various explanations for the known evidence, striving to reduce the size of inferential leaps by accounting for as much evidence as possible.

Review of Relevant Research

Prior to commencing the evaluation, the expert will have reviewed research relevant to the particulars of the case for which he or she was retained (see Chapter 3). That research needs to be reviewed and updated prior to interpreting the results of the evaluation, to try to ensure that the evaluator accurately incorporates the nomothetic data into the case specific analysis. If any significant aspects of the case came to light during the evaluation that have not been researched, that review should be undertaken before the interpretation of the data commences. Often this will occur between the first and second days of the evaluation. In addition, the evaluator should have been checking on research published during the course of the evaluation, for the same reason. The goal of having an assessment that is truly state of the art should always be kept in mind. Note that after an expert's deposition, any additional relevant information that the expert becomes aware of and intends to testify about must be made known to the opposing counsel.

For example, one clear area needing monitoring of ongoing research is with regard to whether the Fake Bad ("Symptom Validity") Scale of the MMPI-2 is a valid measure of feigning that should be utilized in assessing whether an individual may be malingering. At the time this book was written, in our opinion, the data remain equivocal. A psychologist who wishes to utilize that scale must continually monitor the ongoing research as it is published, to decide whether there is sufficient research support to justify the use of that scale in the evaluation.

BEST PRACTICE

It is important to continually update your research review prior to the evaluation and through the time you are ready to interpret the results. This ensures the most up-to-date information is included and utilized.

If the psychologist anticipates difficulty justifying the use of the FBS during testimony, it should probably not be included in the report. On the other hand, if the psychologist feels that use of the FBS is scientifically justified, he or she should be able to respond to the predictable questions that arise from professional literature criticizing the scale.

Principles of Forensic Mental Health Assessment

Heilbrun et al. (2009) specified 38 principles of forensic mental health assessment. Several of these are specifically relevant to interpretation of the data collected. If the evaluation was conducted in a situation that did not provide privacy, quiet, and freedom from distractions, that should be taken into consideration in the interpretation, and noted in the report. (See also Pope & Vasquez, 2007). If there is any question regarding whether the plaintiff understood the nature and purpose of the evaluation, that should be considered and noted as well. Third-party information (including records) and psychological testing should be used to assess response style. The plaintiff's clinical condition is assessed utilizing case-specific information, while nomothetic (group) data is used to compare the plaintiff's functioning, clinical status, and causality with norms from relevant groups. The method for addressing causality is scientific reasoning, based on idiographic (i.e., individual, idiosyncratic) and nomothetic (i.e., group) data. By following these guidelines, the quality of the interpretation is maximized.

Impairment vs. Disability

The expert in a personal injury case must rule in one or more specific causes of the impairment and disability, not simply rule out some number of possible causes and outcomes. As indicated in Chapter 2, an expert who does not specify the likely cause(s) of impairment and disability may not be permitted to testify. The evaluator needs to ensure that he or she is clear regarding any impairments identified and the degree to which they have contributed to a disability.

Schultz (2003a) indicates eight common problems or misconceptions in addressing "impairment" and "disability," which, she notes, are frequently confused.

(1) Impairment refers to the presence of a diagnosable disorder that makes it harder for an individual to function at full capacity. Impairment is assessed by a clinician who carefully addresses the person's difficulty with normal functioning. "Disability," by contrast, refers to how that impairment affects actual work situations, including both physical and psychological demands of the job, and the qualities needed by the individual to perform a particular job (e.g., skills, education, flexibility, and/or experience).

(2) There is not necessarily a direct relationship between psychological impairment and vocational disability. A work environment that reminds the plaintiff of the traumatic event may cause a substantial vocational disability (e.g., a fireman who becomes phobic about fires, or a construction worker who becomes fearful of heights), while a work situation that does not relate in any way to the traumatic event may cause minimal vocational impairment.

(3) Minimal data from the psychological tests and clinical assessments used by clinical and forensic psychologists address actual or potential work performance. While clinical and forensic psychologists could learn to use appropriate instruments to assess actual disability and work performance, few do so. The degree of predictive validity of a typical psychological assessment depends on precisely which instruments are utilized and the ability of those instruments to predict vocational disabilities. If the nature of the evaluation only requires a general, broad conclusion, the forensic expert who is not also a vocational rehabilitation or

occupational therapy expert may be able to offer it. For example, it might be said that "the plaintiff was able to return to his old job three months prior to the evaluation, and his supervisor indicated that his performance was about the same as prior to his accident." In contrast, if there is a need for a detailed vocational or occupational assessment, and the forensic expert is not knowledgeable about conducting such an assessment, he or she should seriously consider retaining, or asking the retaining attorney to retain, a vocational rehabilitation or occupational therapy expert to do a formal vocational assessment.

(4) The psychologist and attorney need to identify the occupational disability questions that are relevant to the particular legal case. Among the issues to be addressed: loss of ability to work at the plaintiff's former job or occupation; lessened ability to earn what he or she previously earned; the expected duration of the disability and when the plaintiff is expected to return to work; whether the plaintiff is employable at any job at close to pre-trauma levels; whether there are any accommodations the workplace could offer to permit the plaintiff to return to work; whether the person must change jobs; what other jobs the person may be able to handle; and whether the plaintiff is capable of any gainful employment.

(5) The expert must estimate the plaintiff's degree of disability, if any, prior to the trauma, and contrast that with the degree of disability after the traumatic event.

(6) The objectively-assessed disability must be distinguished from the plaintiff's perception of his or her disability.

(7) If pain is an issue, there must be an assessment of its role in the impairment and determination of disability. There should be discussion of the ways that pain, anxiety and depression interact in the given case.

(8) Motivation must be assessed, since it can play a major role in the plaintiff's ability to return to work and in other areas of recovery of functioning. While motivation can only be assessed indirectly, its assessment is essential. Note, however, that a lack of motivation does not necessarily preclude a finding that the traumatic event caused the disability; depression is a common cause of poor motivation, and itself might be attributable to the traumatic event. It is thus incumbent upon the expert to carefully parse out the various consequences of the traumatic event, and in some cases how they interact.

Avoiding Misinterpretations or Going Beyond the Data

One of the most difficult tasks for an evaluator is to ensure that all statements are adequately supported by the data obtained during the evaluation. The evaluator needs to clearly identify statements that are at best marginally supported by the data, separating them from the statements that are firmly data based. By doing so, the evaluator is making clear statements that are relatively unlikely to be misinterpreted by the reader. In addition, such clear statements are less likely to take on exaggerated importance as part of a deposition or in court testimony. Inferential opinions must be based on more than speculation. In every case, experts must clearly label the degree of inference associated with each opinion, as well as the evidentiary and logical basis for it.

BEST PRACTICE

Always distinguish information that is only marginally supported by data from information that is firmly data based. Your opinion must not be inferred on speculation. You must have evidence to support it.

6
chapter

Computerized Scoring

Research has established that hand scoring of psychological tests often leads to errors (Simons, Goddard & Patten, 2002). Hand scoring in one study indicated error rates of over five percent on four tests, leading to significantly different results in over 42 percent of these tests. If there is a computer program available from a recognized vendor of psychological tests to score a test, the computer program should be used.

However, as discussed in Chapter 3, computer-based test *interpretations* should either not be used at all, or should be used only as one of several sources of data regarding the meaning of the test results (Otto, 2002). This is particularly true for multiscale tests like the MMPI-2, for which some computerized interpretations are based on the scores on the two highest clinical scales, regardless of how many scales are elevated. An interpretation based on only two of several scales is very unlikely to be an adequate reflection of the information available from the test (Butcher & Pope, 1993). Some psychologists also copy sections of a computer-based interpretation directly into their reports, implying that the information presented is the psychologist's own work product. This is unethical for several reasons. First, it would be plagiarism if the source were not identified. In addition, the psychologist would have no knowledge of the algorithm used by the test author, or the empirical research supporting each opinion, and, therefore, no basis for going beyond the computer printout's limited data to examine those test results that may be quite specific to the instant case. Finally, many interpretive statements generated by computer are so vague as to be of little use. For example, "this person may be depressed" does not specify the relative likelihood that the person is (or is not) depressed, and would add little value to an evaluation.

A sampling of the members of the Society for Personality Assessment found that more than 80 percent of the sample considered

BEWARE
It is best to avoid using computer programs to interpret test data. If you do, make sure you do not include the computer-based interpretation in your report and present it as your own work. This is unethical.

computer-based scoring to be ethical, and to use computer-based data to supplement the psychologist's other clinical methodology. However, more than 80 percent of the sample responded that it was not ethical to use computer-based test interpretations as the primary source of information from a test (McMinn, Ellens, & Soref, 1999).

An additional problem for a psychologist who uses a computer-based interpretation will occur if the cross-examining attorney has a copy of the computerized interpretation. That attorney can note that the psychologist failed to consider more than the two primary scale elevations, rather than considering all scale elevations. Even if the psychologist did consider all of the scale elevations, the attorney may question the psychologist regarding why he or she did not include every significant point from the computer-based interpretation. Finally, the attorney may question the expert regarding the empirical basis for inferences contained in the computerized interpretation.

We therefore recommend that the MMPI-2 and other tests that have validated computer-based *scoring* programs use those programs, but that computer-based *interpretations* be used as only one source or not be used at all to test hypotheses or as evidence supporting the expert's opinion. The forensic expert should be familiar with recommendations for interpretation of tests from several well-respected authors, whenever possible, and to consider the interpretations each author would suggest for a given test profile. Ideally, the expert would also identify relevant research from the professional literature on personal injury evaluations or on specific claimed symptoms for each major test utilized. At the minimum, it should be understood that "one size fits all" actuarial interpretation is a potential criticism of all objective tests that the expert should be prepared to address during testimony. The expert should be able to indicate how the interpretation applies to the particular context of the type of case, to the particular population being addressed, and in light of the totality of the data obtained in the evaluation (Heilbrun, personal communication, February 11, 2010).

The Importance of Transparency

The evaluator who reports both positive and negative findings, who provides data in the report to make it clear how conclusions are supported, and who provides the logical progression from the referral question to the conclusions drawn has gone a long way toward enhancing the transparency of the interpretive process. This strengthens the credibility of the report and testimony. The reader should be able to tell how the evaluator went from the referral question through the data collection to the conclusions based on this description.

The primary area in which there remains contention is whether it is acceptable to audio- or videotape the interview. One of the present authors believes that taping is important because it enhances transparency. The other is more concerned about the evidence from social facilitation research that taping, or any presence of a third party, is likely to change the evaluatee's responses (e.g., less openness, trying to avoid embarrassment). At this time, both positions have substantial support in the professional literature.

Differential Diagnosis

The evaluator should indicate each diagnosis considered, how well the data support each potential diagnosis, and why each final diagnosis was made. One method of doing so is to quote the diagnostic requirements from DSM-IV-TR (American Psychiatric Association, 2000) and, under each element, indicate whether it is present or absent—and, if present, the nature of the evidence supporting that portion of the diagnosis. For example, for a diagnosis of Posttraumatic Stress Disorder, the evaluator might indicate:

Diagnostic criteria for 309.81 Posttraumatic Stress Disorder

A. The person has been exposed to a traumatic event in which both of the following were present:

(1) the person experienced, witnessed, or was confronted with an event or events that involved actual or threatened death or serious injury, or a threat to the physical integrity of self or others

Plaintiff John Jones was in a motor vehicle accident in which his life could have been in danger.

(2) the person's response involved intense fear, helplessness, or horror. Note: In children, this may be expressed instead by disorganized or agitated behavior

By self-report and according to the responding police officers, Mr. Jones was extremely fearful, felt helpless, and had a severe anxiety reaction.

B. *The traumatic event is persistently reexperienced in one (or more) of the following ways:*

(1) recurrent and intrusive distressing recollections of the event, including images, thoughts, or perceptions. Note: In young children, repetitive play may occur in which themes or aspects of the trauma are expressed.

Mr. Jones reports thinking about the accident many times a day, has intrusive images of the accident, and is afraid to travel in a car even two years after the accident. This is consistent with numerous family and friends who report that Mr. Jones has declined trips because they would have required him to travel by car.

(2) recurrent distressing dreams of the event. Note: In children, there may be frightening dreams without recognizable content.

Mr. Jones and his wife report that he has nightmares about the accident at least once a week, even though it is two years post-accident at the time this is written.

(3) acting or feeling as if the traumatic event were recurring (includes a sense of reliving the experience, illusions, hallucinations, and dissociative flashback episodes, including those that occur on awakening or when intoxicated). Note: In young children, trauma-specific reenactment may occur

When riding in or driving a car, Mr. Jones reports reacting to any potential accident as if the motor vehicle accident two years ago was recurring, including having a panic attack. This was confirmed by hospital records of 4 trips to an emergency room because Mr. Jones reported that he thought he was having a heart attack. In each, he was diagnosed with a panic attack.

(4) intense psychological distress at exposure to internal or external cues that symbolize or resemble an aspect of the traumatic event

Mr. Jones reports having a panic attack any time he thinks about the accident two years ago, or he believes an accident could occur, or if he drives past the location at which his accident occurred. This was consistent with hospital records confirming panic attacks. (Note: Objectively, he may or may not have a full panic attack on every occasion, but his report is that he does. The expert should question the plaintiff regarding the actual frequency of such attacks, and may wish to specify both that this is the plaintiff's report and that it has not been objectively confirmed to be "always.")

(5) physiological reactivity on exposure to internal or external cues that symbolize or resemble an aspect of the traumatic event

Mr. Jones reports that he shakes, sweats, and becomes dizzy if exposed to thoughts or dreams about his accident, or if he believes that an accident could happen while he was in a car, or if he drives past the place his accident occurred. This was confirmed by his wife, and by one police report where Mr. Jones was pulled over because an officer believed him to be in medical distress.

C. Persistent avoidance of stimuli associated with the trauma and numbing of general responsiveness (not present before the trauma), as indicated by three (or more) of the following:

(1) efforts to avoid thoughts, feelings, or conversations associated with the trauma

Mr. Jones reports that he tries to avoid any discussion about cars or traveling in cars, and does not watch the news on TV because there are often videos or pictures of car accidents.

(2) efforts to avoid activities, places, or people that arouse recollections of the trauma

Mr. Jones does not go to places that would require that he drive or be driven to get there to the degree he can avoid such places. (Confirmed by several collateral informants.)

(3) inability to recall an important aspect of the trauma

This is not a factor for Mr. Jones. He remembers the accident very well, and his recollections are generally consistent with police reports of the incident.

(4) markedly diminished interest or participation in significant activities

Mr. Jones reports that he no longer goes to baseball or basketball games he used to enjoy attending because he would have to get there by car, whether he drove or was driven. This was confirmed by his wife, and by his personal calendar.

(5) feeling of detachment or estrangement from others

This is not a factor for Mr. Jones.

(6) restricted range of affect (e.g., unable to have loving feelings)

Mr. Jones reports that he is afraid to get too emotionally close to anyone since the accident, fearing that he or that person may be involved in an accident, causing a permanent loss.

(7) sense of a foreshortened future (e.g., does not expect to have a career, marriage, children, or a normal life span)

Mr. Jones reports that he feels as though he "lucked out" in his accident two years ago, but that he won't be so lucky next time – so he doesn't expect that he will live long. This is consistent with a review of Mr. Jones' spending habits, as indicated by a review of his check register and credit card receipts.

D. Persistent symptoms of increased arousal (not present before the trauma), as indicated by two (or more) of the following:

(1) difficulty falling or staying asleep

Mr. Jones reports that he no longer has difficulty falling asleep, but he reports that he frequently awakens as a result of a nightmare about the accident; or, if he awakens to go to the bathroom, he has difficulty falling back to sleep because of intrusive thoughts about the accident.

(2) irritability or outbursts of anger

Mr. Jones reports that he has had a short fuse since the accident, causing him to get upset much more easily than he did prior to the accident. This was confirmed by several friends and co-workers.

(3) difficulty concentrating

According to Mr. Jones, he is able to concentrate adequately to do his job and to interact with other people, so long as he does not have a reminder or an intrusive thought about the accident. If he does have a reminder or intrusive thought, his concentration is severely disrupted. His co-workers report that his concentration is usually good, but is sometimes disrupted for no obvious reason.

(4) hypervigilance

Mr. Jones reports hypervigilance anytime he's in a place at which a car could go out of control or there could be an accident. There is no evident hypervigilence if he is indoors and is not looking out a window. This is confirmed by his wife.

(5) exaggerated startle response

Mr. Jones reports that any hint that there could be a car accident causes him to be startled. While this is not an issue indoors, it is sometimes an issue outdoors. His wife confirms his exaggerated startle responses.

E. Duration of the disturbance (symptoms in Criteria B, C, and D) is more than 1 month.

Duration is now two years.

F. The disturbance causes clinically significant distress or impairment in social, occupational, or other important areas of functioning.

Mr. Jones reports some difficulty with his job, including difficulty driving there every day. He is much less social, since getting together with other people involves driving or being driven. He avoids being around cars or streets to the degree he's able. He has panic attacks at least once a week related to his perception there could be an accident.

On the basis of the above data, the plaintiff clearly meets the diagnostic criteria for a Posttraumatic Stress Disorder.

The evaluator could repeat this process for each diagnosis seriously considered or, if PTSD were the only diagnosis that comes close to fitting the plaintiff's symptoms, could specify the other diagnoses considered and comment briefly on why each was not appropriate for the plaintiff.

Malingering

Because malingering is a question in any tort action, the evaluator must draw a conclusion regarding whether there is evidence of malingering. If the most common psychological test, the MMPI-2, was utilized, what do the validity scales of that test indicate? If the MMPI-2 is not sufficiently definitive, did the evaluator also administer the SIRS and/or one or more cognitive symptom validity tests? If so, what did those other tests indicate?

Equally important, the evaluator must consider the extent to which collateral reports are consistent or inconsistent with those of the plaintiff. This is especially useful if claimed impairment is contradicted by credible reports of observed behavior. See Chapters 2 and 3 for a more complete discussion of assessment of malingering.

The Role of Stress Engendered by the Litigation Process

As discussed earlier, the litigation process itself causes anxiety and/or depression in many people, as well as interfering with their getting on with their lives. The role of stress from the litigation process should be addressed in the interpretation of the results of the evaluation.

Prognosis, Treatment Needs, Timetable, and Costs

On the basis of the interpretation of the data, it should be possible to make a reasonable statement about the prognosis for the plaintiff. Given his or her pre-trauma status, the affect of the trauma on the plaintiff, the progress made by the plaintiff since the traumatic event, and the expert's knowledge of the affect of treatment on people like the plaintiff, what progress would be expected? How likely is a complete recovery, and what factors would maximize the benefit the plaintiff receives from treatment? In effect, the expert is predicting the plaintiff's future adjustment if certain interventions are attempted to try to reduce or eliminate the negative consequences of the tort (Melton et al., 2007).

The plaintiff's response to treatment to date is important. Did the plaintiff avail himself or herself of psychotherapy, medication, physical therapy, occupational therapy, vocational counseling, or any other services that might reasonably mitigate the damages? If so, how effective were the services at returning the plaintiff to his or her pre-trauma status? What evidence suggests that the plaintiff can or cannot return to the pre-trauma status? If the plaintiff did not seek important services, why not? What affect might that have on his or her future functioning? Depending on the answers to these questions, what kind of timetable could be suggested for the plaintiff's recovery?

Finally, what costs could be estimated for the process of attempting to return to his or her pre-trauma status? Having specified the plaintiff's current status, pre-trauma status, treatment needed and utilized, and remaining treatment needs, at current community rates what might it cost to maximize the recovery of the plaintiff?

For example, assume that plaintiff John Jones was in good physical health when he was involved in a motor vehicle accident. He had occasional problems in functioning at various times in his life, but never to the degree that he sought psychological help or medication to address his symptoms—and never resulting in an inability to work. After the accident, he was diagnosed with Posttraumatic Stress Disorder and moderate depression. Lacking health insurance with mental health coverage, and not thinking of himself as needing mental health services, he resisted recommendations to seek psychotherapy. He did receive appropriate medical care, including physical therapy. He was able to return to his job, but did not function as well as he had prior to the accident. He was talked into taking antidepressant and anti-anxiety medication by his primary care physician. When those proved insufficient to reduce his anxiety and depression adequately, he began to see a psychologist for Cognitive Behavioral Therapy a year after the accident—but could only afford to go to therapy twice a month. His symptoms slowly abated as his therapy continued, permitting him to function better in his job and to begin to enjoy life again. At the time of the trial, however, he was still not recovered from his PTSD and depression. The expert recommended that Mr. Jones receive weekly psychotherapy sessions for one year, tapering off to bi-weekly in the second year and monthly in the third year, until the therapist and patient agreed he was no longer benefiting from the therapy. At community rates of $150–200 per psychotherapy hour, the first year (50 psychotherapy sessions) would cost $ 7,500–$10,000. The second year would cost half that amount, $3,750–$5,000. If the full third year of therapy was conducted, it would cost $1,800– $2,400. The total amount anticipated for therapy would, therefore, be $13,050–$17,400. An additional amount could be added for visits to Mr. Jones' physician for as long as Mr. Jones remained on his antidepressant and anti-anxiety medications. This process gives the attorneys and fact finder enough information to assess the amount of money that Mr. Jones should be awarded for psychotherapy and related services if he prevails in the litigation.

Guides to the Evaluation of Permanent Impairment, Sixth Edition

The American Medical Association's *Guides* (2007) are an attempt to provide standardized criteria for rating impairments and disabilities. According to Babitsky and Mangraviti (2009), it places each diagnosis into one of five categories: no problem, mild, moderate, severe, or complete. A range of impairment percentages is given for each category, with the evaluator to adjust the percentage based on history, physical findings, and test results. However, there are a number of problems with its use for mental disorders in personal injury cases. According to its preface, it is a combination of evidence-based and consensus criteria, but it does not specify the data for any specific diagnosis. Only some mental illnesses are

The AMA's *Guides* are designed to provide standardized criteria for rating impairments and disabilities. They are not useful in cases of personal injury claims involving psychological injuries, however. You should avoid using them in these cases unless they are an expected part of one's report in the jurisdiction in which the case will be tried.

included: mood disorders, anxiety disorders, and psychotic disorders. It does not include ratings for somatoform disorders, factitious disorders, nor most others in DSM-IV-TR. It also fails to assign a rating to the psychological component of physical injuries on the basis that psychological distress has already been incorporated in the rating of the physical injury. No exceptions are acknowledged. No rating or guidance is given if a disorder, for example, anxiety or depression, is the result of a physical injury. For those diagnoses that are ratable, the evaluator scores three scales: the Brief Psychiatric Rating Scale, the Global Assessment of Functioning Scale, and the Psychiatric Impairment Rating Scale. The impairment rating is the median score on the three scales. Given the lack of a clear empirical basis for its inclusion of diagnoses and ratings, the lack of a clear rationale for using the median score of three scales, and the lack of a separate rating for the psychological component of a physical injury, the *AMA Guides* are of minimal utility in personal injury evaluations involving psychological injuries.

Drawing Conclusions

Occasionally, there will be significant and contradictory evidence about a key fact at issue in the case. For example, a defendant may deny that an assault ever took place. Such factual determinations are the role of the trier of fact. However, some diagnoses (especially PTSD) require a factual determination of the cause of the person's distress. Our recommendation in such cases is to offer our findings about the person's functioning before and after the time of the alleged event, followed by conditional explanations of our conclusions. In some cases, evidence of the allegedly traumatic event is uncontroverted, in which case we recommend treating it as factual. In other cases, there is a plethora of evidence suggesting that the event happened, even if it is denied by the defendant.

In those cases, one may state that the weight of the evidence convinces the evaluator that the event occurred, and that statements in one's report are predicated on that conclusion. In yet other cases, the evidence is equivocal, with little or no objective evidence to belie or affirm either the plaintiff's or defendant's versions of the event. There may, however, be substantial evidence that the plaintiff has experienced a significant, psychologically traumatic injury. In these cases, the evaluator states the conclusion that the evidence for causality is equivocal, but that the plaintiff did suffer traumatization by some event or events. If possible, state some of the possible or probable causes of the plaintiff's traumatic injury. It will be up to the plaintiff's and defendant's attorneys to try to make their cases, while the fact finder weighs the evidence and draws its own conclusion. Thus, it is possible to communicate one's beliefs about what happened, as required for diagnosis, without overstepping onto the role of the trier of fact.

Conclusion

Once the expert has made a determination of diagnosis, the nature of any impairment, and the degree to which it has caused disability in the plaintiff, it will be necessary to communicate these findings, in the form of inferential opinions, first to the retaining attorney, and later to the parties, the court, and the trier of fact. In Chapter 7, we turn to the means of communicating opinions, specifically oral and written forensic reports and oral testimony.

Report Writing and Testimony $\quad$ 7

The Report

Having carefully considered the legal context, forensic mental health concepts, the empirical foundations and limits of an evaluation, and having conducted a comprehensive, biopsychosocial evaluation and interpreted the resulting data, the evaluator is ready to provide the retaining attorney with a verbal report. If the verbal report is not favorable to the attorney's case, the psychologist may be asked to stop working on the case, and to not write a formal report (Melton et al., 2007). In most cases the expert will be asked to write a report of his or her findings, however. If the expert is not identified as a testifying expert, he or she is a consultant to the attorney, and his or her work falls under the attorney work-product privilege (Weiner, 2006). With the possible exception of "duty to warn or protect" situations (see Chapter 4), the consulting expert is bound by the attorney work-product privilege.

In some cases, the verbal report will suggest that the expert's opinion on some questions might be deemed helpful to the attorney's case. In other cases, it will not. It is acceptable for the attorney to narrow the scope of the psychologist's testimony by eliminating certain referral questions at this stage. However, the answer to each question that remains must be objective, impartial, and complete. Given that every evaluation has limits, experts are not expected to testify to an absolute certainty, but, rather, only to a "reasonable degree" of psychological, medical, scientific, or professional certainty, as appropriate. See the discussion of "reasonable psychological/medical certainty," below, for a discussion of the meaning of this term.

As a testifying expert, the psychologist must remember that he or she is to be impartial, advocating for his or her data but not for either side in the case (Heilbrun, 2001; Melton et al., 2007). Although most evaluations will lead the psychologist to conclude that the data support one side more than the other, both sides should be presented and the reasoning of the psychologist should be provided as each hypothesis is evaluated and each conclusion drawn.

Although the psychologist has discussed statutes, case law, and the referral question(s) with the referring attorney, it remains essential that the report accurately and appropriately addresses all three. Therefore, when the psychologist has a complete draft of his or her report, it is appropriate to send the referring attorney a copy with a request for feedback regarding "errors and omissions" to ensure that the legal standards and referral question are adequately addressed. **This is not a "working draft," and the psychologist must not change anything in the report that is not based on an error or omission.** Opposing counsel may ask if there are any prior drafts of the report, and in most cases will be entitled to discover them. Thus, it will be necessary to be able to explain any changes; the only acceptable response is factual errors or additional information that was brought to the psychologist's attention after the report was drafted. The attorney must not be permitted to shade any part of the report in a direction more favorable to his or her client. It is important that the expert's conclusions be as fully developed as possible before presenting them to the attorney, to minimize the affect of any discussion on those conclusions (Saks & Lanyon, 2007). However, the requirement that the report accurately reflect statutes, case law, and the referral question(s) makes it important for the psychologist to get feedback regarding any errors in the report or anything important that was omitted.

It should be noted that, at the time this is being written, the Supreme Court has announced changes in Rule 26 of the Federal Rules of Civil Procedure to protect drafts from discovery as work product in federal court cases. It is anticipated that most state courts will eventually follow suit, either by statute or case law. The expert

needs to determine the requirement in the jurisdiction in which he or she will be testifying.

The psychologist should remember that the
direct examination by the retaining attorney will
be primarily based on the report, as will the
cross-examination by opposing counsel. Thus, it
is essential that the psychologist be able to both
explain and defend in testimony what is written
in the report (Weiner, 2006). Further, in our experience, a well-
written and complete report facilitates preparation for deposition
and trial testimony.

BEWARE Never
change anything in your
report at the referral
source's request
unless there are
factual errors or
errors of omission.

There are a number of models for writing reports (e.g.,
Heilbrun, 2001; Melton et al., 2007), but no specific model that
must be followed. Every report should contain a number of elements, however, if it is to be valuable to the court.

The quality of the written presentation may significantly influence the impact of the report (Griffith, Stankovic & Baranoski,
2010; Appelbaum, 2010). Griffith, Stankovic and Baranoski
(2010) recommend that the forensic expert construct their reports
as narratives, as stories, designed to help the reader understand the
subject of the report (the plaintiff) and to "answer questions posed
by the law," with answers that "turn on the explication of individuals' thinking and their behavior, on the creation of stories
about how individuals came to carry out their actions" (p. 36).
This approach makes sense to us, and we therefore recommend
that forensic experts consider inclusion of a narrative about the
plaintiff within their reports.

If the expert's thoughts are not communicated well to the
reader, in grammatically correct fashion, then some of the impact
of the report will be lost. Similarly, incorrect spelling and other
errors can reduce the perceived quality and credibility of the presentation. Every report should be carefully written and proofread,
to maximize the quality of the presentation of the information and
to avoid embarrassment associated with the attorney for the other
side reading aloud a statement that doesn't make sense—or that
conveys an unintended message. The written report may also be

entered into evidence, preserving any errors as part of the court record (Weiner, 2006). Weiner (2006) recommends that reports be written in a conversational tone, making them easy to read and explain. Groth-Marnat (2009b) recommends that reports "increase readability, connect interpretations to the person's context, integrate interpretations around relevant domains, include client strengths, and provide clear links between referral questions and the answers to those questions" (p. 303). Wettstein (2010) recommends that the writing of forensic reports should be considered a core competency in forensic training.

Structure of the Report

Heilbrun et al. (2009) suggest that the report be broken into sections relevant to the forensic principles in a case: "referral…, procedures…, relevant history…, current clinical condition…, forensic capacities…, [and] conclusions and recommendations" (pp. 115–116). Breaking down these categories further, or adding variations on these themes, is useful if it helps the expert explain what was done and clarifies the conclusions. In our experience, well written forensic reports can significantly reduce the time needed to prepare for deposition or court testimony. Heilbrun (2001) suggests that a report that is well written and organized will facilitate testimony by making information accessible when needed to respond to questions asked by an attorney.

Karson (2005) describes three ways to address the information that should go into a report: "procedure by procedure, issue by issue, and point by point" (p.4). The first involves organizing the data according to the methodology used to obtain it. Sections might be labeled "record review," "clinical interviews," "psychological testing," and so forth. The advantage of this method is that the database upon which the expert bases his or her opinions is clearly explicated.

BEST PRACTICE
Organize your report into sections creating a logical path from presentation of data collected to the formulation of your opinion. You may wish to organize your report by method used to obtain information, psychological constructs, or according to the referral question.

The disadvantage is that people tend to skip to the end of the report to see the conclusions.

Writing a report issue-by-issue refers to identifying psychological constructs such as "intelligence, impulse control…, and the components of the Five Factor model of personality," (p. 4) as well as person- and case-specific issues, and addressing each in turn. The same data are presented as in the "procedure by procedure" method, but under the topical headings. The advantage of this method is that it presents a clearer portrait of the person's psychological makeup than the procedure by procedure method.

The point-by-point method addresses the referral question by discussing the psychological issues related to each component of that referral question. The same data as would be cited in either of the above methods would still be cited, but within the categories directly related to the referral question. The advantage, Karson (2005) indicates, is that the psychologist's impact is maximized. The disadvantage is that it minimizes the ability of the reader to make up his or her mind about the meaning of the data presented by the evaluator and the conclusions linked to the data by the reasoning of the evaluator. Karson also indicates that point-by-point reports tend to be shorter than the other types, which may be an advantage or disadvantage.

Karson (2005) also recommends that the report be organized in a manner that will make sense to readers, suggests that topic sentences be used, recommends that one builds one's arguments rather than building suspense, that each paragraph be self-contained, that hearsay be clearly identified, that one carefully avoid making statements that are false and defamatory, and that the expert ensure that statements made and conclusions drawn are more probative than prejudicial. An example of the last, he indicates, is that one should use the abbreviations for the MMPI-2's original validity and major clinic scales, not the original names of the scales, since scale names such as "Lie" and "Psychopathic Deviate" are clearly prejudicial, while "L Scale" and "Scale 4" are not.

Melton et al. (2007) indicate that a variety of formats are appropriate, but that several areas need to be addressed in all

BEWARE ⚠
Failure to identify the reasoning behind your opinion leaves the door open for a Daubert or Mohan hearing.

reports: "circumstances of the referral…, date and nature of clinical contacts…, collateral data sources…, relevant personal background information…, clinical findings…, [and] psychological-legal formulation" (pp. 583–584).

Wettstein (2005) indicated that the primary problem area identified by empirical research on forensic reports is the evaluator's failure to identify the reasoning behind the opinions given in the report. It is also common for evaluators to fail to identify connections among psychopathology, psychological test results, diagnosis, relevant functional impairments, and disability. Evaluators who fail to present their reasoning and to connect the key parts of their reports are inviting a *Daubert* or *Mohan* hearing, in addition to the likelihood of their conclusions being discounted by the trier of fact. On the other hand, presenting this information in the report makes a *Daubert/Mohan* hearing less likely.

Grisso (2010) reviewed a national sample of forensic reports submitted as part of the requirements for candidacy as a Diplomate of the American Board of Forensic Psychology (ABFP) that failed to be acceptable to the reviewers. The sample contained 62 reports submitted by 36 forensic mental health professionals. The ten most-frequent problems with the reports, and the percentages of reports in which the reviewers mentioned them, were:

1. Opinions without sufficient explanations (56%)
2. Forensic purpose unclear (53%)
3. Organizational problems (36%)
4. Irrelevant data or opinions (31%)
5. Failure to consider alternate hypotheses (30%)
6. Inadequate data (28%)
7. Data and interpretation mixed [in sections that were meant to focus on data] (26%)
8. Over-reliance on single source of data (22%)
9. Language problems (19%)
10. Improper test uses (15%)
(pp. 110–111)

We recommend that the report should contain information in six domains:

(1) The first section should include the identifying information, a list of records reviewed, the tests and other instruments utilized, and an indication of who retained the psychologist and the purpose for which the psychologist was retained. As an example of the last area, the evaluator might report, "I was retained by Attorney John Jones for the purpose of identifying whether, and, if so, to what degree, the motor vehicle accident of June 4, 2008 caused psychological harm to the plaintiff, Henry Smith." This is the referral question, and provides the context for everything presented in the balance of the report.

(2) Next, we recommend a presentation and discussion of the information culled from the records reviewed. Medical, employment, school and other records that address the functioning of the plaintiff prior to the accident or other tort provide a baseline against which the accident or other tort and its affect on the plaintiff can be assessed. This may be a summary of the most salient information on the timeline. While the timeline should provide quotations from documents as much as possible, the report should generally use summary statements based on those documents.

> **BEST PRACTICE**
> Suggested sections and order for the personal injury claim report:
>
> - Identifying information
> - Sources of information
> - Assessment data
> - Assessment of malingering
> - Clinical opinions
> - Summary and conclusions

(3) Third, the evaluator should describe the assessment process and the data obtained from the plaintiff and collaterals. It is important to describe the process of informed consent or notification of purpose that was utilized, so that it is clear that the plaintiff was appropriately informed about the considerations relevant to participating, and understood the nature and purpose of the evaluation, that the evaluation was not confidential, and that he or she had a right to consult with his or her attorney at any point in the evaluation. See the sample informed consent form in Appendix B. Each test or other instrument should be identified, and the relevant data obtained from its administration should be presented. Observations by the psychologist should be noted. Plausible interpretations should be stated, and all information upon which one's conclusions are based must be included. Information that is not relevant to the instant case should not be reported, since it adds nothing to the quality of the report while potentially confusing the reader. Inferences should be distinguished from facts (Heilbrun, 2001; Heilbrun et al., 2009; Melton et al., 2007; Weiner, 2006). Speculation should be avoided.

Psychologists also have ethical and specialty requirements for focusing on the essential components of their evaluations. The Ethical Principles of Psychologists and Code of Conduct, Ethical Standard 4.04, indicates that psychologists are to "include in written and oral reports and consultations only information germane to the purpose for which the communication is made" (APA, 2002). Specialty Guideline V.F.2. indicates that "forensic psychologists avoid offering information from their investigations or evaluations that does not bear directly upon the legal purpose of their professional services and that is not critical as support for their product, evidence or testimony, except where such disclosure is required by law" (Committee on Ethical Guidelines for Forensic Psychologists, 1991, p. 662). This is especially important when the information is potentially prejudicial. For example, the fact that a plaintiff in a car accident case once was incarcerated for manslaughter might have no relevance to the instant claim, but could result in a jury viewing the plaintiff in an unfavorable light.

(4) Because allegations of malingering are usually part of the defense in a personal injury case, the evaluator should specify what was done to assess the possibility of malingering, and the conclusions of that assessment.

(5) Statements should be made regarding the conclusions drawn that are relevant to the referral question(s), including:

(a) The pre-trauma psychological status of the individual;

(b) The data from the evaluation (across all sources) that describe the current psychological status of the plaintiff;

(c) Data relevant to whether the plaintiff was psychologically injured by the actions or failures to act of the defendant;

(d) Evidence of proximate cause, if any;

(e) If relevant, discussion of "thin skulled man" issues, i.e., did the plaintiff have a preexisting condition (physical or psychological) that may have increased the degree of harm;

(f) Data indicating what the plaintiff did to mitigate the damage from the accident, including various kinds of therapies;

(g) Damages (including input from the psychologist and, if indicated, other experts);

(h) Prognosis, including the basis for statements made regarding the plaintiff's degree of recovery to date and expected recovery in the future;

(i) Treatment needs, including a timetable (if possible) and projected costs of that treatment;

(j) Limitations of the evaluator's opinions.

(6) A brief summary of the evaluation and the conclusions. If the report is especially long, this may best be presented as an executive summary at the end of the first section of the report, to provide a context for the information in the balance of the report.

Within this outline of the report's structure, numerous suggestions are made by forensic experts for how the information should be presented. We recommend that the evaluator seriously consider all of the following suggestions.

One of the most valuable tools in a personal injury evaluation is a timeline of significant events in the plaintiff's life. The timeline is most useful if it quotes sections of the records reviewed, making it a source of concrete information identified by the records that can be a reference for information in the report, in a deposition, and in court. All of the information in the timeline (and in the report) should be explicitly attributed to its source (Heilbrun, 2001).

Judge David Bazelon offered excellent advice when he wrote, "Behavioral scientists who appear in the public arena all too often focus on little more than making conclusory pronouncements. Either they omit any real discussion of underlying observations and methods of inference, or they drown such discussion in a sea of jargon…. Legal and policy questions are multidimensional. They involve scientific, moral, and social judgments….What the public needs most from any expert, including the psychologist, is a wealth of intermediate observations and conceptual insights that are adequately explained" (1982, p. 116).

Technical jargon should be avoided, to the degree possible, in the report (Heilbrun, 2001; Melton et al., 2007; Weiner, 2006). When it is necessary to include professional terminology,

BEST PRACTICE

Keep your reports jargon free. If it is necessary to include clinical terms, be sure to clarify their meaning and relevance.

it should be explained in as simple terms as possible, so it's readily understood by the non-mental-health-professionals who will read the report. Diagnoses may be the primary exception to the recommendation to avoid technical jargon, but the principle of explaining terminology as simply as possible holds true. As noted earlier, it may be helpful to present the full DSM-IV-TR criteria for each diagnosis considered, specifying which criteria are met and explaining why.

Writing the report in sections also contributes to helping the reader understand what is being presented and why it is being presented (Heilbrun, 2001; Melton et al., 2007). If the case goes to trial, a well-structured report also contributes to the ability of the psychologist to present the evaluation and its conclusions in a cogent manner (Heilbrun, 2001). A report that is sufficiently comprehensive and well-written may facilitate a settlement of the case, eliminating the need for court testimony altogether (Melton et al., 2007).

The best reports are generally the ones that state what hypotheses were investigated, indicating the ones that were supported and those that were not, and why. The psychologist who is candid about the findings is likely to be able to present credibly during direct examination, and to avoid surprises during cross-examination. These psychologists strive for objectivity, whether retained by the plaintiff, the defendant, or the court. Their work is consistent with the forensic specialty guideline specifying that "forensic psychologists are aware that their essential role as expert to the court is to assist the trier of fact to understand the evidence or to determine a fact in issue" (Specialty Guideline VII.F, Committee on Ethical Guidelines for Forensic Psychologists, 1991, p. 665).

Experts must be able to identify relevant learned treatises (professional articles and books) that support their methodology,

Include test scores in your report if they were used to test hypotheses. If scores were used only to generate hypotheses, they need not be included.

if asked. It may be appropriate for the expert to include that information in the report (Baer & Neal, 2000). If it is included in the report, it is also appropriate to cite one or more examples of contrary articles, indicating why one found them to be less persuasive than the supportive literature, for example, when the contrary article was based upon a dissimilar population.

Two additional questions involve whether and how to report test results and scores (as opposed to raw test data) as part of the report. In our experience, a minority of psychologists includes no test scores at all, while the majority includes selected test data. In part, this depends upon how one uses test data. For those who use psychometric scores only to generate hypotheses, they need not be included. However, if some of the test scores and interpretations are relied upon in forming inferential opinions—that is, they are used to <u>test</u> hypotheses—then the scores should be included. Some psychologists do not include test scores even when they have used those scores to test hypotheses, instead simply including all or part of the interpretation of those scores. We recommend against this practice, as interpretations of test scores are seldom unambiguous, and the opposing attorney and expert should have the opportunity to offer competing interpretations of the scores.

Length of the Report

Melton et al. (2007) recommend avoiding "information over (and under) kill" (p. 585). They note that some psychologists prefer brief reports that are primarily conclusory, leaving out the information on which the conclusions are based, while others prefer long reports that include excessive and irrelevant detail, making them difficult to read. The proper goal is a happy medium. The report "should be comprehensive; relevan[t] to the factfinder, [avoid] tactical considerations (such as minimizing information to be scrutinized for cross-examination), [and] should guide the clinician in condensing the data. Indeed, the clinician is ethically obliged to make known all sources of data and to present a balanced account of the evaluation.... [F]indings essential to the clinical formulations advanced must be included" (p. 586).

BEST PRACTICE
Be sure your reports are detailed and balanced. The length of your report should depend on the facts and complexity of the case.

Some psychologists we know write relatively short reports, looking forward to presenting substantially more information during their court testimony and parrying with the attorney on the other side during cross examination. We strongly recommend against this tactic, especially since reports are often used for other purposes, such as pre-trial motions, settlement discussions, etc. Further, many courts will not allow experts to testify about any opinion that is not explicitly included in the written report. The report should be long enough to present all of the essential information from the case, with no significant issues saved for the trial. As indicated earlier, a well-written and convincing report may facilitate settlement of the case, something obviously impossible if all of the relevant data is not in the report.

Occasionally, an attorney may request a "brief report." In that case, the expert should first inquire with more specificity exactly what is being requested. For example, the attorney may wish to narrow the scope of the report by asking fewer questions on direct examination. We view this as permissible. On the other hand, if the attorney is asking for incomplete responses to questions, the expert should either refuse or should clearly indicate that the brief report is not a complete report of his or her findings and conclusions. Without question, if a briefer report would be likely to mislead the trier of fact, we would regard the expert as acting unethically if he or she were to offer such a report.

BEWARE
Do not write short reports with the intention of presenting more comprehensive information in court. Many courts do not allow experts to testify about an opinion that is not included in the written report.

BEWARE
It is unethical to agree to the referring attorney's request for a briefer report if the briefer report is likely to mislead the judge or jury.

7
chapter

Prognosis, Treatment Needs, Timetable, and Costs

As indicated in Chapter 6, the expert should make statements regarding prognosis, psychological treatment needs, the expected time period during which treatment would be necessary, and the costs of that treatment. The figures should be good faith estimates based on the expert's personal experience as a clinician, on the anticipated treatment period as suggested by the professional literature, and on current community rates.

Expert Testimony

Depositions and Court Testimony

The primary task of the testifying expert is educating the fact finder, as well as the attorneys and the judge (Gutheil & Bursztajn, 2003; Saks and Lanyon, 2007; Van Dorsten, 2002; Dvoskin and Guy, 2008). The expert who consistently remembers this is likely to do relatively well, including taking questions as requests for information rather than as challenges.

The presentation to the fact finder is likely to be most effective if it involves a thorough description of how the plaintiff's life has changed as a result of the alleged tort, including symptoms apparently resulting from the tort, and how they affect the plaintiff's ability to function on a day-to-day basis (Melton et al., 2007).

Most personal injury cases will involve one or more depositions well before a trial is scheduled to occur. The expert has typically issued a report prior to the scheduling of the deposition. The questioning, primarily by the opposing attorney(s), tests the ability of the expert to testify about the plaintiff and the specifics of the case, particularly focusing on the issue of causality. It is often an opportunity as well for the expert to learn of the theory of the case of that attorney, as the expert is asked to respond to questions regarding alternative interpretations of the data. Because the deposition is an opportunity for "the other side" to test the mettle, competence, and credibility of the expert, and because deposition testimony is a part of the record, it is essential that the expert be as well-prepared as if he or she were going to the trial itself.

Part of what is assessed by the attorneys is the degree of knowledge the expert has about the specifics of the case, and how well organized the expert is. It is strongly recommended that the expert overlearn the case-relevant information (Bank & Packer, 2007). The documents reviewed—

BEST PRACTICE
As a testifying expert, your expertise is likely to be questioned by the opposing attorney. Make sure you are well-organized and knowledgeable about the case and present your findings in a professional manner that instills confidence in your knowledge and skills.

for example, the records, tests and other information, and depositions—should be in binders that are labeled and indexed so that documents can be quickly found if and when needed. An alternative, if the expert is adept at doing so, is to scan all of the records into one's laptop computer, and to have it available to the expert in that manner. The effectiveness of the expert is contingent not only on what the expert knows and can convey in words; it also includes the presentation of expertise in a manner that helps convince the other attorneys at a deposition or the judge and jury at a trial that the expert is knowledgeable and skilled. That includes the willingness of the expert to change his or her opinion(s) if provided with convincing new data during testimony (Dvoskin & Guy, 2008; Greenberg et al., 2007).

If the expert is permitted to review the transcript of the deposition for errors, this should always be done (Hess, 2006). We have seldom seen a transcript without errors, some of which have been quite significant.

The Value and Skills of the Expert

Haney and Smith (2003), in reviewing a number of cases, found that those involving psychological or psychiatric testimony had a greater likelihood of involving compensatory, rather than only nominal, damages when there was an allegation of violation of constitutional rights. Further, when psychological or emotional injuries are alleged, both judges and juries expect the plaintiff to present testimony by psychologists and/or psychiatrists, and are highly skeptical when plaintiffs do not present such expert evidence (Shuman, 2005).

The expert's task is to educate the judge and/or jury about the methods used in the evaluation, the data derived from the evaluation, the conclusions drawn from the data, and the opinions formed based on the conclusions. However, the expert needs to keep from boring the trier of fact by presenting too many details, without omitting any essential details. Visual aids (e.g., flip charts, PowerPoint) may be utilized to help the judge and jury learn and understand the information presented (Rogers & Shuman, 2005). Many attorneys prefer experts who regularly teach graduate or undergraduate courses, since they are practiced in conveying information to students on many occasions, honing their skill at presentation.

The testifying expert is most likely to come across well to the jury if he or she (1) has credentials that support his or her experience and knowledge base; (2) appears trustworthy; (3) explains technical terms and processes in lay terms (minimizing jargon); (4) addresses the pros and cons of each significant interpretation of the data; (5) summarizes his or her conclusions; and (6) is consistent and concise (Dvoskin & Guy, 2008; McGaughey & Walker, 2002).

Reasonable Psychological/Medical Certainty

Since every evaluation has some limits, psychologists and psychiatrists must generally testify to a "reasonable degree of certainty" regarding their statements and conclusions. There is no definition of the term that is universally accepted (Heilbrun et al., 2009). According to Koocher (1998, p. 512), "As used in personal injury lawsuits, a term implying that more than mere conjecture, possibility, consistency with, or speculation; similar to a probability, more likely than not, 50.1%, but an overwhelming likelihood or scientific certainty is not required." Melton et al. (2007, p. 605) indicate that such statements "relate more to the clinician's subjective confidence in his or her findings than to a firm basis in science...." If the expert merely states that the relationship is *possible*, rather than probable to a reasonable degree of certainty, the court may exclude the opinion as lacking the required degree of certainty (Shuman, 2005). Heilbrun et al. (2009) suggest that opinions be based on all of the sources of information utilized in the evaluation (interviews, tests, records and so forth), in addition to a review of relevant, peer-reviewed professional literature, analysis of consistencies and inconsistencies, and consideration of alternative opinions. They also recommend that "opinions should incorporate sources with established reliability, and with validity for purposes con-

BEST PRACTICE
In order for your testimony to be accepted by the trier of fact, you must demonstrate that your opinion is probable to a "reasonable degree of certainty." Facilitate this by basing your opinion on all sources of information used in the evaluation, reviewing the professional literature, and considering alternative opinions.

sistent with the present evaluation" (p. 55). Ideally, the expert's opinions should flow so naturally from the evidence and logic upon which they are based that the trier of fact will come to the same conclusion as the expert, but without having to "take the expert's word" for it.

Ultimate Issue Testimony

The task of the expert is to provide the trier of fact with the information that will permit decisions regarding whether the defendant owed the plaintiff a duty, whether that duty was breached, whether the plaintiff was harmed as a direct result of that breach, whether, but for that breach, the defendant would not have sustained the psychological injury that was sustained, and what damages the expert can identify that could be assessed to the defendant if responsible for the plaintiff's injury. The expert may reasonably state conclusions regarding his or her data and the conclusions drawn on the basis of those data, including hypotheses that were either accepted or rejected.

Missing from the expert's database, but an essential part of the court process, are legal and policy issues that are addressed by the jury and/or judge. According to Judge David Bazelon (1982, p. 116), these issues "involve scientific, moral and social judgments…. What the public needs most from any expert, including the psychologist, is a wealth of intermediate observations and conceptual insights that are adequately explained. Only then can his or her contributions be combined with the communal sense of right and wrong to produce a decision."

Despite one's best efforts to avoid testifying as to the ultimate issue in a case, courts will occasionally press the expert for such an opinion. Whether or not to resist this pressure is an individual decision that is based in part upon the expert's level of comfort with legal (as opposed to psychological) questions. Often, the issues at bar are so clear and unambiguous that there is virtually no way to avoid exposing one's opinion about the ultimate issue. In other cases, an expert may feel quite strongly that legal questions are beyond his or her expertise, and simply refuse to provide an ultimate issue opinion. As with so many issues, this question should be discussed in some detail with the retaining attorney prior to testimony being offered. In our experience, the best course in most cases is to answer any question that is not successfully objected to, unless doing so would violate the expert's oath or ethical obligations. Sometimes, however, the only truthful answer will be, "I don't know."

Base Testimony on a Well-Conducted Assessment and Interpretation

The psychologist who has performed an appropriate assessment, and who has accurately and fairly interpreted the data from the assessment, should have no difficulty testifying about what was done, the results of the assessment, and the meaning of the results. The thoroughness of the expert will be evident from the quality of the information furnished in the report and testimony, and the accuracy of the interpretation will follow from the logic of the conclusions drawn.

Utilize the Timeline

It is not unusual to have a thousand pages or more of records, depositions, and other documents to review for a personal injury case, in addition to results from tests and other instruments, as well as notes from interviews. Because the goal is to identify and explain the changes in the plaintiff's functioning that relate to the allegedly traumatic incident(s), it is necessary to organize the information in the records in a meaningful way. The timeline allows the expert to see every major life event, including the allegedly traumatic incident(s), in context, and to continue to add to that perspective up to the day of a deposition or trial. The timeline also provides a concise source of information to help answer questions during a deposition or trial. If the expert has done a good job of preparing it, the timeline will significantly facilitate the provision of quality testimony.

Conclusion

A thorough evaluation consisting of multiple methods of data gathering, including careful review of medical and other records, interviews of the plaintiff and collateral informants, questionnaires, and psychological testing (especially the MMPI-2 and symptom validity testing) provides a best practice basis for identifying what the plaintiff experienced, what the experience meant to him or her, the degree of feigning (if any), and the long-term consequences of the trauma. This information should prepare the expert well for testifying regarding the relevant aspects of the emotional trauma experienced by the plaintiff, whether proximate cause was present, and what damages, if any, are recommended.

References

Ackerman, M. J., & Kane, A. W. (1998). *Psychological experts in personal injury actions.* New York, NY: Aspen Law and Business.

Ackerman, M. J., & Kane, A. W. (2005). *Psychological experts in divorce actions.* New York, NY: Aspen Law and Business.

Advisory Committee on the Federal Rules of Evidence. (2000). Notes of advisory committee on proposed rules. Washington, DC: Judicial Conference of the United States. Retrieved April 13, 2011 from http://federalevidence.com/advisory-committee-notes

American Academy of Psychiatry and the Law. (2005). *Ethics guidelines for the practice of forensic psychiatry.* Retrieved November 25, 2009 from http://www.aapl.org/ethics.htm.

American Bar Association. (2009). *ABA model rules of professional conduct.* Retrieved October 25, 2009 from http://www.abanet.org/cpr/mrpc/rule_3_3.html

American Educational Research Association. (1999). *Standards for educational and psychological testing.* Washington, DC: Author.

American Medical Association. (2007). *Guides to the evaluation of permanent impairment* (6th ed.). Chicago, IL: Author.

American Psychiatric Association. (2000). *Diagnostic and statistical manual of mental disorders: Text revision* (4th ed.). Washington, DC: Author.

American Psychiatric Association. (2009). *The principles of medical ethics with annotations especially applicable to psychiatry.* Retrieved October 3, 2009 from http://www.psych.org/MainMenu/PsychiatricPractice/Ethics/ResourcesStandards/Principlesof MedicalEthics.aspx

American Psychological Association. (2002). Ethical principles of psychologists and code of conduct. *American Psychologist, 57,* 1060–1073.

American Psychological Association. (2007). Record keeping guidelines. *American Psychologist, 62,* 993–1004.

American Psychological Association Ethics Committee. (1993). *Policy statement of the APA Ethics Committee regarding "take home" tests.* Washington, DC: Author.

American Psychological Association Ethics Committee. (1994). "Take home" tests. *American Psychologist, 49,* 665–666.

Anderson, A., Barenberg, L., & Trembley, P. R. (2007). Professional ethics in interdisciplinary collaboratives: Zeal, paternalism and mandated reporting. *Clinical Law Review, 13, 659.* Retrieved November 25, 2009 from http://ssrn.com/abstract=921590

Antoine-Tubbs v. Local 513, Air Transport Division, 50 F. Supp. 2d 608 (N.D. Texas, 1998).

APA concise dictionary of psychology. (2009). Washington, DC: American Psychological Association.

Arbisi, P. A., & Butcher, J. N. (2004). Psychometric perspectives on detection of malingering of pain: Use of the Minnesota Multiphasic Personality Inventory-2. *Clinical Journal of Pain, 20,* 383–391.

Association of State and Provincial Psychology Boards. (2005). *ASPPB code of conduct.* Retrieved November 25, 2009 from http://www.asppb.net/i4a/pages/index.cfm?pageid=3353

Athey v. Leonati, 3 S.C.R. 458. (1996).

Babitsky, S., & Mangraviti, J. J., Jr. (2009). *Understanding the AMA guides in workers' compensation.* New York, NY: Aspen Law and Business.

Baer, L. G., & Neal, J. K. (2000). Admissibility of medical causation expert opinions in federal courts, part I: The current state of the law. *The Trial Lawyer, 23,* 323–334.

Bank, S. C., & Packer, I. K. (2007). Expert witness testimony: Law, ethics, and practice. In A. M. Goldstein (Ed.), *Forensic Psychology: Emerging Topics and Expanding Roles* (pp. 421–445). Hoboken, NJ: Wiley.

Barefoot v. Estelle, 463 U.S. 880. (1983).

Barnett, J. E. (2009). Security necessary for test validity. *The National Psychologist, 18,* 10–11.

Barth, R. J. (2007). Observation compromises the credibility of an evaluation. *The Guides Newsletter, July/August,* 1–3, 8–9.

Bazelon, D. L. (1982). Veils, values and social responsibility. *American Psychologist, 37,* 115–121.

Bender, S. D. (2008). Malingered traumatic brain injury. In R. Rogers (Ed.), *Clinical assessment of malingering and deception* (3rd ed.), (pp. 69–86). New York, NY: Guilford.

Ben-Porath, Y. S., Greve, K. W., Bianchini, K. J., & Kaufmann, P. M. (2009a). The MMPI-2 Symptom Validity Scale (FBS) is an empirically validated measure of overreporting in personal injury litigants and claimants: Reply to Butcher et al. (2008). *Psychological Injury and Law, 2,* 62–85.

Ben-Porath, Y. S., Greve, K. W., Bianchini, K. J., & Kaufmann, P. M. (2009b). The MMPI-2 Symptom Validity Scale (FBS) is an empirically-validated measure of over-reporting in personal injury litigants and claimants: Reply to Williams et al. (2009). *Psychological Injury and Law, 2,* retrieved October 6, 2009 from http://springerlink.com/content/l603n1n896w518k6/fulltext.pdf

Berry, D. T. R., & Schipper, L. J. (2008). Assessment of feigned cognitive impairment using standard neuropsychological tests. In R. Rogers (Ed.), *Clinical assessment of malingering and deception* (3rd ed.) (pp. 237–252). New York, NY: Guilford.

Bianchini, K. J., Greve, K. W., & Glynn, G. (2005). On the diagnosis of malingered pain related disability: Lessons from cognitive malingering research. *The Spine Journal, 5,* 404–417.

Bianchini, K. J., Etherton, J. L., Greve, K. W., Heinly, M. T., & Meyers, J. E. (2008). Classification accuracy of MMPI-2 validity scales in the detection of pain-related malingering. *Assessment, 15,* 435–449.

Binder, L., & Rohling, M. L. (1996). Money matters: A meta-analytic review of the effects of financial incentives on recovery after closed-head injury. *American Journal of Psychiatry, 153,* 7–10.

Binder, L., & Willis, S. C. (1991). Assessment of motivation after financially compensable minor head trauma. *Psychological Assessment, 3,* 175–181.

Binder, R. L., Trimble, M. R., & McNeil, D. E. (1991). The course of psychological symptoms after resolution of lawsuits. *American Journal of Psychiatry, 148,* 1073–1075.

Black, H. C. (1979). *Black's law dictionary* (5th ed.). St. Paul, MN: West Publishing.

Blake, D. D., Weathers, F. W., Nagy, L. M., Kaloupek, D. G., Gusman, F. D., Charney, D. S., & Keane, T. M. (1995). The development of a clinician-administered PTSD scale. *Journal of Traumatic Stress, 8,* 75–90.

Blanchard, E. B., Hickling, E. J., Taylor, A. E., Buckley, T. C., Loos, W. R., & Walsh, J. (1998). Effects of litigation settlements on posttraumatic stress symptoms in motor vehicle accident victims. *Journal of Traumatic Stress, 11*(2), 337–354.

Boccaccini, M. T., & Brodsky, S. L. (1999). Diagnostic test usage by forensic psychologists in emotional injury cases. *Professional Psychology: Research and Practice, 30,* 253–259.

Bond, C. F., Jr. (2000). Social facilitation. In A. E. Kazdin (Ed.), *Encyclopedia of psychology,* vol. 7 (pp. 338–340). Washington, DC: American Psychological Association.

Bowman, M. (2003). Problems inherent to the diagnosis of posttraumatic stress disorder. In I. Z. Schultz & D. O. Brady (Eds.), *Psychological injuries at trial* (pp. 820–849). Chicago, IL: American Bar Association.

Breslau, N., Chilcoat, H., Kessler, R. C., & Davis, G. C. (1999). Previous exposure to trauma and PTSD effects of subsequent trauma: Results from the Detroit Area Survey of Trauma. *American Journal of Psychiatry, 156,* 902–907.

Briere, J. (1995). *Trauma Symptom Inventory professional manual.* Odessa, FL: Psychological Assessment Resources.

Briere, J. (2001). *Detailed Assessment of Posttraumatic Stress (DAPS).* Odessa, FL: Psychological Assessment Resources.

Briere, J. (2004). *Psychological assessment of adult posttraumatic states* (2nd ed.). Washington, DC: American Psychological Association.

Briere, J., Elliott, D. M., Harris, K., & Cotman, A. (1995). Trauma Symptom Inventory: Psychometrics and association with childhood and adult victimization in clinical samples. *Journal of Interpersonal Violence, 10,* 387–401.

Bryant, R. A., & Harvey, A. G. (2003). The influence of litigation on maintenance of posttraumatic stress disorder. *Journal of Nervous and Mental Disease, 191,* 191–193.

Butcher, J. N. (1995). Personality patterns of personal injury litigants: The role of computer-based MMPI-2 evaluations. In Y. S. Ben-Porath, J. R. Graham, G. C. N. Hall, R. D. Hirschman, & M. S. Zaragoza (Eds.), *Forensic applications of the MMPI-2*. Thousand Oaks, CA: Sage.

Butcher, J. N., & Miller, K. B. (2006). Personality assessment in personal injury litigation. In I. B. Weiner & A. K. Hess (Eds.), *The handbook of forensic psychology* (3rd ed.). (pp. 140–166). Hoboken, NJ: Wiley.

Butcher, J. N., & Pope, K. S. (1993). Seven issues in conducting forensic assessments: Ethical responsibilities in light of new standards and new tests. *Ethics and Behavior, 3,* 267–288.

Butcher, J. N., Gass, C. S., Cumella, E., Kally, Z., & Williams, C. L. (2008). Potential bias in MMPI-2 assessments using the Fake Bad Scale (FBS). *Psychological Injury and Law, 1,* 191–209.

Butcher, J. N., Dahlstrom, W. G., Graham, J. R., Tellegen, A., & Kaemmer, B. (1989). *Minnesota Multiphasic Personality Inventory (MMPI-2). Manual for administration and scoring*. Minneapolis, MN: University of Minnesota Press.

Butcher, J. N., Graham, J. R., Ben-Porath, Y. S., Tellegen, A., Dahlstrom, W. G., & Kaemmer, B. (2001). *MMPI-2 Manual for administration, scoring, and interpretation* (Rev. ed.). Minneapolis, MN: University of Minnesota Press.

Call, J. A. (2003). Liability for psychological injury: History of the concept. In I. Z. Schultz & D. O. Brady (Eds.), *Psychological injuries at trial* (pp. 40–64). Chicago, IL: American Bar Association.

Camara, W. J., Nathan, J. S., & Puente, A. E. (2000). Psychological test usage: Implications in professional psychology. *Professional Psychology: Research & Practice, 31,* 141–154.

Campbell, D. S., & Montigny, C. (2004). Psychological harm and tort law: Reassessing the legal test for liability. In T. Archibald & M. Cochrane (Eds.), *Annual review of civil litigation: 2003* (pp. 133–155). Toronto, ON: Thomson/Carswell.

Cato, M. A., Brewster, J., Ryan, T., & Giuliano, A. J. (2002). Coaching and the ability to simulate mild traumatic brain injury symptoms. *The Clinical Neuropsychologist, 16,* 524–535.

Child Welfare Information Gateway. (2008). Mandatory reporters of child abuse and neglect. Retrieved November 25, 2009 from http://www.childwelfare.gov/systemwide/laws_policies/statutes/manda.cfm

Cohen, F. L. (2004). The expert medical witness in legal perspective. *The Journal of Legal Medicine, 25,* 185–209.

Committee on Ethical Guidelines for Forensic Psychologists. (1991). Specialty guidelines for forensic psychologists. *Law and Human Behavior, 15,* 655–665.

Committee on Psychological Tests and Assessment. (2007a). *Statement on third party observers in psychological testing and assessment: A framework for decision making*. Washington, DC: American Psychological Association.

Committee on Psychological Tests and Assessment. (2007b). *Recent developments affecting the disclosure of test data and materials: Comments regarding the 1996 statement on the disclosure of test data.* Washington, DC: American Psychological Association.

Constantinou, M., Ashendorf, L., & McCaffrey, R. J. (2002). When the 3rd party observer of a neuropsychological evaluation is an audiorecorder. *The Clinical Neuropsychologist, 16,* 407–412.

Constantinou, M., & McCaffrey, R. J. (2003). The effects of 3rd party observation: When the observer is a video camera. *Archives of Clinical Neuropsychology, 18,* 788–789.

Craig, R. J. (1999). Testimony based on the Millon Clinical Multiaxial Inventory: Review, commentary, and guidelines. *Journal of Personality Assessment, 73,* 290–304.

Craig, R. J. (2005). *Personality-guided forensic psychology.* Washington, DC: American Psychological Association.

Daller, M. F. (Ed.). (2009). *Tort law desk reference: A fifty-state compendium.* New York, NY: Aspen Law and Business.

Daubert v. Merrell Dow Pharmaceuticals, Inc., 509 U.S. 579, 113 S.Ct. 2786. (1993).

Daubert v. Merrell Dow Pharmaceuticals, Inc., 43 F.3d 1311. (1995).

Dean, B. P. (2004). Discovery in scientific evidence cases. In J. J. Brown (Ed.), *Scientific evidence and experts handbook* (2004 cumulative supplement) (pp. 137–229). New York, NY: Aspen Law and Business.

Deatherage v. Board of Psychology, 134 Wn.2d 131, 948 P.2d 828. (Wn. Sup. Ct. 1997).

Demaré, D., & Briere, J. (1996). *Validation of the Trauma Symptom Inventory with abused and nonabused university students.* Paper presented at the 104th Annual Convention of the American Psychological Association, Toronto, ON, Canada.

Detroit Edison Co. v. NLRB, 440 U.S. 301. (1979).

Dillon v. Legg, 441 P.2d 912. (Cal. 1968).

Douglas, K. S., Huss, M. T., Murdoch, L. L., Washington, D. O., & Koch, W. J. (1999). Posttraumatic stress disorder stemming from motor vehicle accidents: Legal issues in Canada and the United States. In E. J. Hickling & E. B. Blanchard (Eds.), *The international handbook of road traffic accidents and psychological trauma: Current understanding, treatment and law* (pp. 271–289). New York, NY: Elsevier Science.

Drob, S. L., Meehan, K. B., & Waxman, S. E. (2009). Clinical and conceptual problems in the attribution of malingering in forensic evaluations. *Journal of the American Academy of Psychiatry and the Law, 37,* 98–106.

Dvoskin, J. A. (2007). Presidential Column. *AP-LS Newsletter, 27,* 2–3.

Dvoskin, J. A., & Guy, L. S. (2008). On being an expert witness: It's not about you. *Psychiatry, Psychology and Law, 15,* 202–212.

Edens, J. F., Otto, R. K., & Dwyer, T. J. (1998). Susceptibility of the Trauma Symptom Inventory to malingering. *Journal of Personality Assessment, 71*, 379–392.

Eisendrath, S. J., & McNiel, D. E. (2002). Factitious disorders in civil litigation: Twenty cases illustrating the spectrum of abnormal illness-affirming behavior. *Journal of the American Academy of Psychiatry and the Law, 30*, 391–392.

Elhai, J. D., Gold, P. B., Sellers, A. H., & Dorfman, W. I. (2001). The detection of malingered posttraumatic stress disorder with MMPI-2 Fake Bad Indices. *Assessment, 8*, 221–236.

Elhai, J. D., Naifeh, J. A., Zucker, I. S., Gold, S. N., Deitsch, S. E., & Frueh, B. C. (2004). Discriminating malingered from genuine civilian posttraumatic stress disorder: A validation of three MMPI-2 infrequency scales (F, FP, and FPTSD). *Assessment, 11*, 139–144.

Estelle v. Smith, 451 U.S. 454. (1981).

Ewing, C. P. (2003). Expert testimony: Law and practice. In I. B. Weiner (Series Ed.) & A. M. Goldstein (Vol. Ed.), *Handbook of psychology: Vol. 11, Forensic psychology* (pp. 55–66). Hoboken, NJ: Wiley.

Faigman, D. L., & Monahan, J. (2005). Psychological evidence at the dawn of the law's scientific age. *Annual Review of Psychology, 56*, 631–659.

Faust, D. (2003). Alternatives to four clinical and research traditions in malingering detection. In P. W. Halligan, C. Bass, & D. A. Oakley (Eds.), *Malingering and illness deception* (pp. 107–121). New York, NY: Oxford University Press.

Faust, D., & Heard, K. V. (2003a). Objectifying subjective injury claims. In I. Z. Schultz & D. O. Brady (Eds.), *Psychological injuries at trial* (pp. 1686–1705). Chicago, IL: American Bar Association.

Faust, D., & Heard, K. V. (2003b). Biased experts: Some practical suggestions for identifying and demonstrating unfair practices. In I. Z. Schultz & D. O. Brady (Eds.), *Psychological injuries at trial* (pp. 1706–1739). Chicago, IL: American Bar Association.

Federal Rules of Civil Procedure, December 1, 2009, retrieved April 13, 2011 from http://www.utd.uscourts.gov/forms/civil2009.pdf

Federal Rules of Evidence, December 1, 2009, retrieved April 13, 2011 from http://www.utd.uscourts.gov/forms/evid2009.pdf

First, M. B., Spitzer, R. L., Gibbon, M., & Williams, J. B. W. (1997). *Structured Clinical Interview for DSM-IV Axis I Disorders (SCID-I), Clinician Version.* Arlington, VA: American Psychiatric Press.

Fishbain, D. A., Cutler, R., Rosomoff, H. L., & Rosomoff, R. S. (1999). Chronic pain disability exaggeration/malingering and submaximal effort research. *Clinical Journal of Pain, 15*, 244–274.

Fishbain, D. A., Cutler, R., Rosomoff, H. L., & Rosomoff, R. S. (2003). Chronic pain disability exaggeration/malingering and submaximal effort research. In I. Z. Schultz, & D. O. Brady (Eds.), *Psychological injuries at trial* (pp. 1064–1122). Chicago: American Bar Association.

Fisher, C. (2003). *Decoding the ethics code: A practical guide for psychologists.* Thousand Oaks, CA: Sage.

Fleishman, W., Jackson, J. R., & Rothschild, M. (1999). Defensive litigation strategy in scientific evidence cases. In J. J. Brown (Ed.), *Scientific evidence and experts handbook* (pp. 305–385). New York, NY: Aspen Law and Business.

Foa E. B. (1995). Posttraumatic Stress Diagnostic Scale manual. Minneapolis, MN: National Computer Systems, Inc.

Foa, E. B., Tolin, D. F., Ehlers, A., Clark, D. M., & Orsillo, S. M. (1999). The Posttraumatic Cognitions Inventory (PTCI): Development and validation. *Psychological Assessment, 11,* 303–314.

Franz, V. A., Glass, C. R., Arnkoff, D. B., & Dutton, M. A. (2009). The impact of the September 11th terrorist attacks on psychiatric patients: A review. *Clinical Psychology Review, 29,* 339–347.

Frueh, B. C., Elhai, J. D., & Kaloupek, D. G. (2004). Unresolved issues in the assessment of trauma exposure and posttraumatic reactions. In G. M. Rosen (Ed.), *Posttraumatic stress disorder: Issues and controversies.* West Sussex, England: Wiley.

Frye v. United States, 293 F. 1013, 34 ALR 145. (D.C. Cir. 1923).

Gabbay, V., & Alonso, C. M. (2004). Legal aspects related to PTSD in children and adolescents. In R. R. Silva (Ed.), *Posttraumatic stress disorder in children and adolescents: Handbook* (pp. 60–82). New York, NY: Norton.

Garb, H. N. (2003). Incremental validity and the assessment of psychopathology in adults. *Psychological Assessment, 15,* 508–520.

Gatchel, R. J., & Kishino, N. (2006). Influence of personality characteristics of pain patients: Implications for causality in pain. In G. Young, A. W. Kane, & K. Nicholson (Eds.), *Psychological knowledge in court: PTSD, pain and TBI* (pp. 149–162). New York, NY: Springer SBM.

Gavett, B. E., Lynch, J. K., & McCaffrey, R. J. (2005). Third party observers: The effect size is greater than you might think. *Journal of Forensic Neuropsychology, 4,* 49–64.

Geier, P. (2006). Emerging med-mal strategy: 'I'm sorry'. *The National Law Journal Online,* July 24, 2006. Retrieved July 23, 2006 from www.nlj.com

General Electric Company v. Joiner, 118 S.Ct. 512, 522 U.S. 136. (1997).

Goldstein, A. M. (2007). Forensic psychology: Toward a standard of care. In A. M. Goldstein (Ed), (2007). *Forensic psychology: Emerging topics and expanding roles* (pp. 3–41). Hoboken NJ: John Wiley & Sons Inc.

Gouvier, W. D., Hayes, J. S., & Smiroldo, B. B. (2003). The significance of base rates, test sensitivity, test specificity, and subjects' knowledge of symptoms in assessing TBI sequelae and malingering. In I. Z. Schulze & D. O. Brady (Eds.), *Psychological injuries at trial* (pp. 641–671). Chicago, IL: American Bar Association.

Graham, J. R. (2006). *MMPI-2. Assessing personality and psychopathology* (4th ed.). New York, NY: Oxford University Press.

Green, P. (2003). *Memory Complaints Inventory.* Edmonton: Green's Publishing.

Green, P. (2005). *Green's Word Memory Test user's manual.* Edmonton: Green's Publishing.

Green, P., Allen, L. M., & Astner, K. (1996). *The Word Memory Test: A manual for the oral and computerized forms.* Durham, NC: CogniSyst, Inc.

Greenberg, S. A. (2003). Personal injury examinations in torts for emotional distress. In I. B. Weiner (Series Ed.) & A. M. Goldstein (Vol. Ed.), *Handbook of psychology: Vol. 11, Forensic psychology* (pp. 233–257). Hoboken, NJ: Wiley.

Greenberg, S. A., Otto, R. K., & Long, A. C. (2003). The utility of psychological testing in assessing emotional damages in personal injury litigation. *Assessment, 10,* 411–419.

Greenberg, S. A., Shuman, D. W., Feldman, S. R., & Middleton, C. (2007). Lessons for forensic psychology practice drawn from the law of malpractice. In A. M. Goldstein (Ed.), *Forensic Psychology: Emerging Topics and Expanding Roles.* Hoboken, NJ: Wiley.

Greenberg, S. A., Shuman, D. W., & Meyer, R. G. (2004). Unmasking forensic diagnosis. *International Journal of Law and Psychiatry, 27,* 1–15.

Greene, R. L. (2000). *The MMPI-2: An interpretive manual* (2nd ed.). Needham Heights, MA: Allyn & Bacon.

Greene, R. L. (2008). Malingering and defensiveness on the MMPI-2. In R. Rogers (Ed.), *Clinical assessment of malingering and deception* (3rd ed.) (pp. 159–181). New York, NY: Guilford.

Greene, R. L. (2011). *The MMPI-2/MMPI-2-RF: An interpretive manual* (3d ed.). Boston: Allyn & Bacon.

Greiffenstein, M. F., Fox, D., & Lees-Haley, P. R. (2007). The MMPI-2 Fake Bad Scale in detection of noncredible brain injury claims. In K. B. Boone (Ed.), *Assessment of feigned cognitive impairment: A neuropsychological perspective.* (pp. 210–235). New York, NY: Guilford.

Grisso, T. (2003). *Evaluating competencies* (2nd ed.). New York, NY: Kluwer/Plenum.

Grisso, T. (2010). Guidance for improving forensic reports: A review of common errors. *Open Access Journal of Forensic Psychology, 2,* 102–115. Retrieved June 6, 2010 from HYPERLINK "http://www.forensicpsychologyunbound.ws/" www.forensicpsychologyunbound.ws/

Groth-Marnat, G. (2009a). *Handbook of psychological assessment.* Hoboken, NJ: Wiley.

Groth-Marnat, G. (2009b). The five assessment issues you meet when you go to heaven. *Journal of Personality Assessment, 9,* 303–310.

Gutheil, T. G. (2006). Commentary: Systems, sensitivity, and "sorry." *Journal of the American Academy of Psychiatry and Law, 34,* 101–102.

Gutheil, T. G., & Brodsky, A. (2010). Commentary: Tarasoff duties arising from a forensic independent medical examination. *Journal of the American Academy of Psychiatry and Law, 38,* 57–60.

Gutheil, T. G., & Bursztajn, H. (2003). Avoiding *ipse dixit* mislabeling: Post-*Daubert* approaches to expert clinical opinions. *Journal of the American Academy of Psychiatry and the Law, 31,* 205–210.

Hall, H. V., & Poirier, J. G. (2001). *Detecting malingering and deception* (2nd ed.). New York, NY: CRC Press.

Hansen, L. (2004). Attorneys' duty to report child abuse. *Journal of the American Academy of Matrimonial Lawyers, 19,* 59–76.

Harris v. Forklift Systems, Inc., 114 S.Ct. 367. (1993).

Hartlage, L. C. (1989). *Behavior Change Inventory.* Branden, VT: Clinical Psychology Publishing Company.

Health Canada. Health Canada homepage. Retrieved January 25, 2004 from http://www.hc-sc.gc.ca/index-eng.php

Heilbrun, K. (2001). *Principles of forensic mental health assessment.* New York, NY: Kluwer/Plenum.

Heilbrun, K., Marczyk, G. R., & DeMatteo, D. (Eds.). (2002). *Forensic mental health assessment: A casebook.* New York, NY: Oxford University Press.

Heilbrun, K., DeMatteo, D., Marczyk, G., & Goldstein, A. (2008). Standards of practice and care in forensic mental health assessment: Legal, professional, and principles-based considerations. *Psychology, Public Policy, and Law, 14,* 1–26.

Heilbrun, K., Marczyk, G., DeMatteo, D. & Mack-Allen, J. (2007). A principles-based approach to forensic mental health assessment: Utility and update. In A. M. Goldstein (Ed), (2007). *Forensic psychology: Emerging topics and expanding roles* (pp. 45–72). Hoboken, NJ: John Wiley & Sons.

Heilbrun, K., Warren, J., & Picarello, K. (2003). Third party information in forensic assessment. In I. B. Weiner (Series Ed.) & A. M. Goldstein (Vol. Ed.), *Handbook of psychology, Vol. 11, forensic psychology* (pp. 69–86). Hoboken NJ: Wiley.

Heilbrun, K., Grisso, T., & Goldstein, A. M. (2009). *Foundations of forensic mental health assessment.* New York, NY: Oxford University Press.

Heilbrun, K., Yasuhara, K., & Shah, S. (2010). Violence risk assessment tools: Overview and critical analysis. In R. Otto & K. Douglas (Eds.), *Handbook of violence risk assessment* (pp. 1–17). New York: Routledge.

Heilbronner, R. L. (1993). Factors associated with postconcussion syndrome: Neurological, psychological, or legal? *Trial Diplomacy Journal, 16,* 161–167.

Heilbronner, R. L. (Ed.). (2005). *Forensic neuropsychology casebook.* New York, NY: Guilford.

Heilbronner, R. L., Sweet, J. J., Morgan, J. E., Larrabee, G. J., & Millis, S. R. (2009). American Academy of Clinical Neuropsychology consensus conference statement on the neuropsychological assessment of effort, response bias, and malingering. *The Clinical Neuropsychologist, 23,* 1093–1129.

Hertenstein v. Kimberly Home Health Care, Inc. 189 F.R.D. 620. (Kan. 1999).

Hess, A. (1998). Millon Clinical Multiaxial Inventory-III. In J. C. Impara & B. S. Plake (Eds.), *The thirteenth mental measurements yearbook* (pp. 665–667). Lincoln, NE: University of Nebraska-Lincoln.

Hess, A. K. (2006). Defining forensic psychology. In I. B. Weiner & A. K. Hess (Eds.), *The handbook of forensic psychology* (3rd ed.) (pp. 28–58). Hoboken, NJ: Wiley.

Howard v. Drapkin, 271 Cal.Rptr. 893. (Ct.App. 1990).

Hunsley, J. (2003). Introduction to the special section on incremental validity and utility in clinical assessment. *Psychological Assessment, 15,* 443–445.

Hunsley, J., & Meyer, G. J. (2003). The incremental validity of psychological testing and assessment: Conceptual, methodological, and statistical issues. *Psychological Assessment, 15,* 446–455.

Hyler, S. E., Williams, J. B., & Spitzer, R. L. (1988). Where in DSM-III-R is "compensation neurosis"? *American Journal of Forensic Psychology, 6,* 13–22.

Hynan, D. J. (2004). Unsupported general differences on some personality disorder scales of the Millon Clinical Multiaxial Inventory-III. *Professional Psychology: Research and Practice, 35,* 105–110.

In re air crash at Taipei, Taiwan, on October 31, 2000, 01-MDL-1394-GAF (Rcx). (C.D. Cal. 2003).

Inman, T. H., Vickery, C. D., Berry, D. T. R., Lamb, D., Edwards, C., & Smith, G. T. (1998). Development and initial validation of a new procedure for evaluating adequacy of effort given during neuropsychological testing: The Letter Memory Test. *Psychological Assessment, 10,* 128–139.

Iverson, G. L., & Lange, R. T. (2006). Detecting exaggeration and malingering in psychological injury claims. In W. J. Koch, K. S. Douglas, T. L. Nicholls, & M. L. O'Neill, *Psychological injuries: Forensic assessment, treatment, and law.* Oxford, UK: Oxford University Press.

Kane, A. W. (2007a). Basic concepts in psychology and law. . In G. Young, A. W. Kane, & K. Nicholson, *Causality of psychological injury: Presenting evidence in court* (pp. 261–292). New York, NY: Springer SBM.

Kane, A. W. (2007b). Conducting a psychological assessment. In G. Young, A. W. Kane, & K. Nicholson, *Causality of psychological injury: Presenting evidence in court* (pp. 293–323). New York, NY: Springer SBM.

Kane, A. W. (2007c). Other psycho-legal issues. In G. Young, A. W. Kane, & K. Nicholson, *Causality of psychological injury: Presenting evidence in court* (pp. 325–367). New York, NY: Springer SBM.

Karson, M. (2005). Ten things I learned about report writing in law school (and the eighth grade). *The Clinical Psychologist, 58,* 4–11.

Kaufmann, P. M. (2005). Protecting the objectivity, fairness, and integrity of neuropsychological evaluations in litigation. *Journal of Legal Medicine, 26,* 95–131.

Kaufmann, P. M. (2009). Protecting raw data and psychological tests from wrongful disclosure: Primer on the law and other persuasive strategies. *The Clinical Neuropsychologist, 23,* 1130–1159.

Kehrer, C. A., Sanchez, P. N., Habif, U., Rosenbaum, J. G., & Townes, B. D. (2000). Effects of a significant-other observer on neuropsychological test performance. *The Clinical Neuropsychologist, 14,* 67–71.

Kimerling, R., Prins, A., Westrup, D., & Lee, T. (2004). Gender issues in the assessment of PTSD. In J. P. Wilson & T. M. Keane (Eds.), *Assessing psychological trauma and PTSD* (2nd ed.) (pp. 565–599). New York, NY: Guilford.

Kirkpatrick, L. C., & Mueller, C. B. (2003). *Evidence: Practice under the rules.* New York, NY: Aspen Law and Business.

Kraus, D. A., & Sales, B. D. (2003). Forensic psychology, public policy, and the law. In I. B. Weiner (Series Ed.) & A. M. Goldstein (Vol. Ed.), *Handbook of psychology: Vol. 11, Forensic psychology* (pp. 543–560). Hoboken, NJ: Wiley.

Koch, W. J., O'Neill, M., & Douglas, K. S. (2005). Empirical limits for the forensic assessment of PTSD litigants. *Law and Human Behavior, 29,* 121–149.

Koch, W. J., Douglas, K. S., Nicholls, T. L., & O'Neill, M. L. (2006). *Psychological injuries: Forensic assessment, treatment, and law.* Oxford, UK: Oxford University Press.

Koocher, G. P. (1998). Glossary of legal terms of special interest in mental health practice. In G. P. Koocher, J. C. Norcross, & S. S. Hill III (Eds.), *Psychologist's desk reference* (pp. 509–513). New York, NY: Oxford University Press.

Kumho Tire Co. v. Carmichael, 526 U.S. 137, 119 S.Ct. 1167. (1999).

Lees-Haley, P. R. (1992). Psychodiagnostic test usage by forensic psychologists. *American Journal of Forensic Psychology, 10,* 25–30.

Lees-Haley, P. R. (1997). *Challenges to validity and reliability in neurotoxic assessment of mass injuries.* Presentation at the 17th Annual Conference of the National Academy of Neuropsychology, Las Vegas, NV.

Lees-Haley, P. R., & Brown, R. S. (1993). Neuropsychological complaint base rates of 170 personal injury claimants. *Archives of Clinical Neuropsychology, 8,* 203–209.

Lees-Haley, P. R., English, L. T., & Glenn, W. J. (1991). A Fake Bad Scale on the MMPI-2 for personal injury claimants. *Psychological Reports, 68,* 203–210.

Lees-Haley, P. R., Smith, H. H., Williams, C. W., & Dunn, J. T. (1995). Forensic neuropsychological test usage: An empirical survey. *Archives of Clinical Neuropsychology, 11,* 45–51.

Levy, M. I., & Rosenberg, S. E. (2003). The "eggshell plaintiff" revisited: Causation of mental damages in civil litigation. Retrieved April 22, 2003 from www.apanet.org/disability/reporter/feature.html

Lezak, M. D., Howieson, D. B., & Loring, D. W. (2004). *Neuropsychological assessment* (4th ed.). Oxford, UK: Oxford University Press.

Linley, P. A., & Joseph, S. (2005). The human capacity for growth through adversity. *American Psychologist, 60,* 262–264.

Lowes, R. L. (2009). Liability means never saying you're sorry. An interview with Nancy Berlinger, Ph.D., of the Hastings Center. Retrieved October 18, 2009 from www.medscape.com/viewarticle/709743_print

Macartney-Filgate, M. S., & Snow, G. W. (2004). The practitioner as expert witness. In D. R. Evans (Ed.), *The law, standards, and ethics in the practice of psychology* (2nd ed.) (pp. 287–309). Toronto, ON: Edmond Montgomery Publications.

MacDonald, N., & Attaran, A. (2009). Medical errors, apologies and apology laws. *Canadian Medical Association Journal, 180,* 11.

Maddi, S. R. (2005). On hardiness and other pathways to resilience. *American Psychologist, 60,* 261–262.

Martelli, M. F., Nicholson, K, Zasler, N. D., & Bender, M. C. (2007). Assessment of response bias in clinical and forensic evaluations of impairment following brain injury. In N. D. Zasler, D. I. Katz, & R. D. Zafonte (Eds.), *Brain injury medicine: Principles & practice.* New York, NY: Demos.

McDonnell, W. M., & Guenther, E. (2008). Narrative review: Do state laws make it easier to say "I'm sorry"?. *Annals of Internal Medicine, 149,* 811–815.

Medical Protection Society. (2008). Patients are less likely to sue if they receive an apology, finds new survey. Retrieved November 6, 2009 from http://www.medicalprotection.org/uk/press-release/Patients-are-less-likely-to-sue-if-they-receive-an-apology

Mayer, J. L., & Farmer, R. F. (2003). The development and psychometric evaluation of a new measure of dissociative activities. *Journal of Personality Assessment, 80,* 185–196.

McCaffrey, R., Lynch, J. K., & Yantz, C. L. (2005). Third party observers: Why all the fuss? *Journal of Forensic Neuropsychology, 4,* 1–15.

McGaughey, B. D., & Walker, J. D. (2002). The scientific expert's approaches to litigation testimony. In J. J. Brown (Ed.), *Scientific evidence and expert's handbook* (1999, 2002 cumulative supplement) (pp. 43–67). New York, NY: Aspen Law and Business.

McLearen, A. M., Pietz, C. A., & Denney, R. L. (2004). Evaluation of psychological damages. In W. T. O'Donohue & E. R. Levensky (Eds.), *Handbook of forensic psychology* (pp. 267–299). Amsterdam, The Netherlands: Elsevier.

McMinn, M. R., Ellens, B. M., & Soref, E. (1999). Ethical perspectives and practice behaviors involving computer-based test interpretation. *Assessment, 6,* 71–77.

Melton, G. B., Petrila, J., Poythress, N. G., & Slobogin, C. (2007). *Psychological evaluations for the courts: A handbook for mental health professionals and lawyers* (3rd ed.). New York, NY: Guilford.

Melzack, R. (1975). The McGill Pain Questionnaire: Major properties and scoring methods. *Pain, 1,* 277–279.

Mendelson, D. (1992). The defendants' liability for negligently caused nervous shock in Australia quo vadis? *Monash University Law Review, 18,* 16–69.

Mendelson, G., & Mendelson, D. (2004). Malingering pain in the medicolegal context. *The Clinical Journal of Pain, 20,* 423–432.

Meyers, J. E., Millis, S. R., & Volkert, K. (2002). A validity index for the MMPI-2. *Archives of Clinical Neuropsychology, 17,* 157–169.

Miller, L. (2001). Crime victim trauma and psychological injury: Clinical and forensic guidelines. In E. Pierson (Ed.), *2001 expert witness update* (pp. 173–207). New York, NY: Aspen Law and Business.

Miller, W. (2003). Evidentiary issues in the psychological injury case. In I. Z. Schulze & D. O. Brady (Eds.), *Psychological injuries at trial* (pp. 202–235). Chicago, IL: American Bar Association.

Millon, T. (1997). *Millon Clinical Multiaxial Inventory-III Manual* (3rd ed.). Minneapolis, MN: NCS Pearson.

Miramon v. Bradley, 701 S.2d 475. (La. App. 1 Cir., 9/23/97).

Mooney, R. L., & Gordon, L. V. (1950). *Mooney Problem Check List.* [manual]. Oxford, UK: Psychological Corporation.

Morel, K. R. (2009). Test security in medicolegal cases: Proposed guidelines for attorneys utilizing neuropsychology practice. *Archives of Clinical Neuropsychology, 24,* 635–646.

Morey, L. C. (1991). *The Personality Assessment Inventory professional manual.* Odessa, FL: Psychological Assessment Resources.

Morey, L. C. (2003). *Essentials of PAI assessment.* Hoboken, NJ: Wiley.

Morgan, L. (2004). Does the mandatory reporting law trump attorney-client privilege? *American Psychology-Law Society News, 24,* 12–13.

Mullen, K. L., & Edens, J. F. (2008). A case law survey of the Personality Assessment Inventory: Examining its role in civil and criminal trials. *Journal of Personality Assessment, 90,* 300–303.

Murphy, J. P. (2000). Expert witnesses at trial: Where are the ethics? *Georgetown Journal of Legal Ethics, 14.* Retrieved December 1, 2009 from http://findarticles.com/p/articles/mi_qa3975/is_200010/ai_n8913474/

National Association of Social Workers. (1999). Code of ethics. Retrieved November 25, 2009 from http://www.socialworkers.org/pubs/code/default.asp

Nelson, N. W., Hoelzle, J. B., Sweet, J. J., Arbisi, P. A., & Demakis, G. J. (2010). Updated meta-analysis of the MMPI-2 Symptom Validity Scale (FBS): verified utility in forensic practice. *The Clinical Neuropsychologist, 24,* 701–724.

Nichols, D. S. (2001). *Essentials of MMPI-2 assessment.* New York, NY: Wiley.

Nichols, D. S., & Greene, R. L. (1997). Dimensions of deception in personality assessment: The example of the MMPI-2. *Journal of Personality Assessment, 68,* 251–266.

Nicholson, K., & Martelli, M. F. (2007a). Malingering: Overview and basic concepts. In G. Young, A. W. Kane, & K. Nicholson, *Causality of psychological injury: Presenting evidence in court* (pp. 375–409). New York, NY: Springer SBM.

Nicholson, K., & Martelli, M. F. (2007b). The effect of compensation status. In G. Young, A. W. Kane, & K. Nicholson, *Causality of psychological injury: Presenting evidence in court* (pp. 411–426). New York, NY: Springer SBM.

Nicholson, K., & Martelli, M. F. (2007c). Malingering: Traumatic brain injury. In G. Young, A. W. Kane, & K. Nicholson, *Causality of psychological injury: Presenting evidence in court* (pp. 427–475). New York, NY: Springer SBM.

Nicholson, K., & Martelli, M. F. (2007d). Malingering: Chronic pain. In G. Young, A. W. Kane, & K. Nicholson, *Causality of psychological injury: Presenting evidence in court* (pp. 477–500). New York, NY: Springer SBM.

Nicholson, K., & Martelli, M. F. (2007e). Malingering: Posttraumatic stress disorder and depression. In G. Young, A. W. Kane, & K. Nicholson, *Causality of psychological injury: Presenting evidence in court* (pp. 501–508). New York, NY: Springer SBM.

Nicholson, K., & Martelli, M. F. (2007f). Malingering: Summary and conclusions. In G. Young, A. W. Kane, & K. Nicholson, *Causality of psychological injury: Presenting evidence in court* (pp. 509–514). New York, NY: Springer SBM.

Niland, J. (2004). Expert opinion: Does the mandatory reporting law trump attorney-client privilege? *American Psychology-Law Society News, 24,* 10–12.

Norris, F. N., & Hamblen, J. L. (2004). Standardized self-report measures of civilian trauma and PTSD. In J. P. Wilson & T. M. Keane (Eds.), *Assessing psychological trauma and PTSD* (2nd ed.) (pp. 63–102). New York, NY: Guilford.

Norris, F., & Perilla, J. (1996). The Revised Civilian Mississippi Scale for PTSD: Reliability, validity and cross-language stability. *Journal of Traumatic Stress, 8,* 285–298.

O'Donnell, M. L., Creamer, M., Bryant, R. A., Schnyder, U., & Shalev, A. (2006). Posttraumatic disorders following injury: Assessment and other methodological considerations. In G. Young, A. W. Kane, & K. Nicholson (Eds.), *Psychological knowledge in court: PTSD, pain, and TBI* (pp. 70–84). New York, NY: Springer SBM.

Otto, R. K. (2002). Use of the MMPI-2 in forensic settings. *Journal of Forensic Psychology Practice, 2,* 71–91.

Otto, R. K. (2008). Challenges and advances in assessment of response style in forensic examination contexts. In R. Rogers (Ed.), *Clinical assessment of malingering and deception* (3rd ed.) (pp. 365–375). New York, NY: Guilford.

Otto, R. K., & Krauss, D. A. (2009). Contemplating the presence of third party observers and facilitators in psychological evaluations. *Assessment, 16,* 362–372.

Otto, R. K., Slobogin, C., & Greenberg, S. A. (2007). Legal and ethical issues in accessing and utilizing third-party information. In A. M. Goldstein (Ed), (2007). *Forensic psychology: Emerging topics and expanding roles* (pp. 190–205). Hoboken, NJ: John Wiley & Sons.

Pearson Assessments. (2009). Legal policies. Retrieved October 5, 2009 from http://www.pearsonassessments.com/cgi-bin/MsmGo. exe?grab_id=0&page_id=9&query=trade%20secret&hiword= SECRECY%20SECRETS%20TRADERS%20TRADES%20secret %20trade

Pitt, S. E., Spiers, E. M., Dietz, P. E., & Dvoskin, J. A. (1999). Preserving the integrity of the interview: The value of video tape. *Journal of Forensic Sciences, 44,* 1287–1291.

Polusny, M., & Arbisi, P. A. (2006). Assessment of psychological distress and disability after sexual assault in adults. In G. Young, A. W. Kane, & K. Nicholson (Eds.), *Psychological experts in court: PTSD, pain, and TBI* (pp. 97–125). New York, NY: Springer SBM.

Pope, K., & Vasquez, M. J. T. (2007). *Ethics in psychotherapy and counseling* (3rd ed.). San Francisco, CA: Jossey-Bass.

Pope, K. S., Butcher, J. N., & Seelen, J. (2000). *The MMPI, MMPI-2 & MMPI-A in court* (2nd ed.). Washington, DC: American Psychological Association.

Pope, K. S., Butcher, J. N., & Seelen, J. (2006). *The MMPI, MMPI-2 & MMPI-A in court* (3rd ed.). Washington, DC: American Psychological Association.

Posthuma, A., Podrouzek, W., & Crisp, D. (2002). The implications of *Daubert* on neuropsychological evidence in the assessment of remote mild traumatic brain injury. *American Journal of Forensic Psychology, 20,* 21–37.

Prohaska, M., & Martin, D. P. (2007). Obtaining neuropsychological test data: Why is this so hard? *The Alabama Lawyer, 68,* 216–223.

R. v. Mohan, 2 S.C.R. (1994).

Rabin, L. A., Barr, W. B., & Burton, L. A. (2005). Assessment practices of clinical neuropsychologists in the United States and Canada: A survey of INS, NAN, and APA Division 40 members. *Archives of Clinical Neuropsychology, 20,* 33–65.

Ragge v. MCA/ Universal Studios, 165 F.R.D. 605. (C.D. Cal. 1995).

Resnick, P. J. (1988). Malingering of posttraumatic disorders. In R. Rogers (Ed.), *Clinical assessment of malingering and deception* (pp. 84–103). New York, NY: Guilford.

Resnick, P. J. (1997). Malingering of posttraumatic disorders. In R. Rogers (Ed.), *Clinical assessment of malingering and deception* (2nd ed.) (pp. 130–152). New York, NY: Guilford.

Resnick, P. J., West, S., & Payne, J. W. (2008). In R. Rogers (Ed.), *Clinical assessment of malingering and deception* (3rd ed.) (pp. 109–127). New York, NY: Guilford.

Risinger, D. M., Saks, M. J., Thompson, W. C., & Rosenthal, R. (2002). The *Daubert/Kumho* implications of observer effects in forensic science: Hidden problems of expectation and suggestion. *California Law Review, 90,* 1–56.

Rogers, R. (1992). *Structured Interview of Reported Symptoms.* Odessa, FL: Psychological Assessment Resources.

Rogers, R. (2008a). An introduction to response styles. In R. Rogers (Ed.), *Clinical assessment of malingering and deception* (3rd ed.) (pp. 3–13). New York, NY: Guilford.

Rogers, R. (2008b). Detection strategies for malingering and defensiveness. In R. Rogers (Ed.), *Clinical assessment of malingering and deception* (3rd ed.) (pp. 14–35). New York, NY: Guilford.

Rogers, R. (2008c). Structured interviews and dissimulation. In R. Rogers (Ed.), *Clinical assessment of malingering and deception* (3rd ed.) (pp. 301–322). New York, NY: Guilford.

Rogers, R. (2008d). Current status of clinical methods. In R. Rogers (Ed.), *Clinical assessment of malingering and deception* (3rd ed.) (pp. 391–410). New York, NY: Guilford.

Rogers, R., & Bender, S. D. (2003). Evaluation of malingering and deception. In I. B. Weiner (Series Ed.) & A. M. Goldstein (Vol. Ed.), *Handbook of psychology: Vol. 11, Forensic psychology* (pp. 109–129). Hoboken, NJ: Wiley.

Rogers, R., & Shuman, D. W. (2005). *Fundamentals of forensic practice: Mental health and criminal law.* New York, NY: Springer SBM.

Rogers, R., Salekin, R. T., & Sewell, K. W. (1999). Validation of the Millon Clinical Multiaxial Inventory for Axis II disorders: Does it meet the *Daubert* standard? *Law and Human Behavior, 23,* 425–443.

Rogers, R., Salekin, R. T., & Sewell, K. W. (2000). The MCMI-III and The *Daubert* standard: Separating rhetoric from reality. *Law and Human Behavior, 24,* 501–506.

Rogers, R., Sewell, K. W., & Salekin, R. T. (1994). A meta-analysis of malingering on the MMPI-2. *Assessment, 1,* 227–237.

Rogers, R., Payne, J. W., Berry, D. T. R., & Granacher, R. P., Jr. (2009). Use of the SIRS in compensation cases: An examination of its validity and generalizability. *Law and Human Behavior, 33,* 213–224.

Rogers, R., Sewell, K. W., Martin, M. A., & Vitacco, M. (2003). Detection of feigned mental disorders: A meta-analysis of the MMPI-2 and malingering. *Assessment, 10,* 160–177.

Romano, J., & Romano, R. (1993). How to avoid the traps of expert witnesses: The seven deadly sins. *Trial Diplomacy Journal, 16,* iv–viii.

Rubenzer, S. (2009). Posttraumatic stress disorder: Assessing response style and malingering. *Psychological Injury and Law, 2,* 114–142.

Ryan, L. M., & Warden, D. L. (2003). Post concussion syndrome. *International Review of Psychiatry, 15*, 310–316.

Sageman, M. (2003). Three types of skills for effective forensic psychological assessments. *Assessment, 10*, 321–328.

Saks, M. J., & Lanyon, R. I. (2007). Pitfalls and ethics of expert testimony. In M. Costanzo, D. Krauss, & K. Pezdek (Eds.), *Expert psychological testimony for the courts* (pp. 277–295). Mahwah, NJ: Erlbaum.

Sales, B. D., & Shuman, D. W. (2005). *Experts in court: Reconciling law, science, and professional knowledge.* Washington, DC: American Psychological Association.

Samra, J., & Connolly, D. A. (2004). Legal compensability of symptoms associated with posttraumatic stress disorder: A Canadian perspective. *International Journal of Forensic Mental Health, 3*, 55–66.

Samra, J., & Koch, W. J. (2002). The monetary worth of psychological injury: What are litigants suing for? In J. R. P. Ogloff (Ed.), *Taking psychology and law into the twenty-first century* (pp. 285–321). New York, NY: Kluwer/Plenum.

Samuel, S. E., DeGirolamo, J., Michaels, T. J., & O'Brien, J. (1995). Preliminary findings on the MMPI "cannot say" responses with personal injury litigants. *American Journal of Forensic Psychiatry, 16*, 59–72.

Schultz, I. Z. (2003a). The relationship between psychological impairment and occupational disability. In I. Z. Schultz & D. O. Brady (Eds.), *Psychological injuries at trial* (pp. 65–101). Chicago, IL: American Bar Association.

Schultz, I. Z. (2003b). Psychological causality determination in personal injury and workers' compensation contexts. In I. Z. Schultz & D. O. Brady (Eds.), *Psychological injuries at trial* (pp. 102–125). Chicago, IL: American Bar Association.

Schultz, I. Z., & Brady, D. O. (Eds.). (2003a). *Psychological injuries at trial.* Chicago, IL: American Bar Association.

Schutte, James W. (2000). Using the MCMI-III in forensic evaluations. *American Journal of Forensic Psychology, 19*, 5–20.

Scrignar, C. B. (1996). *Post-traumatic stress disorder: Diagnosis, treatment, and legal issues* (3rd ed.). New Orleans, LA: Bruno Press.

Sears v. Rutishauser, 466 N.E.2d 210. (1984).

Sella, G. (1997). Causation. *Forensic Examiner, 32*, 32.

Sellbom, M., & Bagby, R. M. (2008). Response styles on multiscale inventories. In R. Rogers (Ed.), *Clinical assessment of malingering and deception* (3rd ed.) (pp. 182–206). New York, NY: Guilford.

Sheehan v. Daily Racing Form, Inc., 104 F.3d 940. (7th Cir. 1997).

Sherman, J. J., & Ohrbach, R. (2006). Objective and subjective measurement of pain: Current approaches for forensic assessments. In G. Young, A. W. Kane & K. Nicholson, *Psychological knowledge in court: PTSD, pain and TBI* (pp. 193–211). New York, NY: Springer SBM.

Shirsat v. Mutual Pharmaceutical Co., 169 F.R.D. 68. (E.D. Pa. 1996).

Shuman, D. W. (1994a). Psychiatric and psychological evidence (2nd ed.). Deerfield, IL: Clark, Boardman, Callaghan. [Supplemented 2002, 2003, 2004.]

Shuman, D. W. (1994b). The psychology of compensation in tort law. *Kansas Law Review, 43,* 39–77. Retrieved April 6, 2003 from www. lexis.com.

Shuman, D. W. (1995a). Persistent reexperiences in psychiatry and law. In R. I. Simon (Ed.), *Posttraumatic stress disorder in litigation.* Washington, DC: American Psychiatric Press.

Shuman, D. W. (1995b). Reporting of child abuse during forensic evaluation. *American Psychology-Law Society News, 15*(3), 5.

Shuman, D. W. (2000a). When time does not heal: Understanding the importance of avoiding unnecessary delay in the resolution of tort cases. *Psychology, Public Policy, and Law, 6,* 880–897.

Shuman, D. W. (2000b). The role of apology in tort law. *Judicature, 83,* 180–189.

Shuman, D. W. (2002a). Retrospective assessment of mental states and the law. In R. I. Simon & D. W. Shuman (Eds.), *Retrospective assessment of mental states in litigation* (pp. 21–45). Washington, DC: American Psychiatric Association.

Shuman, D. W. (2005). *Psychiatric and psychological evidence* (3rd ed.). Eagen, MN: West Publishing.

Shuman, D. W., & Daley, C. E. (1996). Compensation for mental and emotional distress. In D. B. Sales & D. W. Shuman (Eds.), *Law, mental health, and mental disorder* (pp. 294–308). Pacific Grove, CA: Brooks/Cole.

Shuman, D. W., & Greenberg, S. A. (2003). The expert witness, the adversary system, and the voice of reason: Reconciling impartiality and advocacy. *Professional Psychology: Research and Practice, 34,* 219–224.

Shuman, D. W., & Hardy, J. L. (2007). Causation, psychology and law. In G. Young, A. W. Kane, & K. Nicholson, *Causality of psychological injury: Presenting evidence in court* (pp. 517–548). New York, NY: Springer SBM.

Siharath v. Sandoz Pharmaceuticals Corp, 131 F. Supp.2d 1347. (N.D.Ga. 2001).

Simon, R. I., & Wettstein, R. M. (1997). Toward the development of guidelines for the conduct of forensic psychiatric examinations. *Journal of the American Academy of Psychiatry and Law, 25,* 17–30.

Simons, R., Goddard, R., & Patton, W. (2002). Hand-scoring error rates in psychological testing. *Assessment, 9,* 292–300.

Slick, D. J., Sherman, E. M. S., & Iverson, G. L. (1999). Diagnostic criteria for malingered neurocognitive dysfunction: Proposed standards for clinical practice and research. *Clinical Neuropsychologist, 13,* 545–561.

Slick, D. J., Hopp, G. Strauss, E., & Thompson, G. B. (1997). *Victoria Symptom Validity Test*. Odessa, FL: Psychological Assessment Resources.

Slovenko, R. (1988). The role of the expert (with focus on psychiatry) in the adversarial system. *Journal of Psychiatry and Law, 16*, 333–373.

State Justice Institute. (1999). The bench: Companion to a judge's deskbook on the basic philosophies and methods of science. Retrieved November 6, 2004 from www.unr.edu/bench/

Strasburger, L. H. (1999). The litigant-patient: Mental health consequences of civil litigation. *Journal of the American Academy of Psychiatry and Law, 27*, 203–211.

Susan A. v. County of Sonoma, 3 Cal.Rptr.2d 27. (Ct. App. 1991).

Sweet, J. J.,Condit, D. C., & Nelson, N. W. (2008). Feigning amnesia and memory loss. In R. Rogers (Ed.), *Clinical assessment of malingering and deception* (3rd ed.) (pp. 218–236). New York, NY: Guilford.

Tombaugh, T. N. (1996). *Test of Memory Malingering*. Toronto, ON: Multi-Health Systems, Inc.

Tomlin v. Holocek, 150 F.R.D. 628. (D. Minn. 1993).

Tyler, T. R. (1984). The role of perceived injustice in defendants' evaluations of their courtroom experience. *Law & Society Review, 18*, 51–74.

U.S. Centers for Medicare and Medicaid & National Center for Health Statistics. (1979, updated annually). *International classification of diseases, 9th edition, clinical modification* (ICD-9-CM). Washington, D.C.: Author.

U.S. Department of Health and Human Services. (1999). *Mental health: A report of the surgeon general*. Rockville, MD: Author.

Van Dorsten, B. (2002). Forensic psychology: Decades of progress and controversy. In B. Van Dorsten (Ed.), *Forensic psychology: From classroom to courtroom* (pp. 1–16). New York, NY: Kluwer Academic/ Plenum.

Vitacco, M. J. (2008). Syndromes associated with deception. In R. Rogers (Ed.), *Clinical assessment of malingering and deception* (3rd ed.) (pp. 39–50). New York, NY: Guilford.

Vore, D. A. (2007). The disability psychological independent medical evaluation: Case law, ethical issues, and procedures. In A. M. Goldstein (Ed), *Forensic psychology: Emerging topics and expanding roles* (pp. 489–510). Hoboken NJ: John Wiley & Sons.

Walfish, S. (2006). Conducting personal injury evaluations. In I. B. Weiner & A. K. Hess, (Eds.), *The handbook of forensic psychology* (3rd ed.) (pp. 124–139). Hoboken NJ, US: John Wiley & Sons.

Warner, J. (2003). 9/11 lingers in mind and body. Retrieved 11/28/09 from http://www.webmd.com/a-to-z-guides/features/psychological-effects-of-a-post-september-cleventh-new-york

Watkins, C. E., Campbell, V. L., Nieberding, R., & Hallmark, R. (1995). Contemporary practice of psychological assessment by clinical psychologists. *Professional Psychology: Research and Practice, 26*, 54–60.

Wayte, T., Samra, J., Robbennolt, J. K., Heuer, L., & Koch, W. J. (2002). Psychological issues in civil law. In J. R. P. Ogloff, (Ed.), *Taking psychology and law into the twenty-first century* (pp. 323–369). New York, NY: Kluwer/Plenum.

Weathers, F. W., Huska, J. A., & Keane, T. M. (1991). *PCL-C for DSM-IV.* Boston, MA: National Center for PTSD-Behavioral Science Division.

Weathers, F. W., Keane, T. M., & Davidson, J. R. T. (2001). Clinician-Administered PTSD Scale: A review of the first ten years of research. *Depression and Anxiety, 13*, 132–156.

Weiner, I. B. (2006). Writing forensic reports. In I. B. Weiner & A. K. Hess (Eds.), *The handbook of forensic psychology* (3rd ed.) (pp. 631–651). Hoboken, NJ: Wiley.

Weinstock, R., & Garrick, T. (1995). Is liability possible for forensic psychiatrists? *Bulletin of the American Academy of Psychiatry & Law, 23*, 183–193.

Weiss, D. S., & Ozer, E. J. (2006). Predicting who will develop posttraumatic stress disorder. In G. Young, A. W. Kane & K. Nicholson (Eds.), *Psychological knowledge in court: PTSD, pain and TBI* (pp. 85–96). New York, NY: Springer SBM.

Wetter, M., & Corrigan, S. (1995). Providing information to clients about psychological tests: A survey of attorneys' and law students' attitudes. *Professional Psychology: Research and Practice, 26*, 474–477.

Wettstein, R. M. (2005). Quality and quality improvement in forensic mental health evaluations. *Journal of the American Academy of Psychiatry and the Law, 33*, 158–175.

Widows, M., & Smith, G. P. (2005). *Structured Inventory of Malingered Symptomatology (SIMS) and professional manual.* Odessa, FL: Psychological Assessment Resources.

Williams, C. L., Butcher, J. N., Gass, C. S., Cumella, E., & Kally, Z. (2009). Inaccuracies about the MMPI-2 Fake Bad Scale in the reply by Ben-Porath, Greve, Bianchini, and Kaufmann. (2009). *Psychological Injury and Law, 2*, 182–197.

Wilson, J. P. (2004). PTSD and complex PTSD. In J. P. Wilson & T. M. Keane (Eds.), *Assessing psychological trauma and PTSD* (2nd ed.) (pp. 7–44). New York, NY: Guilford.

Wilson, J. P., & Moran, T. A. (2004). Forensic/clinical assessment of psychological trauma and PTSD in legal settings. In J. P. Wilson & T. M. Keane (Eds.), *Assessing psychological trauma and PTSD* (2nd ed.) (pp. 603–636). New York, NY: Guilford.

World Health Organization. (1992). *International classification of diseases, injuries, and causes of death, 10th edition* (ICD-10). Geneva, Switzerland: Author.

Worley, C. B., Feldman, M. D., & Hamilton, J. C. (2009). The case of factitious disorder versus malingering. *Psychiatric Times, 26,* retrieved November 25, 2009 from www.psychiatrictimes.com/print/article/10168/1482349?verif

Youngjohn, J. R. (1995). Confirmed attorney coaching prior to neuropsychological evaluation. *Assessment, 2,* 279–283.

Young, G. (2007). Causality: Concepts, issues, and recommendations. In G. Young, A. W. Kane, & K. Nicholson. *Causality of psychological injury: Presenting evidence in court* (pp. 49–86). New York, NY: Springer SBM.

Young, G., & Kane, A. W. (2007). Causality in psychology and law. In G. Young, A. W. Kane, & K. Nicholson (Eds.). *Causality of psychological injury: Presenting evidence in court* (pp. 13–47). New York, NY: Springer SBM.

Young, G., Kane, A. W., & Nicholson, K. (2007). Causality, psychological injuries, and court: Introduction. In G. Young, A. W. Kane, & K. Nicholson (Eds.). *Causality of psychological injury: Presenting evidence in court* (pp. 1–10). New York, NY: Springer SBM.

Young, G., Kane, A. W., & Nicholson, K. (2007). *Causality of psychological injury: Presenting evidence in court.* New York, NY: Springer SBM.

Youngstrom, E. A., & Busch, C. P. (2000). Expert testimony in psychology: Ramifications of Supreme Court decision in Kumho Tire Co., Ltd. v. Carmichael. *Ethics & Behavior, 10,* 185–193.

Zatzick, D., Jurkovich, J. G., Rivara, F. P., Wang, J., Fan, M.-Y., Joesch, J., MacKenzie, E. (2008). A national US study of posttraumatic stress disorder, depression, and work and functional outcomes after hospitalization for traumatic injury. *Annals of Surgery, 248,* 429–437.

Appendix A: Forensic Services Contract

(The reader is invited to adapt this model document
for his or her own professional use.)

[Phone number of expert] [Fax number of expert]
[e-mail address of expert]

Forensic Mental Health Expert

1234 Any Street
Anytown, Any State 99999-9999

FORENSIC SERVICES CONTRACT

Retaining Attorney(s): _____

Case: _____

(1) Fees: Dr. Expert's professional time is billed @ $XXX/hour or
YYYY/day. This rate applies to evaluations, testimony, meetings with
attorneys, telephone calls, review of documents, travel time, and all
other professional or related activities. Because the attorney is my
client, all fees are to be paid to Dr. Expert by the retaining attorney
or insurance company, not by the attorney's client.

During the course of my provision of services, it may be
advisable or necessary for me to retain a third party to provide
services on behalf of your or your client, for example, consultation
with a child psychologist or a neuropsychologist, or my hiring a
research assistant. If this occurs, I will advise you of the nature and
purpose of my retaining this third party, and will advise you of the
cost of doing so. The services of this individual will be billed along
with my other expenses.

(2) Expenses: Expenses will be billed at actual cost, if known, or at
an approximate cost if unknown at the time of the billing. As
indicated above, expenses may include retaining an expert or an
assistant to assist with a particular portion of this consultation.

(3) Retainer: An estimate will be made of the anticipated charge for
review of documents, conducting of an evaluation, or other services,
and initial billing will be made against this retainer. This amount must
be paid prior to any evaluation or review of materials, unless a
different contract is entered into in writing with the attorney. If the
initial retainer has been largely exhausted, the attorney will be
notified that an additional amount must be paid in order for the
professional services to continue.

(4) <u>Minimum fees</u>: (a) The minimum fee for a trial, hearing, deposition or similar proceeding is $ZZZZ, based on an anticipated six-hour-minimum for preparation and time available for testimony. This amount <u>must be paid at least one week</u> prior to Dr. Expert's scheduled testimony. If an attorney wishes Dr. Expert to reserve more than six hours for preparation and testimony, Dr. Expert would be happy to do so, provided the amount (at $XXX/hour) is paid <u>at least one week in advance</u>. <u>If the minimum fee is not paid one week in advance, Dr. Expert will remove the scheduled event from his calendar</u>. If the minimum is not sufficient to cover the time necessary for preparation and testimony, the balance will be billed, and is due and payable upon receipt of the statement.

(b) "Out of town" services: If I must travel more than one hour by car in each direction, or if the consultation or testimony cannot be completed in one eight-hour day, this provision may apply. In general, these services will be billed in half-day increments, with it being likely that the minimum charge will be for one full day ($ZZZZ), plus expenses. If I must travel on the day prior to the consultation or testimony, and/or must return on the day after the consultation or testimony, the likely minimum charge will be for 1.5 days ($AAAA) plus expenses. The anticipated minimum fee will be specified prior to the consultation or testimony. Payment of that fee must be made at least seven (7) days prior to the scheduled consultation or testimony or the planned activity will be removed from my calendar.

(c) Consultations: Because case consultations preclude my being retained by another party in a case, there is a non-refundable (specify amount) engagement fee for a case consultation. The consultation may occur as soon as the attorney's check has been received. If the consultation (and related work) exceed (specify number) hours, additional time will be billed at $XXX/hour.

(5) <u>Payments</u>: (a) Payment for <u>evaluations and consultations</u> must be made in full <u>prior to furnishing a report</u> to the attorney or Court. A written guarantee of payment by an attorney may be accepted in lieu of actual payment at my discretion. Statements are due and payable upon receipt. If they are not paid in full within seven (7) days of the billing date, and no acceptable alternative arrangement has been put in place, Dr. Expert reserves the right to suspend services until payment is received.

(b) <u>Payment for all services rendered, plus payment for time reserved for court</u>, must be made at least <u>one week</u> in advance of a scheduled court appearance. This benefits the attorney and his/her client by avoiding the appearance that Dr. Expert's testimony is in any way contingent upon the success of the case. The charges indicated below apply if the scheduled hearing or other event is postponed or canceled.

(c) <u>All payments are to be made by the retaining attorney if he/she represents the plaintiff</u>, not by the attorney's client. If the retaining attorney represents the defense, payment may be made by the attorney or by an insurance company, and the responsible party must be clearly stated in advance.

   (6) <u>Cancellations/Refunds</u>: (a) If scheduled <u>office time</u> is canceled/postponed with at least <u>96 hours</u> notice, there is no charge. If canceled/postponed with less than 96 hours' notice, a refund will be made only for those hours that can be filled with other income-producing work.

(b) If scheduled <u>testimony</u> (deposition or court) is canceled <u>more than seven days</u> in advance, there will be a full refund of any amount paid in advance. If canceled with <u>less than seven but more than four days'</u> notice, a refund will be only made for those hours that can be filled with other income-producing work. If <u>less than four days'</u> notice is given, the minimum fee for preparation and testimony is not refundable. Any refund will be made immediately after the originally-scheduled date for testimony.

(7) <u>Balances</u>: If fees paid in advance exceed the actual charges, a refund will be made within seven days of the final statement. If fees paid in advance are not sufficient to cover the actual charges, the undersigned guarantees that payment in full will be made <u>within 30 days</u> of the date of billing. If for any reason payment in full is not made within 30 days, interest shall accrue at the rate of one percent (1%) per month (12%/annum) from the date of original billing, and the retaining attorney agrees to pay this accrued interest in addition to the balance due for professional services.

(8) <u>Billing health insurance</u>: Plaintiffs often request that their health insurance be billed for a forensic psychological evaluation and related services. However, health insurance is normally meant to cover treatment services, not forensic services, and it would be unethical for Dr. Expert to bill health insurance for services that are not intended to be part of the client's treatment. <u>However</u>, if your client believes that his or her health insurance <u>will</u> cover at least a portion of the evaluation and/or other services, <u>your client</u> may consult with the insurance company and is free to submit a claim for reimbursement for any portion of the evaluation that is covered. The situation in which this is most likely to occur is when the results of an evaluation are made available to your client's psychotherapist, who may then use that information to facilitate the treatment process.

(9) <u>Attorney's provision of information to me</u>: You will provide me with factual information and materials that are necessary if I am to perform the task for which you have retained me. You will ensure that I have that information and those materials on a timely basis, so that I can meet your case schedule. <u>You will also ensure</u> that I have

<u>all information relevant to my role</u> in this case, since I cannot adequately perform my work without this information.

(10) <u>If I am evaluating an individual, he or she will be asked to sign an informed consent/assent document.</u> Please note that the document indicates that Dr. Expert "is free to disclose any information necessary to protect the public safety, including but not limited to child abuse, or a plan I may have to hurt myself or someone else." I am required by statute, administrative code, and/or case law to so report. A copy of that informed consent/assent document may be found at the end of this document. [Note to reader: see Appendix B for a draft statement of understanding with the plaintiff.]

(11) <u>Re-evaluation</u>: Depending on the type of case and the exact circumstances, it may be necessary to update the evaluation prior to deposition or court testimony. Data from both psychological tests and interviews generally becomes stale after a period of time. As a rough guideline, psychological tests other than intelligence tests may be considered valid for six months. Unless IQ is at issue in the case, intelligence tests may not need to be readministered. Interview data may be considered valid for perhaps a month, with at least an update needed prior to testimony. I will decide, for each source of data, whether updated information is essential. If a substantial period of time has passed since the evaluation, a re-evaluation is likely to be necessary, to update the data from assessment instruments and interviews. Without that re-evaluation, I could testify at length about the individual's status as of the date of the evaluation, but could not state to a reasonable degree of certainty that that testimony would remain accurate at the time of the deposition, court hearing, or other testimony. The terms of this contract apply equally to any reassessment that must be done.

(12) <u>Reasonableness of fees</u>: If you believe that the bill is not reasonable, you will notify me in writing within ten (10) calendar days of receiving the bill, and you and I will review the bill together. If no notice is received, it is understood that the billing statement is accepted as correct, accurate, and reasonable.

(13) <u>Subpoena</u>: I would be happy to accept a subpoena by fax, which I will acknowledge by faxing it back to you, or by faxing back a "notice and acknowledgment of receipt," indicating it was received, with my signature. Alternatively, I will accept a subpoena by mail to my office (address above), will sign a "notice and acknowledgment of receipt" and return the original, signed notice and acknowledgment to you by fax or mail. I prefer not having to have my signature notarized, since I will have to take time to do so, and will therefore have to charge for that time.

(14) <u>Termination of contract</u>: This contact may be terminated at will by either party, subject to ethical restraints and your payment of all fees and costs that are due at the time of termination.

(15) <u>Federal Tax Identification Number</u>: For payment purposes, our Federal Tax Identification Number is: 00-0000000.

AGREED TO THIS _____ DAY OF _____, 20___ BY:

Attorney's Signature: _____

Please print name: _____

Appendix B: Statement of Understanding for an Evaluation, and Release of Information

(The reader is invited to adapt this model document for his or her own professional use.)

[Phone number of psychologist] [Fax number of psychologist] [e-mail address of psychologist]

Forensic Psychology Experts

1234 Any Street
Anytown, Any State 99999-9999

Statement of Understanding for an Evaluation, and Release of Information

The undersigned _____ hereby certifies and
[print name]
agrees that:

(1) I understand that the results and interpretations of psychological testing, interviews, and other services related to this evaluation are <u>not confidential</u>. Information will be available to my attorney and may also be given to the Court, other attorneys, and, possibly, other parties, and **CONSENT IS HEREBY GIVEN** for the release of this information to appropriate parties. [Note: If consent is irrelevant because, e.g., the individual has been court-ordered to undergo the evaluation, the second sentence in this item could be deleted.]

(2) I further understand that <u>I do not have a "doctor-patient relationship" with Dr. Expert</u>, that I am here for an evaluation and not for treatment, and that the laws on the confidentiality of a "doctor-patient relationship" <u>do not</u> apply to this evaluation.

(3) I further understand that Dr. Expert relies upon my telling the truth, and that I am responsible for telling Dr. Expert <u>everything</u> that may be relevant to this legal matter. If it is discovered that I have not done so, it may work very strongly against me. However, I do not have to tell Dr. Expert anything I have been told by my attorney.

(4) However, Dr. Expert cannot force me to answer questions. In speaking with Dr. Expert, I do not have to answer every question he asks me. If I do not answer a question, Dr. Expert will make a note of my not answering. He will probably ask me why I do not want to answer that question. I do not have to tell him why. If I do tell him why, he will write down what I say. I must make my own decisions about what to answer and what not to answer, what to tell him and what not to tell him.

(5) I further understand and agree that Dr. Expert is free to disclose any information necessary to protect the public safety, including but not limited to child abuse or a plan that I may have to hurt myself or someone else. [Note: if the evaluation occurs in one of the few jurisdictions without a "duty to warn or protect" mandate, that part of this item could be deleted.]

(6) I further understand that I may be entitled to feedback about the results of this psychological evaluation, but that I am not entitled to a copy of the raw data or of Dr. Expert's report. Dr. Expert will, however, gladly forward copies to any licensed psychologist I choose.

(7) I further understand that any information I wish to give to Dr. Expert after the formal evaluation is completed must be in writing. It should be mailed, faxed, or e-mailed to the above address.

(8) I further understand that I must try to do my best on each of the tests and other instruments administered to me, and promise to do so.

(9) Because psychological tests and other instruments are meant to be used only under conditions that did not include audio taping or video taping of the test or other instrument being given, Dr. Expert's administration of these tests and other instruments must not be recorded. Recording them would potentially invalidate their results. By my signature below, I certify that I am not taping any part of this evaluation in any way. [Note: evaluators who will permit recording of the interview(s) should change "evaluation" to "testing."]

(10) A psychological evaluation generally remains valid (accurate, reliable) for six to twelve months unless there has been a significant change of some kind involving me or my circumstances. If the court case for which this evaluation is being done extends beyond that six- to twelve-month period, it may be necessary to repeat some part(s) of the evaluation in order to update both information and conclusions. A relatively brief interview may be necessary after even two or three months, to try to be sure that Dr. Expert is up-to-date regarding my condition and circumstances.

(11) I may use my cell phone during breaks, but not at any other time during the evaluation.

(12) I have a right to consult my attorney regarding my legal rights and/or what I should sign or do.

I have read, understand, and agree to all of the above, have asked Dr. Expert any questions I may have about the above, and acknowledge receiving a copy of this form:

Signature: _____

Print name: _____

Date: _____/_____/_____

Appendix C: Request for Collateral Interviews

(The reader is invited to adapt this model document for his or her own professional use.)

Request for Collateral Interviews

Please indicate below the names, telephone numbers, and information on your relationship with each individual who has known you since before the accident or incident and who, therefore, can help me understand how you've changed.

Please also <u>tell each person that I may call him or her to talk about you</u>, and that you want the person to speak with me, and to be completely open and honest with me in response to any questions I ask. Please also tell the person that the interview will not be confidential, since it is relevant to a legal matter.

Your name:_____ Signature:_____ Date: ___/___/___

Name of person	Telephone number(s)	Person's relationship to you, how long you've known the person, any important information for me to ask about
1		
2		
3		
[Etc.]		

Cases

Acosta v. Tenneco Oil Company, 913 F.2d 205 (5th Cir.1990)

Antoine-Tubbs v. Local 513 Air Transp. Div., 50 F.Supp.2d 601 (N.D. Texas, 1998)

Athey v. Leonati [1996] 3 S.C.R. 458

Barefoot v. Estelle, 463 U.S. 880 (Sup.Ct. 1983)

Daubert v. Merrell Dow Pharmaceuticals, Inc., 509 U.S. 579, 113 S.Ct. 2786, 125 L.Ed.2d 469 (Sup.Ct. 1993)

Daubert v. Merrell Dow Pharmaceuticals, 43 F.3d 1311 (9th Cir. 1995)

Davidson v. Strawberry Petroleum et al., Case No. 05-4320 (Fla. 2007)

Deatherage v. Washington Examining Board of Psychology 134 Wn.2d 131, 948 P.2d 828 (Wn. Sup.Ct. 1997)

Detroit Edison Co. v. NLRB, 440 U.S. 301 (Sup.Ct. 1979)

Dillon v. Legg, 441 P.2d 912 (Cal. 1968)

Dziwanoski v. Ocean Carriers Corporation, 26 F.R.D. 595 (D.Md.1960)

Estelle v. Smith, 451 U.S. 454 (Sup.Ct. 1981)

Frye v. United States, 293 F. 1013, 34 ALR 145 (D.C. Cir. 1923)

General Electric Co. v. Joiner, 522 U.S. 136, 118 S.Ct. 512 (Sup. Ct. 1997)

Harris v. Forklift Systems, Inc., 114 S.Ct. 367 (1993)

Hayes v. District Court, 854 P.2d 1240 (Colo.1993)

Hertenstein v. Kimberly Home Health Care, Inc., 189 F.R.D. 620 (Kan. 1999)

Holland v. United States, 182 F.R.D. 493 (D.S.C. 1998)

Howard v. Drapkin, 222 Cal.App.3d 843 (1990)

In re air crash at Tapei, Taiwan on October 31, 2000 (C.D. Cal. 2003)

Kumho Tire Co. v. Carmichael, 526 U.S. 137, 119 S.Ct. 1167 (Sup. Ct. 1999)

Langfeldt-Haaland v. Saupe Enterprises, Inc., 768 P.2d 1144 (Alaska 1989)

Key Terms

Bystander rule The principle that an individual could recover for psychological damage if he or she observed an accident or other trauma and had a relationship with the person who suffered a physical injury as a result of the accident, even though the bystander did not suffer any physical injury and was not in the zone of danger.

Causation

    General causation: Whether an event *can* cause a disorder.

    Specific causation: Whether an event *did* cause a specific disorder in a specific person.

Compensation neurosis The notion that an individual is likely to become free of psychological symptoms soon after the end of litigation. That notion has been thoroughly debunked by research.

Crumbling skull In Canada and at least one state, the principle that the tortfeasor need not improve the plaintiff beyond the condition the plaintiff was in at the time of the tort. For example, if the plaintiff was wheelchair bound prior to an accident, the tortfeasor need not fund treatment beyond that required to permit the individual to use a wheelchair again.

Damages Compensation for a loss or impairment suffered by an individual as a direct result of negligence or another tortious act. Compensation may include special damages, e.g., to pay for psychotherapy needed by the plaintiff.

Falsifiability From *Daubert v. Merrell Dow Pharmaceuticals* (1993). It addresses the question, "How would you know if the assertion were not true?"

Idiographic evidence Data obtained through the investigation of one individual, or applicable to one individual, usually the individual under consideration.

Impact rule The principle that a plaintiff may not recover for psychological damage unless there has also been a physical injury, e.g., as the result of an accident.

Malpractice A legal term indicating that a professional has failed to meet the standard of care, and that an individual has been harmed by that failure.

Motion *in limine* A motion to exclude "matters which are irrelevant, inadmissible and prejudicial" (*Black's Law Dictionary*, 1979, p. 914).

Negligence A basis for a legal suit alleging that an individual (the tortfeasor) had a duty to another individual, that the tortfeasor breached that duty, that that breach proximately caused an injury to another individual, and that the individual who was injured should be compensated for that injury. *Negligence* includes the notion that the tortfeasor has not behaved as a reasonable and prudent person would behave under identical or similar circumstances.

Nomothetic (group) evidence Data obtained through the investigation of groups similar to the population to which the evaluatee belongs. Such data would be no more applicable to a particular individual than to any other member of the group.

Peer review A process by which presumably knowledgeable/expert professionals critically review the work (e.g., articles, books) of an author or researcher prior to publication, in an attempt to improve the quality of the science included in the publication. As indicated in this book, peer review is no guarantee of increased validity or trustworthiness.

Personal injury: See *tort*.

Proximate cause Also known as the 'legal cause', this term refers to the primary, independent and direct cause of injuries. With regard to tort claims, the plaintiff must establish that without the wrongdoing of the defendant, the injuries or loss would not have been sustained and that the wrongdoing was the direct cause of the alleged harm. Also known as "but for" causation, i.e., *but for* the incident the individual would not have been damaged.

Punitive damages Monetary compensation intended to punish or deter the wrongdoer. These damages may be awarded to the plaintiff in addition to compensatory damages.

Standard of Care Judicial determinations that establish minimally acceptable standards of professional conduct or practice. The California Supreme Court defined it as "that reasonable degree of skill, knowledge, and care ordinarily possessed and exercised by members of [that professional specialty] under similar circumstances" in *Tarasoff v. Regents of the University of California*, 551 P.2d 334 (1976) at fn. 6.

Standard of Practice The customary or best practice in a given field, as established by the particular field itself. This may be informal, based on what most practitioners do, or may be formalized in a document like the *Specialty Guidelines for Forensic Psychologists*. Standards of practice are aspirational, not mandatory, unless they have been incorporated into law by statute, administrative rule, or case law.

Symptom Validity Testing (SVT) A means of addressing whether an individual's test responses are valid, usually by comparing the individual's performance with the performance of people known to have a specific disorder, e.g., a traumatic brain injury. Alternatively, many SVTs use a forced choice method in which an individual who scores significantly below chance (i.e., well below 50% when there are two choices) is seen as likely to be malingering unless a specific cause can be determined for the below-chance performance (e.g., poor reading comprehension, culturally inappropriate tests, fatigue, disinterest in the task, or headaches or other problems that interfere with performance).

Thin skull Whether the defendant caused an injury in an otherwise healthy person or worsened a preexisting condition, the defendant is responsible for any impairments and disabilities that resulted. In many cases, there will be a combination of the two: both a direct traumatic injury and an acute exacerbation of any existing psychological or emotional problems. Also referred to as an "eggshell skull" or by other, similar, terms.

Tort From the French word 'tort' meaning wrongdoing or wrongful conduct. In law, refers to a civil wrong: an intentional or accidental (negligent) act causing harm to another person that does not solely breach a contract. Tort laws outline the criteria for legal responsibility or liability for causing harm or injury to another.

Tort claim A civil claim for compensation based on damage or injury caused by another person's negligent or intentional conduct comprising a tort, or wrongdoing.

Tortfeasor The individual who commits a tort.

Zone of danger test The principle that an individual may not recover for psychological damage unless he or she was in a situation in which there *could have been* a physical injury, even though there was not in the particular case.

Index

About the Authors

Andrew W. Kane, Ph.D., ABAP is a clinical and forensic psychologist in private practice in Milwaukee, WI. Dr. Kane is a Diplomate of the American Board of Assessment Psychologists. He is a Professor at the Wisconsin School of Professional Psychology, an Adjunct Clinical Professor in the Department of Psychology at the University of Wisconsin-Milwaukee, and an Associate Clinical Professor in the Department of Psychiatry and Behavioral Medicine at the Medical College of Wisconsin. He is the author or co-author of ten professional books and more than 60 professional papers and chapters. He is the Associate Editor for Psychology and the chair of the Forensic Psychology Section of the journal, *Psychological Injury and Law*. He is the Associate Vice President of the Association for Scientific Advancement in Psychological Injury and Law (ASAPIL). He served as a member of the Expert Panel on Psychiatric and Psychological Evidence of the Commission on Mental and Physical Disability Law of the American Bar Association, which helped produce the National Benchbook on Psychiatric and Psychological Evidence and Testimony, published by the ABA. He holds a Certificate of Professional Qualification (CPQ) from the Association of State and Provincial Psychology Boards. He is a former president of the Wisconsin Psychological Association and of its Division of Forensic and Correctional Psychologists. He served for 10 years as a member of the Ethics Committee of the Wisconsin Psychological Association. Dr. Kane founded the Wisconsin Coalition on Sexual Misconduct by Psychotherapists and Counselors, a national model program.

Joel A. Dvoskin, Ph.D., ABPP (Forensic) is a clinical psychologist, licensed in Arizona and New Mexico. He is a Diplomate in Forensic Psychology of the American Board of Professional Psychology, and a Fellow of the American Psychological Association (APA) and the American Psychology-Law Society. Dr. Dvoskin is a former President of Division 18 of the American Psychological Association (Psychologists in Public Service), 2000–2001, and a

Former President of the American Psychology-Law Society, Division 41 of the APA. He holds a Certificate of Professional Qualification and an Interjurisdictional Practice Certificate from the Association of State and Provincial Psychology Boards. He is the author of more than 60 articles and chapters in professional journals and texts, and frequently serves as a consultant, expert witness, and trainer on the treatment and risk assessment of persons with serious mental illness and/or substance abuse disorders, and assessing the risk of violence to self and others. He served as Acting Commissioner of Mental Health for the State of New York, prior to which he served as its Director of Forensic Services and Associate Commissioner, overseeing the forensic and correctional mental health systems for the State of New York. He has served as a mediator and monitor of Federal Court settlement agreements over psychiatric hospitals and prisons and has testified in numerous class action lawsuits regarding treatment and suicide prevention for persons with mental health and substance use disorders in hospitals, prisons, and jails throughout the United States. Dr. Dvoskin has consulted to state and local governments in more than half of the United States and the Civil Rights Division of the U.S. Department of Justice regarding the provision of mental health services in public settings, and has served as the architectural design consultant for a number of psychiatric hospital and prison construction and suicide prevention projects in the U.S. and Puerto Rico. He is the winner of the Arizona Psychological Association's 2010 "Distinguished Contribution to the Science of Psychology Award." Dvoskin is also the Editor (with Jennifer Skeem, Raymond Novaco, and Kevin Douglas) of *Using Social Science to Reduce Violent Offending*," to be published by Oxford University Press in 2011.